Con Comdon

1988

GUINNESS

# AUSTRALIAN FIRSTS

## Patrick Robertson

GUINNESS

# AUSTRALIAN FIRSTS

*Patrick Robertson*

COLLINS
Australia

GUINNESS BOOKS

**The Guinness Book of Australian Firsts**
First published in 1987 by
Collins Australia Pty Ltd and
Guinness Superlatives Ltd

Produced for Collins Australia by
The Watermark Press Pty Ltd

Text © Patrick Robertson
This compilation © Collins Australia and Guinness Superlatives

Australian National Library
Cataloguing-in-Publication Data:
Robertson, Patrick.
Guinness book of Australian firsts.

Includes index.
ISBN 0 00 217812 5.

1. Curiosities and wonders — Australia. 2. Australia — History-Miscellanea.
3. Inventions — Australia. 4. Technological innovations — Australia. I. Title.

032'.02

Typeset by Love Computer Typesetting
Printed by Mandarin Offset, Hong Kong

# CONTENTS

# INTRODUCTION

This is the ultimate sourcebook of Australian firsts documenting in the finest detail well known facts and figures of the past, as well as many of the more obscure. It provides a fascinating insight into the development of Australia.

The early productivity of the film industry may be familiar to many. There are, however, similar achievements and world firsts which are rarely recognised as emanating from Australia.

The black box flight crash recorder, a world first for aircraft safety, was invented by Australian chemist David Warren. Howard Florey first discovered penicillin in 1947. Australian scientists were the first to make artificial rain.

This comprehensive collection of elucidating, startling and sometimes funny, Australian Firsts conveys the extraordinary success of Australians both in their own country and internationally.

# The first . . .

## ABORIGINAL BARRISTER

was Queensland-born Pat O'Shane, called to the bar at Sydney in 1978. Three years later she was appointed head of the NSW State Ministry of Aboriginal Affairs, becoming the first woman to have charge of a NSW Government Department.

## ABORIGINE TO BECOME A COMMISSIONED OFFICER IN THE ARMED SERVICES

was Reginald W. Saunders of Lake Condah, Vic, who won his commission while serving with the Australian Army in 1944. He stayed on in the service after WWII and attained the rank of Captain during the Korean War.

## ABORIGINAL KNIGHT

was Pastor Sir Douglas Nicholls, whose knighthood was granted on 2 June 1972. He was then Director of the Aborigines Advancement League; later he became Governor of South Australia (1976 — 77).

## ABORIGINAL MEMBER OF PARLIAMENT

was Neville Bonner, who filled a casual Senate vacancy in 1971. The following year, standing for the Liberal Party, he was elected as a representative for Queensland. Mr

Bonner's entry in *Who's Who* lists 'boomerang throwing' among his recreations.

## ABORIGINAL PLAYWRIGHT

to have a play performed was Kevin Gilbert, whose *The Cherry Pickers* was staged at the Mews Theatre, Sydney, in 1972. First to have a play published in full was Robert Merritt with *The Cake Man*, published by The Currency Press in 1978. The previous year it was the first play by an aborigine to be performed on television.

## ABORIGINAL STATE GOVERNOR

was Sir Douglas Nicholls, a pastor, who became Governor of South Australia on 1 December 1976. The following month he suffered a stroke and resigned in April 1977.

## ABORIGINAL TO BECOME A UNIVERSITY GRADUATE

was Charles Perkins, who graduated with a BA degree from the University of Sydney in 1964. In 1980 he became the senior ranking Aborigine in the public service with his appointment as Chairman of the Aboriginal Development Commission.

## ABORIGINES, RESERVATION FOR

was established on fertile land at George's Head, near Sydney, early in 1815. Flanagan's *History of New South Wales* (1862) recorded: 'That the sable settlers might be enabled to follow to greater advantage their favourite pursuit of fishing, a boat with the necessary gear was at the same time presented to them. The governor and Lady Macquarie at-

*Neville Bonner, the first aborigine to become a member of Parliament*

Aboriginal Affairs

tended personally at the founding of the settlement, on which occasion a suit of clothes was given to each of the blacks, together with an assortment of implements of husbandry. The settlers comprised sixteen men with their wives and families. At the request of the tribe the governor appointed one of the number to be chief.'

## ABORTION

was legalised in South Australia on 8 January 1970.

## ACCOUNTANT

was Michael Hayes of Sydney, who advertised in August 1803 for a post in a mercantile house or in the brewing and malting business. He subsequently worked for the merchants George Bass and Charles Bishop until sentenced to be removed to Norfolk Island in 1805 for distilling illicit spirits at his house at Farm Cove.

## ACT OF PARLIAMENT

was passed by the Legislative Council of New South Wales on 28 September 1824 and allowed promissory notes and bills of exchange drawn in Spanish dollars (then common currency in Australia) the same legality as those drawn in sterling.

The first Act of Parliament on a policy issue passed by the Federal Parliament (there had been some earlier administrative acts) was the Pacific Island Labourers Act of December 1901. This enshrined the White Australia policy in a measure that allowed for the deportation of the Kanaka labourers of Queensland after a five-year winding down period. It was immediately followed by the Immigration Restriction Act, which imposed an education test deliberately designed to prevent entry of Asians to Australia as immigrants.

## ADOPTION

was first given legal recognition in Australia by Western Australia under the Adoption of Children Act which became law on 23 September 1896.

## ADVANCE AUSTRALIA FAIR

was composed by Scottish songwriter Peter Dodds McCormick and performed for the first time at Sydney on St Andrew's Day, 30 November 1878. In later years it attained something of the status of an unofficial anthem, so much so for some that in 1933 the leader of the Opposition in the NSW Legislative Assembly, J.T. Lang, rebuked a gathering at Lidcombe, NSW, for not standing to attention with their hats off when the band struck up *Advance Australia Fair*. During WWII it was used to introduce ABC news bulletins and was also played in cinemas before or after the performance. It was only on 19 April 1984, however, that it actually succeeded *God Save the Queen* as the Australian national anthem.

## ADVERTISING

The earliest known printed advertisement was a playbill for *The Busybody* and *The Poor Soldier*, to be performed at the Sydney Theatre as a benefit for H. Green on 23 July 1796. The bill was printed by George Hughes on the government printing press. The theatre had opened earlier the same year and it is likely that playbills were produced for the first performance on 16 January.

**The first advertisement in a newspaper** appeared in Vol 1 No 1 of the *Sydney Gazette* on 5 March 1803 and read:

> JOHN JAQUES, Taylor
> At the Back of the General Hospital, Sydney. Respectfully acquaints the Public, that in consequence of the reduction that has lately taken place in the Prices of many Articles of Common Consumption, he has been enabled to make an Abatement in his Charges, and that all Orders with which he may be honoured shall be carefully and punctually honoured.

Advertising rates in the *Sydney Gazette* .romanwere 1s 6d for 12 lines to subscribers and 2s for non-subscribers.

**Classified advertising** in the sense of small advertisements appearing under appropriate headings, was introduced by the *Sydney Morning Herald* on 26 July 1869. There were originally 30 classifications.

**The first branded product to be advertised** regularly and extensively in Australia was the British medicament known as Holloway's Pills. These were being promoted by various retailers as early as 1843 and by J. K. Heydon, who had become sole colonial distributor, in 1850. An advertisement placed by Heydon in *The People's Gazette* for 14 December of that year depicts Professor Holloway in Grecian robes handing out pillboxes to grateful supplicants, while the copy claims that the Secretary of State for the Colonies had instructed the Colonial government, at the behest of the Professor, to legislate against imitations of the celebrated pills. The wonderful cure-all was claimed as sover-

# The first . . .

eign remedy for no less than 33 complaints, some of them terminal. In practice the pills had no value whatsoever except as a placebo, for they consisted of a compound of aloes, ginger and soap.

**The earliest recorded press advertisement illustrated with photography** was for the Grand Natatorium Hotel in Sydney's Pitt Street and appeared in *Truth* for 4 January 1891.

## ADVERTISING AGENCY

was Gordon and Gotch, established in Melbourne probably in 1855. Alexander Gordon had opened a newspaper stand in the Western Market in 1853, and the following year was joined in partnership by John Speechly Gotch. They moved the business to permanent premises at Temple Court, Collins Street West, in 1855 and it seems likely that this was when the advertising agency was added to their wholesale and retail periodical business, though Gordon had acted as agent for the Melbourne *Argus* even in the market stall days. A Sydney branch was founded in 1861, though by this time Edward Greville and already founded the first agency in Sydney. With the founding of the London Branch in 1867, the agency became the first in the world to operate internationally. Other branches followed in South Africa and New Zealand. The London office rapidly became the main advertising agency for British manufacturers seeking to advertise their goods in the colonies.

Advertising agencies had started in Britain as early as 1786 and in America in 1841, but for most of the 19th century they operated more as space brokers than as originators of advertising ideas. It was only in the late 1880s that the British and American agencies began offering a range of creative services, and it would seem that a parallel development was underway in Australia, for the then leading agency, with offices in Sydney, Melbourne and Brisbane, was employing the noted designer Nelson Whitelocke as its art director.

## AERODROME

was established in September 1910 by the Aerial League of Australia on the site of what later became the speedway track at Penrith, NSW. Intended for the use of the League's members, it was described as 'a fine stretch of level ground with a good off-take at one corner.'

## AEROGRAMMES

were issued on 11 September 1944.

## AEROPLANE FLIGHT

in a powered, heavier-than-air machine was made on 9 December 1909 by Colin Defries in a Wright Biplane at Victoria Park Racecourse, Sydney. He flew about 115 yds at heights of 2-15 ft. The speed was about 35 mph.

The first controlled and sustained flight is disputed. It is claimed that on 17 March 1910 F. C. Custance flew for 5 mins 25 secs in a Bleriot from a paddock at Bolivar, nr Adelaide, making three circuits of the paddock totalling about three miles. In the absence of authenticated eye-witness reports of Custance's flight, the rival claim of American magician Harry Houdini, who made three controlled flights in a Voisin at Diggers' Rest, Vic, one day later, must also be considered.

**The first flight in an Australian-built aeroplane** in the presence of witnesses was made by J. R. Duigan in a Farman-type machine at Mia Mia, Vic on 16 July 1910. Duigan had built the entire airframe himself in a shed on a sheep station near Mia Mia called Spring Plains. Powered by a 4 cylinder vertical, air cooled 20 hp engine built by Melbourne engineer J. C. Tilley, the aircraft made two flights before spectators, one of 196 yards at a height of 12 ft and another of 200 yds at a height of 20 ft. Maximum speed was about 20 mph. The original machine is preserved at the National Museum, Melbourne.

**The first cross-country flight** was made in a Bristol Boxkite by New Zealander Joseph J. Hammond of the British Colonial Aircraft Co (later Bristol Aircraft) from Altona Bay, Vic, to Geelong Racecourse, a distance of 42 miles which he covered in 55 mins, on 20 February 1911. The purpose of the flight was to demonstrate to the Australian Government the effectiveness of aircraft for military reconnaissance. On 23 February Mrs Joseph Hammond became the first woman to fly in a powered aeroplane in Australia when she accompanied her husband on a 12 minute circuit of Altona Bay.

**The first England-Australia flight** was made by Ross & Keith Smith, J. M. Bennett and W. H. Shiers in a Vickers Vimy which left Hounslow, Middx, on 12 November 1919 and landed at Darwin, NT, on 10 December.

**The first flight across Bass Strait** was made

by A.L. Lang from Stanley, Tas, to Melbourne on 16 December 1919.

**The first transcontinental flight** was made from south to north by Captain W. N. Wrigley and Sgt A. W. Murphy, who left Point Cook, Vic, in their BE 2e on 16 November 1919 and arrived at Darwin, NT, on 12 December. The flight took almost as long as the concurrent England-Australia flight noted above.

**The first east-west transcontinental flight** was made from Glenroy, Vic, to Perth, WA in a DH4 by F. S. Briggs, C. J. de Garis and J. Howard, leaving on 30 November 1920 and arriving on 2 December. Returning, they made the first west-east flight 14-16 December.

**The first woman to fly from England to Australia** was Mrs K. Miller, accompanying W. N. Lancaster in an Avro Avian, *Red Rose*, which left Croydon on 14 October 1927 and landed at Darwin on 19 March 1928.

**The first trans-Pacific flight** was made from Oakland, California to Brisbane, Queensland, via Honolulu and Suva, by Charles Kingsford Smith, H. Lyon, P. Ulm and J. Warner in the Fokker FV11b-3m *Southern Cross*, leaving the USA on 31 May 1928 and arriving in Australia on 9 June.

**The first non-stop transcontinental flight** was made by Charles Kingsford Smith, H. A. Litchfield, T. H. McWilliam and P. Ulm in the Fokker F VIIb-3m *Southern Cross*, leaving Point Cook, Vic, on 8 August 1928 and arriving at Perth, WA the following day.

**The first flight from Australia to New Zealand** was made by Charles Kingsford Smith, H. A. Litchfield, T. H. McWilliam and P. Ulm in the *Southern Cross*, leaving Richmond, NSW, on 10 September 1928 and landing at Christchurch the following day.

**The first consignment of air freight from England to Australia** was carried by S. J. Moir and H. C. Owen in a Vickers Vellore in 1929. The flight terminated at Cape Don, NT.

**The first west-east trans-Pacific crossing** was made by Charles Kingsford Smith and P. G. Taylor in *Lady Southern Cross*, leaving Australia on 21 October 1932 and arriving in the USA on 4 November.

**The first military aircraft in series production designed and built in Australia** was the Wirraway No 1, produced by the Commonwealth Aircraft Corporation and test flown on 27 March 1939.

**The first flight by a jet aircraft** in Australia was made in June 1946, when the RAAF's newly acquired Gloster Meteor F4 was taken up from Laverton airfield by Squadron Leader D. R. Cumming.

**The first jet aircraft built in Australia** was a DHA Vampire F30, test flown at Bankstown, NSW, on 29 June 1949. It went into service with the RAAF in September of the same year.

**The first supersonic flight in Australia** took place on 11 August 1953, when Flt Lt W. J. Scott broke the sound barrier diving a RAAF Sabre at Avalon, NSW.

*Charles Kingsford-Smith and Charles Ulm made the first trans-Pacific flight and other Australian aviation firsts.*

# The first . . .

## AEROPLANE PILOT

The first Australian to secure a pilot's licence was Lt A. M. Longman of the Royal Navy, originally from St Leonards, Sydney, who received the Federation Aeronautique International's certificate No 72 on 25 April 1911. Longman eventually became Air Chief Marshal of the RAF.

*The first pilot to qualify in Australia* was W. E. Hart, a young Sydney dentist who taught himself to fly and was granted Australian Pilot's Licence No 1 on 5 December 1911.

*The first woman pilot* was Millicent Bryant, who trained at the Australian Aero Club at Mascot and received Pilot Licence No 71 on 23 March 1927. Sadly she was drowned when the Sydney Harbour ferry *Greycliffe* was rammed and sunk.

*The first Australian aeroplane pilot to be killed in warfare* was G. P. Merz while flying a Maurice Farman in Mesopotamia on 30 July 1915.

## AEROPLANE TO TAKE OFF FROM A SHIP

in Australian waters was a Sopwith Pup launched from a revolving platform aboard HMAS *Sydney* on 8 December 1917.

## AGRICULTURAL COLLEGE

was Roseworthy Agricultural College, South Australia, opened on 3 February 1885.

## AGRICULTURAL JOURNAL

was the *Australian Settler's Guide*, Sydney, which began and ended with its first issue in June 1835.

## AGRICULTURAL SHOW

was held by the Agricultural Society of New South Wales at Parramatta on 7 October 1824. Prizes were awarded for the best Australian merino sheep, colonial-bred bulls, heifers, stallions, boars, sows and teams of horses and bullocks, as well as for the best colonial cheese, tobacco and beer. A public testing was held of the latter commodity, with the result that the mob became rowdy — a contemporary newspaper observed, 'reason was dethroned and madness and folly reigned in its stead'. The show continued to be held irregularly at Parramatta until 1867. It then moved to the capital,

where the first Sydney Show was held at Cleveland Paddock (now Prince Albert Park) on 7 May 1869. Attendance during the four days was 37,350.

## AIDS

The first Australian known to have become a victim of AIDS was a 52 year old homosexual who returned to his native country in 1982 after a 10 year absence in the USA and Canada. After several months of unsuccessful treatment, the complaint was identified as AIDS by Dr Harry Michelmore, a practitioner in the Kings Cross area with many gay patients. The sufferer then returned to the USA and died in Florida in May 1983.

*The first person to die of AIDS in Australia* was a middle aged American who had lived on the West Coast for many years. This was the first case to be positively confirmed, the victim dying in hospital in Melbourne on 8 July 1983.

## AIR CHIEF MARSHAL

of the RAAF was Sir Frederick Scherger, promoted on 25 March 1965.

## AIR-CONDITIONED SHOP

for selling perishable foods was a fishmongers opened in Sydney on 15 August 1915 by the NSW State Trawling Industry.

## AIR FORCE

was created by senator G.F. Pearce, Minister for Defence who founded the Australian Aviation Corps on 20 September 1912 with an establishment of four officers and 30 other ranks.

The Corps did not become airborne until 1 March 1914, when L. E. Harrison flew a Bristol Boxkite and Lt H. A. Petre flew a Deperdussin at Point Cook, Vic. These were Australia's first military aircraft. First to be built in Australia was Bristol Boxkite CFS 8, which was flight tested at Point Cook on 10 August 1915.

The Australian Flying Corps, successor to the above, was formed in 1915 in response to a call from the Imperial Army Council for complete squadrons to serve with Britain's Royal Flying Corps. Since the other Dominions allowed their nationals to enlist direct in the RFC, Australia was the only Dominion with its own air force during World War I. No 1 Squadron of the Australian Flying Corps, consisting of 28 officers and 195 other ranks under Lieut. Col. E. H. Reynolds, left Melbourne on 16 March 1916 and served with distinction in Palestine. Nos 2, 3 and 4 Squadrons served in France from the end of 1917. The AFC destroyed a total of 276 enemy aircraft at a cost of 60 of their own machines and 78 killed out of a total flying complement of 563. On returning to Australia in 1919, the AFC was disbanded but replaced the following year by the Australian Air-Corps; this in turn gave way to a permanent Australian Air Force founded 31 March 1921. The prefix 'Royal' was added five months later.

## AIR FORCE COLLEGE

was the Royal Australian Air Force College, founded at Point Cook, near Melbourne, on 1 August 1947.

## AIR RAID

on Australia took place on 19 February 1942, when 128 Japanese aircraft bombed Darwin in two waves, sinking eight ships, destroying 23 aircraft and killing 243 people.

## AIRLINE

was West Australian Airways, founded by Perth pilot Norman Brearley, which inaugurated its Geraldton-Derby run on 4 December 1921. The fleet consisted of six Bristol Tourer

aircraft and there were six pilots, one of them the man who was to become perhaps Australia's greatest long-distance flyer, Charles Kingsford Smith. When one of the aircraft on the first flight crashed, killing pilot and mechanic, Brearley suspended operations until emergency landing grounds could be arranged, and regular passenger service did not begin until 3 March 1922.

NB: Qantas had been founded earlier, on 16 November 1920, but did not start regular operations until November 1922.

**The first daily air service** was operated by Qantas between Brisbane and Toowoomba, commencing 9 May 1928.

**The first Adelaide-Sydney passenger service** was inaugurated by Australian Aerial Services on 1 January 1925 with a DH 50A.

**The first Perth-Adelaide passenger service** was inaugurated by West Australian Airways on 2 June 1929 with DH 66 Hercules airliners.

**The first Melbourne-Sydney passenger service** was inaugurated by Australian National Airways on 1 June 1930 with Avro Tens.

**The first Melbourne-Hobart passenger service** was inaugurated by Australian National Airways on 19 January 1931 with Avro Tens.

**The first passenger service from Australia to England** was inaugurated jointly by Qantas Empire Airways and Imperial Airways on 17

DH.86 "Canberra", on the first overseas passenger service provided by Qantas.

Qantas

# The first ...

April 1935. Qantas flew the Brisbane-Singapore section and Imperial Airways the Singapore-London section of the 12½ day flight.

**The first night flights** undertaken as part of a scheduled airline service began with Australian National Airways' Sydney-Brisbane service aboard the DC-3 *Kyilla* on 29 May 1939.

**The first trans-Pacific passenger service** was inaugurated between Sydney and San Francisco/Vancouver by an Australian National Airways DC-4 on 15 September 1946.

**The first round-the-world passenger service** in the world was inaugurated by Qantas Empire Airways on 14 January 1958, flying the Super Constellation *Southern Aurora* eastbound from Sydney to London via the USA in 5½ days and another Super Constellation, the *Southern Zephyr* westbound from Sydney to London via India and the Middle East in 6½ days.

*The first round-the-world passenger service was by Super Constellations flown by Qantas.*

**The first jet airliner** in service with an Australian airline was a Qantas Empire Airways Boeing 707, which made its inaugural flight from Sydney to San Francisco on 29 July 1959. Jet service from Sydney to London followed on 5 September and the first jet round-the-world service on 27 October.

**The first non-stop service to the USA** was inaugurated by Qantas on 8 March 1965.

**The first Jumbo jet in service with an Australian airline** was the Qantas airliner *City of Canberra*, which made its maiden flight on 16 August 1971.

## AIRLINER

built in Australia was the AAEC B1, a five-seater designed by H.E. Broadsmith and first demonstrated in public at Mascot Airport, Sydney, on 13 March 1922.

## AIRLINER CRASH

took place near the Murchison River between Geraldton and Carnarvon, WA, on 5 December 1921, when an aircraft belonging to West Australian Airways crashed killing the pilot and mechanic. There were no passengers on board. The first airliner disaster involving the death of a number of passengers happened on 21 March 1931, the Avro X *Southern Cloud* disappearing during an Australian National Airways scheduled flight from Sydney to Melbourne. No trace of the aircraft or the eight victims of the crash was ever found.

## AIRMAIL

was flown from Melbourne to Sydney by French aviator Maurice Guillaux in a Bleriot monoplane on 16-19 July 1914. Total flying time, spread out over 2 days 5½ hours, was 9 hrs 33 mins. Guillaux carried 1,785 letters, a consignment of Lipton's Tea and another of O.T. Lemon Squash for delivery in Sydney.

**The first regular airmail service** was inaugurated between Geraldton and Derby, WA by West Australian Airways on 5 December 1921.

Regular airmail service between Adelaide, Melbourne and Sydney began on 4 June 1924. The service was extended to Perth in 1929.

**The first England-Australia airmail** arrived at Darwin aboard Charles Kingsford Smith's *Southern Cross* on 25 April 1931. The mail had been flown out from England on an Imperial Airways DH66, but the plane had crashed at Koepang, Indonesia, on 19 April. Kingsford Smith was commissioned to fly out to Koepang, transfer the mail bags and bring them back to Brisbane via Darwin. The first Australia-England airmail was then flown in the *Southern Cross* to Akyab, leaving Darwin on 27 April, and carried on to London by Imperial Airways, arriving 14 May 1931.

**The first regular New Zealand-Australia airmail** was flown from Plymouth, NZ, to Richmond, NSW, aboard the Avro Ten *Faith in Australia* on 17 February 1934. The first Australia-New Zealand airmail was carried in the same aircraft on 11 April 1934.

**The first regular airmail service to the USA** was inaugurated via Darwin, Hong Kong and Honolulu on 20 April 1937.

## AIR POLLUTION CONTROL

was introduced in Victoria under the Clean Air Regulations which came into force on 1 March 1958.

## AIR RACE

took place on 29 June 1912 between Sydney and Parramatta. The contestants were Sydney dentist Billy Hart, the first pilot to qualify in Australia, and visiting American aviator Eugene 'Wizard' Stone, and the event was billed, very inaccurately, as the 'First International Aviation Contest'. Hart won the race in 23 minutes, his opponent losing the way and landing at Lakemba.

## AIRSHIP

built in Australia was flown over Sydney by A. L. Roberts on 4 July 1914.

## ALUMINIUM

was first produced from imported bauxite by the Australian Aluminium Production Commission at the Bell Bay smelter in Tasmania in 1955. The first aluminium from Australian bauxite was produced by the Alcoa Smelter at Point Henry, near Geelong, Vic, in April 1963.

## AMBULANCE SERVICE

was a sulkie drawn by a white pony which entered service with the Queensland Ambulance Transport Brigade at its headquarters in Queen Street, Brisbane in 1897. The pony was trained to back into harness when an alarm bell rang. No collar was used, merely a chest strap which was strapped smoothly and quickly into place. Before the introduction of horse-drawn ambulances, the only means of transporting sick or injured patients was in a covered litter pushed by stretcher-bearers. The Queensland Ambulance Transport Brigade's pony-drawn sulkies were replaced by motor ambulances in 1908.

## AMERICANS

to visit Australia were the crew of the brigantine *Philadelphia*, under Thomas Patrickson, master, which arrived at Sydney Cove from Philadelphia, Pa, on 1 November 1792. The vessel brought with it the first American imports to reach Australia, chiefly beef, wine, rum, gin, tobacco, pitch and tar.

The first American to establish a business in Australia was the Sydney merchant Prosper de Mestre in 1818.

## AMERICAN CONSUL

was James Hartwell Williams, who took office at Sydney on 15 January 1839.

## AMERICAN FIRM ESTABLISHED IN AUSTRALIA

was the export-import house of Kenworthy & Co; which established a branch in Sydney in 1836.

## ANAESTHETIC

was applied by Dr William Pugh at St John's Hospital, Launceston, Tas, on 7 June 1847, only seven months after ether had first been used in major surgery by Dr Morton of Boston. He removed a tumour and also performed cataract operations, having constructed his own ether spray from an illustration of Morton's apparatus which had appeared in the *Illustrated London News*.

## ANTE-NATAL CLINIC

was established at Adelaide Hospital in June 1910.

## ANTHROPOLOGICAL FILM

made in the field anywhere in the world was shot in 1898 by British zoologist Alfred Cord Haddon of Cambridge University and depicted the life and customs of Torres Strait Islanders. The only earlier anthropological film had been made of African negroes in Paris.

The first anthropological film shot by an Australian was a 3000 ft study of the tribal rites of Aboriginals, taken by University of Melbourne biologist Walter Baldwin Spencer in 1901 with a Warwick Biograph camera at Charlotte Waters, Northern Territory. It was also the first documentary film in the world with sound. The action was accompanied by didgeridoo music, recorded on an Edison wax cylinder as the film was being shot.

## ANTISEPSIS

was introduced to Australia by Crimean War veteran Dr George Pringle of Parramatta, NSW, who treated a young man whose forearm had been flayed in a shooting accident, on 18 October 1867. Pringle had been a colleague of Joseph Lister, the pioneer of antisepsis, at the Royal Infirmary in Edinburgh and had maintained a correspondence with him since coming to Australia. Having swabbed the young man's wound with carbolic 'on Professor Lister's plan', he applied splints and bandages, then a layer of lint soaked in carbolic and a sheet of thin lead to stop the carbolic from evaporating. A month later Pringle triumphantly reported 'No pus whatever has appeared!'.

# The first . . .

## ANZAC DAY

was first observed as a public holiday in Western Australia on 25 April 1919, the fourth anniversary of the landing of the Australasian forces at Gallipoli. New South Wales, Queensland and Tasmania followed suit in 1920 and Victoria and South Australia in 1921.

## APPENDICECTOMY

was performed by M. Russell Nolan at Toowoomba, Queensland, on 11 March 1893. The patient, a 30 year old mother of four, was suffering from acute peritonitis and by the time the operation was performed she was close to death. In 1944, 51 years later, she was reported to be alive and in good health.

## APPLES

were cultivated at Parramatta in 1791. On 3 December of that year Capt. Watkin Tench recorded that he saw at the bottom of the Governor's garden 'several small fruit trees, which were brought in the *Gorgon* from the Cape, and look lively; on one of them a half a dozen apples, as big as nutmegs'.

### The first apples to be exported

— also the first overseas shipment of Australian fruit of any kind — were shipped from Hobart to Edinburgh in 1828.

### The first Granny Smith apples

were propagated by Maria Ann Smith in 1868 and cultivated on a large scale at the government experimental station at Bathurst starting in 1895. Her grandson, Benjamin Spurway of Sarina, Queensland, related the origins of the Granny Smith in the *Australian Post* in 1956:

'From time to time there are short, more or less garbled accounts written about the Granny Smith Apples and as one of her living grandsons, in my seventy ninth year, I think I should relate the story as told to us all, by our mother, her youngest daughter (Maria Anne), and my father, James Spurway.

Granny Smith, her husband and family, emigrated from Sussex about 1837. They settled on the land at what was then North Ryde, now part of Eastwood.

They had a fruit orchard and Granny used to drive into Sydney markets in the early hours of the morning, sell her fruit and return home.

Thomas Lawless, a fruit agent, gave her some green apples, known as Tasmanian French Crabs, and asked her to try them as cookers. She sat at a table, peeled and cored the apples and reaching out of the window, dropped skin and cores underneath, on to a flowerbed. Being out of the way, they were not interfered with.

In due time the Granny Smith Apple was born, the tree growing up, not more than a foot or eighteen inches from the wall of the house. I venture to say that this 'apple' has been and still is, a great asset to Australia.

Strange to say, in the district where it was first raised, it was not so very popular, being a shy bearer, but some years later it was tried at Bathurst and Orange, and so prolific was the crop that the limbs had to be propped up to bear the weight. From then on till now, no general utility apple has proved to be more popular . . .'

ANZAC *troops at Gallipoli using periscopes to observe the enemy.*

## APPOINTMENT OVERSEAS

The first Australian to receive an official appointment overseas was John Macarthur, second son of the pioneer settler of the same name, who was elected Chairman of the Committee of Colonies and Trade in London in 1824.

## AQUEDUCT

was laid between Botany and Sydney, starting in 1827 and finishing in June 1837. The need for an alternative supply of water to Sydney was occasioned not only by the growth of the town — already supporting a population of some 10,000 by the year the aqueduct was started — but also because the cutting down of the trees fringing the Tank Stream had caused its banks to give way and the flow of water to be much diminished. The new tunnel from the Botany swamps was 12,000 feet in length and during the first year of operation, when 27 inches of rain fell in the vicinity, a total of 3,675,375 gallons of water was supplied to the capital. The population having nearly doubled by this time, to 19,729, each inhabitant was able to consume an average of 185 gallons, or 3½ gallons a week.

## ARBITRATION COURT

for the settlement of industrial disputes was established by South Australia under an Act of December 1894. The Commonwealth Arbitration Court was set up under an Act which became law on 15 December 1904.

## ARCHERY

was introduced to Australia by W. F. E. Liardet, proprietor of the Brighton Pier Hotel at Port Melbourne, Vic, who organized the first archery club in October 1840 and the first tournament the following month. The sport failed to take root, but was revived in the 1850s and became very popular in Victoria, New South Wales, Tasmania and South Australia. The first sport in which women could compete on a par with men, it offered ample opportunity not only for healthful exercise of a not too rigorous nature but also for romantic dalliance. When the first major tournament was held at Government House, Melbourne, in 1856, the winner was a woman and it was also in Melbourne that a *Lady's Guide to Archery* was published in 1859.

## ARMED FORCES TO SERVE OVERSEAS

The first unit of the Australian armed forces to engage the enemy in warfare was a detachment of seamen from HMVS *Victoria*, who fought against the Maoris near Kairau, New Zealand, on 29 December 1860. They served with the Naval Brigade under Commodore Seymour, who wrote to the Governor of Victoria that 'I had every reason to be satisfied with their steadiness, and the manner in which they worked in the construction of a redoubt, under heavy fire . . .'

The Victorian seamen were on shore-based active service in New Zealand from 19 December 1860 to 29 January 1861. Although some 2,500 Australians served in the Maori War, these were volunteers who were drafted into New Zealand fighting units. The only Australian servicemen to serve on behalf of their own government were the sailors of Victoria's naval force.

For the first Australian expeditionary force, see Army.

## ARMY

The first military force raised in Australia was 'The Loyal and Associated Corps', founded by Governor Hunter on 6 September 1800 in response to rumours of an uprising among the Irish Convicts sent out after the rebellion in 1798. Their role was 'to protect public and private property and to assist the military in the preservation of order'. There were two units, a Sydney Corps numbering two officers and 49 other ranks under Capt. William Balmain and a Parramatta Corps of 2 officers and 26 other ranks under Richard Atkins. The volunteers received free rations, uniforms and arms, but no pay, and were drilled twice a week until proficient, and thereafter monthly. The Corps was disbanded by Governor King in July 1801 owing to the shortage of suitably qualified officers, but reinstated the following year following the arrival of a further 400 Irish convicts. As the 'Loyal Associations', the volunteers remained in being until 1809.

The oldest existing military unit is the 1st Infantry Battalion (Commando) Royal New South Wales Regiment, The City of Sydney's Own, founded at the time of the Russian invasion scare in 1854 as the 1st New South Wales Rifle Volunteers. This was the first colonial unit raised since the disbandment of the Loyal Association.

**The first Regular Army unit** was the Permanent Garrison Artillery Corps of Victoria, colloquially known as 'Stubbs' Bulldogs', established under the command of Capt. J. A. Stubbs on 1 January 1871 and garrisoned at the Victoria Barracks in St Kilda Road, Melbourne. The force was some 150 strong and recruits, many of whom had served in the British Army, the Royal Irish Constabulary or the Metropolitan Police, were required to be at least 5ft 9ins tall. One early recruit, D. G. O'Donnell, said that at 6ft 1½ ins he was 'considered but a very moderate height, and usually sized about 40 from the right' (i.e. there were 40 men taller than he). Privates were paid 2s a day, and according to O'Donnell, such was the attraction of the uni-

# The first . . .

form with its scarlet-topped busby and plume, that 'many well-educated fellows threw up lucrative positions to serve . . .' (once the attraction wore off, many left for the better paid Victorian Police Force.) Drills and exercises were held from 7 a.m. until 3.30 p.m. and the rest of the day the men had to themselves, many indulging the opportunities for sport to such an extent that by the mid-70s the Garrison had a reputation as 'the greatest school of athletics in Victoria'. Stubbs' Bulldogs were condemned by the Victorian Treasury, who thought public money was being wasted on training athletes to become policemen and the Garrison was disbanded in December 1880, one officer and 12 men being retained for essential military works. It was re-formed at a later date.

**The first Engineer Corps** was the Victorian Engineers, a volunteer unit formed at a meeting held at the *Duke of Rothesay Hotel* in Melbourne on 7 November 1860.

**The first Signal Corps** was the Torpedo and Telegraphs Corps of the Victorian Army, a volunteer unit established on 4 November 1870.

**The first Commonwealth Regiment** the Royal Australian Artillery, created on 24 August 1899 by the amalgamation of the permanent artilleries of NSW, Victoria and Queensland. The new Regiment was the first Federal institution, military or civil, to come into being — 17 months before Federation. Now the Royal Regiment of Australian Artillery, it contains the oldest unit of the Australian Regular Army, 'A' Battery, which was originally founded as the New South Wales Artillery on 1 August 1871.

**The first mechanised unit of the Australian Army** was the Volunteer Automobile Corps, authorised on 9 May 1908 with a section in each State. It was probably a unique corps in that every member of it was an officer. The unit remained operative until 1915, when it was merged with the newly formed Motor Transport Service.

## ARMY CADET CORPS

was established at the King's School, Macquarie Fields, near Liverpool, NSW, under Capt. William Dalmas in 1866. The King's School was an amalgamation of King's School, Parramatta (which had become temporarily defunct in 1864) and St Mark's Collegiate School. Between 60 and 70 boys enrolled, paying 1s a quarter for membership. At first the boys made their own rifles out of broomsticks or whatever wood came to hand — Dalmas recalled that 'some of the fencing suffered in consequence'. They were later armed with police carbines and, when these proved too long for diminutive soldiers, with Lee Enfields. The uniform consisted of blue coat, grey trousers and kepi and this became the King's School uniform when it returned to Parramatta in 1869.

## ARMY EXPEDITIONARY FORCE

to serve overseas was the New South Wales Contingent of 750 men and 225 horses under the command of Col Richardson, which embarked on the troopships *Australasian* and *Iberia* bound for the Sudan on 3 March 1885. Barely three weeks earlier news of General Gordon's death at Khartoum had reached Sydney and the NSW Government immediately cabled Britain with an offer of assistance. This was promptly accepted and the expeditionary force sailed from Circular Quay to the thunderous cheers of a crowd estimated to be 100,000 strong. Having disembarked at Suakin on the Red Sea on 29 March, the Australian troops fought their one and only battle of the war, or more properly a skirmish, in which three were wounded but none killed. After spending the rest of the campaign building a railroad, much to their dissatisfaction, they arrived back in Sydney aboard the *Arab* on 23 June. Six of their number failed to return, having died of fever.

## ART EXHIBITION

was organised by John Skinner Prout and opened at the Legislative Council Chambers, Hobart, Tasmania, on 6 January 1845. The 276 works on show included local pictures by Thomas Bock, F. G. Skimpkinson, Mary Morton, the Bishop of Tasmania and Prout himself, as well as English paintings from private collections in Hobart — views of Gateshead-on-Tyne lent by solicitor John Dobson, scenes of Devon lent by Dr Agnew, and most notable of all, some Turners provided by Bishop Nixon. The Bishop's wife wrote to a friend: ' . . . the Hobartians have proved themselves very unworthy of such an intellectual treat — the receipts have only been £70 — so I fear the committee will be losers by £30. The Governor's liberal donation has been one shilling! The following dialogue was positively overheard between him and Miss Dunn (to whom his son, who came out on the 'Derwent', is engaged): "What is that picture?" quoth the young lady, pointing to the St Sebastian. Governor: "Don't you see, it is a naked man!"'.

**The first one-man show** was *An Artist's Exhibition*, presented by S. T. Gill at Adelaide on 3 February 1847.

**The first overseas exhibition of Australian art** was held at the International Exhibition in Paris, which opened on 15 May 1855. It included paintings by Conrad Martens, F. C. Terry, George French Angas, Adelaide Ironside, William Dexter and C. Abrahams.

**The first exhibition of Australian 'modern art'**, including abstracts, was opened at the Grosvenor Gallery, Sydney on 25 November 1926.

**The first exhibition of Aboriginal art** was held by the National Museum of Victoria in 1929.

**The first exhibition of abstract sculpture** was held by Ola Cohn, a disciple of the English sculptor Henry Moore, at Melbourne in March 1931.

## ART GALLERY

was opened by Robert Vaughan Hood, lithographer, carver, gilder, goldbeater and Australia's pioneer art dealer, in a specially erected building next to his residence in Hobart, on 24 May 1846.

**The first public picture gallery** was the Melbourne Gallery, opened in the north wing of the Melbourne Public Library on 24 December 1864. Works shown at the opening consisted of 13 paintings bought in England at the Victorian Government's expense, a few pictures donated by citizens of Melbourne, and 43 entries for a competition to select an Australian painting for purchase by the gallery. The prize of £200 went to Nicholas Chevalier for 'Buffalo Ranges, Victoria'. The Melbourne Gallery is the oldest art gallery in Australia.

## ART JOURNAL

was *Australian Art* founded by George Collingridge at Sydney in January 1888. It ran for three issues.

## ART SCHOOL

was the Academy of Painting, founded in Sydney in 1812 by John William Lewin, the first artist to settle voluntarily in Australia. The school paid little and his wife was obliged to run a pub, *The Bunch of Grapes*, to keep the Lewin household solvent.

## ARTESIAN BORES

were drilled in 1880 on C. and S. Officers' Killara Station in the Riverina district of New South Wales. One bore yielded 7000 gallons and the other 12000 gallons of water per day.

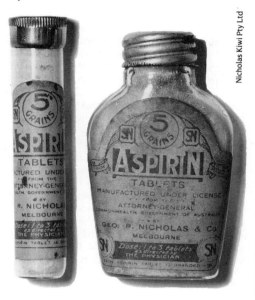

Nicholas Kiwi Pty Ltd

## ASPRO

was developed by George Nicholas of Melbourne in response to the Australian Government's offer of a patent to anyone who could produce a substitute for aspirin — a German product, supplies of which were cut off by the outbreak of World War I. A condition of the offer was that the Australian product had to be of comparable purity. On 12 June 1915 Nicholas perfected a compound which not only equalled but actually surpassed aspirin in purity. The name, adopted in 1917, is not in fact a contraction of aspirin. It is composed of the last two letters of Nicholas and the first three of 'product'. Aspro was exported to Britain in 1925, where it still remains one of the most popular analgesics, and was subsequently marketed in most countries of the world. It is known almost universally by its Australian name, except in Indonesia, where it is sold as 'Naspro'.

## ATHLETICS

The first running races were held in Hyde Park, Sydney, during the town's first Race Week, which commenced 15 October 1810. The *Sydney Gazette* reported: 'Several foot

# The first . . .

races were run on the Course, one of which excited much pleasantry. It was a match for 20 gs made by Dicky Dowling, to carry 14 st on his back 50 yards before his antagonist, a young active man, should run backwards and forwards the same ground, making 100 yards. Dowling won, but had not a foot to spare; and it was generally concluded that his opponent lost considerably more than the ground he was beat by in turning round to double the 50 yards.'

**The first athletic club** was the Sydney Amateur Athletics Club, founded in 1872. It held half-yearly meetings at the Association Cricket Ground (later known as Sydney Cricket Ground). The first State athletics championship was held there under the auspices of the Sydney A.A.A. on 10 May 1888.

**The first sprinter in the world to use the crouch start** was Bobby McDonald of Bourke, NSW, in 1884.

**The first Australian to sprint 100 yards in under 10 seconds** was Billy McPherson in 9.9 secs at the Melbourne athletics championship of 1892.

**The first Australian athlete to achieve a world record** was D. Ross, who threw the hammer 111 ft 5 ins on 2 January 1891.

**The first Australian to hold a world track record** was Nigel Barker, who broke the 440 yds record in a time of 48.5 secs at the Sydney Cricket Ground on 11 November 1905. The new record remained unbroken until 1916.

**The first athletics events for women** were held at the NSW State Championships at Manly in March 1926.

**The first Australian to run a mile in under four minutes** was John Landy of Victoria, who established a new world record of 3 mins 57.9 secs at Turku, Finland on 21 June 1954. This was only 46 days after Britain's Roger Bannister had become the first miler in the world to hear the announcement of his time start with 'Three . . .'.

## ATLAS

of Australia was W. R. Baker's *Australian Atlas*, Sydney, 1843-6.

## AUCTION

was held on 8 December 1794, when a 25 acre farm in the Concord district went under the hammer for £13. The property, which included 'a tolerable hut' as dwelling, had belonged to a soldier called Samuel Crane who was killed when a tree he was cutting fell on him.

**The first regular auctioneer** was Simeon Lord, who was granted a licence by the Sydney magistrates on 19 September 1798. He was appointed 'vendue master' by Governor King in May 1801. Lord charged 5% commission to vendors and there was also a 1½% sales tax which was paid over to the Orphan Fund. Average proceeds were about £30-£40 a month, in addition to his income from other trading activities. Lord, an ex-convict, went on to become the richest of all the emancipists.

The earliest known auction catalogue is a 16 page *Catalogue of the Valuable Library and other effects, the property of Henry Grattan Douglass Esq., which will be sold by auction, by George and John Paul, at their rooms, George-Street, on Monday, the 21st of April 1828*. The only surviving copy is in the Mitchell Library.

**The first wool auctions** were conducted at Sydney by William Lyons, certainly as early as 1834 and possibly before that date. He offered sellers free storage and an advance price on the sale in return for a 5% commission.

**The first tobacco auctions** were held in Queensland in 1932.

## 'AUSTRALIA'

as a name for the continent came into general use after it had been coined by the explorer Matthew Flinders in 1814. In his book *Account of a Voyage to Terra Australis* he wrote: 'Had I permitted myself any innovation upon the original term (Terra Australis), it would have been to convert it into Australia, as being more agreeable to the ear and an assimilation to the name of other great portions of the earth.' Alas, he did not live to see the name in print. He died on the day his book was published, 14 July 1814.

The name 'Australia' was first officially used by Governor Macquarie in correspondence with the Secretary of State on 21 December 1817.

'Australians' as a word to describe people of European stock born in Australia was first used in print by the convict-poet M. M. Robinson in his *Ode for His Majesty's Birthday* published in the *Sydney Gazette* of 10 June 1815.

## AUSTRALIA DAY

was first celebrated as a public holiday on 26 January 1838, the 50th anniversary of settlement, and annually thereafter. It was originally know as Anniversary Day or Foundation Day, but Victoria changed the name to Australia Day in 1931 and the other States subsequently followed this example. In 1934 it was agreed that the first Monday after 26 January would be observed as Australia Day throughout Australia.

## AUSTRALIAN, WHITE

was born to Mrs Whittle, wife of Thomas Whittle of the Royal Marines, as the ships of the First Fleet came up Sydney Harbour for the first time on 26 January 1788. The boy was named Thomas after his father. The elder Whittle elected to stay on in Australia when the Royal Marines returned to England and became a sargeant-major in the New South Wales Corps. In October 1794 he was given a land grant of 30 acres at Lane Cove, so it is possible that this is where young Thomas Whittle spent his formative years. He was subsequently a bugler in the New South Wales Corps.

## AUTOBIOGRAPHY

was *Memoirs of James Hardy Vaux, Written by Himself*, composed by Vaux while serving time at Newcastle in 1812 and published in London in 1819. One of the most picturesque rogues to have decorated the early history of New South Wales, Vaux enjoyed the unique distinction of being the only convict transported to Australia three times. The first occasion was as a youth of 19 in 1801, for stealing a pocket handkerchief. Having returned to England as Governor King's unofficial secretary in 1807, he absconded, was convicted of robbery and sentenced to death, and on remission of this sentence transported again in 1810. In 1827 he escaped from New South Wales and made his way to Dublin, where he was convicted of another robbery and sentenced to transportation for seven years. In the 1850s, when he was over 70, Vaux was still committing fresh crimes and getting caught. The autobiography was written while he was serving as clerk to the Commander of the Newcastle penal station. The coalmines at Newcastle were for persistent offenders like Vaux and conditions there were notorious for the severity of the discipline and lack of the most basic creature comforts. It was typical of Vaux that he succeeded in obtaining a job that released him from the backbreaking labour of the mines and gave him time for the contemplation of literature.

## BADMINTON

was introduced to Australia in 1900 by F. G. Moore, who brought the equipment with him from England, and first played in the Drill Hall at Fremantle, WA.

## BAHA'I TEMPLE

was opened at Mona Vale, Sydney, on 16 September 1961.

## BALLET

performed in Australia was *The Fair Maid of Perth, or The Rival Lovers*, adapted from the novel by Walter Scott, which opened at the Theatre Royal, Sydney, on 17 September 1835. The principal roles were danced by Mrs Jones and Mr Fitzgerald.
**The first romantic ballet** was *La Sylphide*, performed at Melbourne under the title of *The Mountain Sylph* on 25 September 1845. *La Sylphide* had been premiered at the Paris Opera in March 1832 and was the first ballet in which the female dancers wore white tutus.
**The first Australian ballet** was *Turquoisette, or A Study in Blue*, choreographed by Madame Rosalie Phillipini from London and presented by the J. W. Williamson Co at the Princess Theatre, Melbourne on 9 September 1893. The principals were Mlle Catherine Bartho, billed as '*Première Danseuse Assoluta* of the Imperial Theatres of Moscow and St Petersburg', and Signorina Enrichetta D'Argo, of whom the *Argus* sniffed that 'the

# The first . . .

applause ... was less discriminating than ought to have been the case'. The company comprised eight coryphées from London's Empire and Alhambra Theatres and 90 dancers recruited in Australia and New Zealand.

The first overseas ballet company visited Australia in June 1913, when the Danish ballerina Adeline Genée arrived with a company of dancers from the Imperial Russian Ballet. This was augmented by a number of Australian dancers trained by Jennie Brennan. The opening performance of the tour was *Coppélia* at Her Majesty's Theatre, Melbourne, on 21 June 1913. Other ballets in the repertoire included *La Camargo*, *Robert le Diable*, *Les Sylphides* and Volinine's *Arabian Nights*. Volinine was the principal male dancer in the company, billed as '*premier danceur classique* from the Imperial Theatre, Moscow, and the Imperial Russian Ballet'. Genée was billed simply as 'the World's Greatest Dancer'. The tour took the company on from Melbourne to Adelaide, where the opening night had to be postponed because someone had left all the *Coppélia* music behind in Melbourne, and thence to Sydney, enjoying a special triumph when they danced for the sailors of Australia's newly formed battle fleet, which had just sailed in from England on its maiden vogage. On this occasion Adeline Genée forsook the ballet to dance an impromptu hornpipe in their honour. Her tour of Australasia was intended to be Adeline Genée's last overseas appearance prior to retirement after 25 years on the stage. In fact her world farewell was to be postponed for another 20 years, and she finally performed her swan song via the infant medium of television in England in 1933.

**The first ballet company** was the First Australian Ballet, an amateur company founded by Mischa Burlakov, a carpenter by trade, and Louise Lightfoot, which opened at the Savoy Theatre, Sydney, on 4 November 1931 with *Coppélia*. The company produced *Swan Lake*, *Petrouchka*, and *Scheherezade* in Australia before any professional company had done so.

**The first professional classical ballet company** in Australia was founded by Helene Kirsova, formerly of Colonel de Basil's Ballets Russes de Monte Carlo, and gave its first performance in Sydney on 8 July 1941. In addition to a core of de Basil dancers, the company's principals were Peggy Sager, Paul Clementin, Rachel Cameron and Strelsa Heckelman. During its three years of existence the company danced in Sydney, Melbourne and Brisbane, offering a selection of established ballets and no less than 14 new ones created by Kirsova herself, including *A Dream and a Fairytale* and *The Revolution of the Umbrellas*.

**The first Australian ballet company to tour outside Australasia** was the Bodenweiser Ballet, which visited South Africa in 1949.

The Australian Ballet, founded in 1961, made its overseas debut at Covent Garden on 1 October 1965. Its first US tour began at Los Angeles on 26 December 1970, and the first Soviet and East European tour followed in 1973.

**The first full-length contemporary ballet** choreographed in Australia was Graeme Murphy's *Poppy*, presented by the Sydney Dance Co. on 12 April 1978.

## BALLOON ASCENT (*manned*)

was made on 1 February 1858 from Cremorne Gardens, Melbourne by the English aviator William Dean in the 60 ft high *Australasian*. The balloon was inflated with 31,000 cu ft of gas partly at the Melbourne Gas works and partly at the home of its owner, the Hon. George Coppins. The maiden voyage of the *Australasian* was about seven miles.

## BALLPOINT PENS

were imported from England by parcel post in lots of three or six dozen in 1946 by A.W. Birchall & Sons of Launceston, Tas Mr Raymond Tilley, the present Managing Director of Birchall's, recalls:

'Towards the end of World War II "brainstorms" were introduced to our sales promotion meetings and one of the subjects discussed was a news item that the Miles Aeroplane Co was starting to look for an alternative to aircraft construction and had begun producing a "ballpoint" pen. It consisted of a copper tube almost two feet long which was folded back on itself four or five times and fitted with a rotating ball type of point, the whole thing being encased in a rather thick black plastic container with a detachable cap.

'It was guaranteed to write for five years and the price was in the vicinity of £25.

'It performed very effectivly for a while, but eventually the ballpoints wore out the sockets in which they were inserted — the ball dropped out and many customers suffered a flood of several years' supply of ink in their post war double breasted pin striped suits.'

The Miles-Martin ballpoint had originally been patented by Hungarian hypnotist, sculptor and journalist Lasalo Biro in Buenos Aires in 1943. Henry Martin began manufacturing the pen at Reading, England the following year for the use of RAF navigators — fountain pens would not operate at high altitudes.

## BAND

was the Band of the Royal Marines, which gave its first performance on Australian soil on the occasion of the reading of the Governor's Commission at Sydney Cove on 7 February 1788.

The first civilian brass band was formed under the baton of John Agnew of the 96th Regiment by the St Joseph's Total Abstinence Society at Launceston, Tas, in 1845. Despite the Society's raison d'être many of its members were Irish; when the Irish exile John Mitchel came to Launceston in 1851 to see his wife, and was promptly clapped into jail, the St Joseph's band played traditional airs all night below his cell window.

## BANK

was the Bank of New South Wales, which was also the first limited liability company, opened in a cottage in Macquarie Place on 8 April 1817. The first customer was Sargeant Jeremiah Murphy of the 46th Regiment, who deposited the sum of £50. (A considerable sum — a sergeant's pay was 1s 10d a day.) Deposits were placed in a 'strong secure chest', since there was no safe, though the premises were guarded by sentries. The original staff consisted of a cashier, an acountant and a messenger.

## BANK ROBBERY

took place on 13 September 1828, when the Bank of Australia in Sydney was robbed of £20,000.

## BANKCARDS

were introduced throughout Australia in November 1974.

The first international bankcards were Bankcard, Master Charge and Bankcard Visa, introduced on 1 August 1980. Overseas purchases were credited to the existing local Bankcard account. The system also enabled travellers to obtain cash advances of up to $500 each seven days and 30 days interest free terms.

## BANKNOTES

were issued by the Bank of New South Wales from the day of its opening, 8 April 1817. The original denominations were 10s, £1 and £5, followed by a 5s note a few days later. No specimens of the first note issues are known to have survived.

**The first Treasury Notes** were issued in £1 and £5 denominations by the Queensland government on 1 November 1866 following a financial crisis. They were withdrawn in 1869, but Treasury notes were issued in Queensland again from 1893 until the Bank Notes Act of 1910 prohibited further issues.

**The first Commonwealth Notes** were for ten shillings and were issued by the Secretary of the Treasury on 13 July 1913. On this date each member of Parliament was sent two specimens of the note with consecutive numbers. Between 1920 and 1959 the note issue was in the hands of the Commonwealth Bank; since then it has been the responsibility of the Reserve Bank of Australia.

See also Decimal Currency.

## BANQUET

was held at Government House, Sydney, on the occasion of King George III's birthday on 4 June 1788 and attended by the Service Officers and civilian officials of the settlement. Charles Worgan, surgeon of the *Sirius*, recorded: '. . . we sat down to a very good entertainment, considering how far we are from Leadenhall Market. It consisted of Mutton, Pork, Fowls, Fish, Kanguroo, Sallads, Pies and Preserved Fruits. The Potables consisted of Port, Lisbon, Madeira, Teneriffe and good Old English Porter. These went merrily around in bumpers.' The Band of the Royal Marines played during the meal and afterwards the company went out to see the bonfires lit in celebration by the convicts, each of whom had been allowed a pint of grog in which to drink His Majesty's health. Next morning it became apparent that those of the convicts who were not joining in the singing around the bonfire had been busy plundering the houses of the officers attending the banquet.

## BAPTIST SERVICE

was held in the long room of the *Rose and Crown Inn*, Castlereagh Street, Sydney, by

# The first . . .

John McKaeg on 24 April 1831.

**The first Baptist Chapel** was established in Bathurst Street, Sydney on 28 November 1835 by the Rev. John Saunders. The first Baptist minister in Australia, he had arrived on 1 December the previous year.

## BARRACKS

were built at Sydney Cove and completed in February 1789. They consisted of four wooden buildings, each designed to hold one company of soldiers and measuring 68ft by 22ft, and were arranged round a parade ground.

## BASIC WAGE

originated with the celebrated 'Harvester Judgement' of 8 November 1907, delivered by Mr Justice Higgins in the Commonwealth Arbitration Court. The founder of the Sunshine Harvester Works, Hugh McKay, sought a ruling that a wage of 36s a week was 'fair and reasonable'. Mr Justice Higgins made close enquiry into the cost of living and determined that to satisfy 'the normal needs of the average employee regarded as a human being living in a civilized community', a wage of £2 2s a week would be required for a 'family of about five'. This was made up of £1 5s 5d for food, 7s for rent and 7s 7d for sundries. The Harvester Judgement, though later overturned, had in time the effect of establishing the principle of a basic wage, sufficient for all necessities, as a right of the unskilled Australian worker.

## BEAUTY CONTEST

was organized in Sydney by the *Sunday Times* and held at Maroubra Beach on 18 February 1920. Billed as a competition to find 'the most beautiful surfing girl', it was the first in the world where the girls paraded in bathing costumes. (America followed Australia's lead the next year with the inauguration of the Miss America contest.) The winner, who received £25 and a gold medal, was 14 year old Edith Pickup of Manly, who wore a bathing costume sufficiently brief to reveal her thighs, and an exotic slave bangle on her upper right arm. The *Sunday Times* declared that 'she moves naturally daintily, winsomely, modestly' and waxed lyrical about 'the true charm of fresh girlishness that you will seek in vain among the Sennet bath-

*Governor's House, Sydney, the venue of the first banquet, from a watercolour by William Bradley.*

ing beauties and all such professional. types'.

The paper explained that the reason for holding the contest in swimsuits was to promote the idea of the one piece bathing costume, which they were confident 'no sane person could take exception to'. (A lot of people, whether sane or not, were taking grave exception to such scanty attire in 1920). The runners up were Miss Ethel Warren and Miss Dorothy Wooley. The latter, the *Sunday Times* was at pains to explain, could not have been allowed first place as she had but recently 'emerged from childhood'. Given that the winner was only 14, this casts an interesting sidelight on the age at which girls matured 70 years ago — photographs of Miss Pickup portray a young lady who might have been in her 20s. Australia does not appear to have been exceptional in this respect — the first Miss America, elected the following year, was 15.

**The first national beauty contest** was organized by the *Daily Guardian* for the title of 'Miss Australia', seven finalists out of hundreds of hopefuls parading on the stage of the St James' Theatre, Sydney on 25 June 1926. The girls appeared first in black bathing costumes, then in a swimsuit of their own choice, followed by sports dress, street dress — at this juncture they were obliged to take afternoon tea on the stage to demonstrate

Mitchell Library

their social aplomb — and finally in evening dress. No make-up was allowed. The winner was 19 year old brunette Beryl Mills of Geraldton, Western Australia, 5 ft 6½ ins tall and a not inconsiderable 9 stone 11 lbs in weight. (A well-fed look appears to have been what the judges had in mind — none of the finalists was particularly slender.) Miss Mills won about 50 different prizes, most of them donated by sponsors, including 100 guineas and a dress ring of diamonds and platinum, a trip to Atlantic City for her and a chaperon to see the Miss America Contest, together with £500 for expenses, 'sufficient sweets to last Miss Australia until she reaches America' (dieting seems to have had nothing to do with beauty in 1926), soap for the rest of her life, three years of free dental treatment (handy if she ate all the sweets) and a 'florally decorated monster boomerang'. Beryl Mills was married twice and lived most of her life in America, where she died in 1977 aged 70.

## BATHROOM

The first house with baths as fixed installations (as opposed to portable tubs) was Roslyn Hall, Rushcutters Bay, designed by Ambrose Hallen for Thomas Barker c. 1830. The baths, located in the bedrooms, were so constructed that they lay flush with the floor,

so you stepped down into them. The first house with a bathroom was Camden Park, built at Camden, NSW, by John Verge for John Macarthur in 1833.

## BEER

was brewed by John Boston, a free settler who arrived in Sydney in October 1794. He set about building a brewery and in 1796 began producing ale made from 'Indian corn, properly malted and bittered with the leaves and stalks of . . . the Cape gosebery'. It sold for 1s 6d a bottle, undercutting the price of a bottle of London porter by 6d. Boston was a jack of all trades — besides being a brewer he was also a miller, salt maker, fish curer, soap boiler, trader and shipowner. An ardent republican, he hated authority and during the Governorship of Philip Gidley King was wont to drink to 'the damnation of all Kings'. He came to the kind of bad end often predicted for him — in a cannibal's cooking pot in Tonga.

**The first beer brewed from hops** was produced by James Squires of the *Malting Shovel* public house at Kissing Point (near Ryde), NSW, in 1806. Squires had come out with the First Fleet and was the first to cultivate hops successfully, planting a number of vines at Eastern Farm, the site of his pub, in 1804. As a reward for conferring such a boon on the young colony, he was presented with a cow by order of the Governor. Squires' beer became famous throughtout New South Wales, being of a quality far superior to any domestic brew produced before, and he became known by the sobriquet of 'The Whitbread of Australia'. There were some few voices of dissent. It may have been a rival who had an inscription carved on a headstone in St John's Cemetery Parramatta, which read: 'He who drinks Squires' beer, lies here'.

Beer was a great boon in the pioneer days of the colony, as it afforded an alternative to rum, which was drunk in prodigious quantities to the detriment of the general health of the population and to the good order of society generally. It was also a great deal cheaper — Squires' table beer was available at 6d a gallon and strong ale for 1s a gallon.

**Lager beer** was introduced into Australia from Germany by Hamburg-born Bernard Otto Holtermann of Sydney in 1877. Holtermann is better known as the proprietor of the Star of Hope Gold Mine, where the largest ever nugget of gold, weighing 630 lbs, was found in 1872. He is also remembered for the fact that he was born, arrived in

# The first . . .

Australia, and died all on the same day of the same month — 29 April.

Foster's lager was first brewed at Collingwood, Vic, in November 1888 and put on sale on 1 February 1889.

Australia's oldest brewery is the Cascade Brewery in Hobart, which was founded by Peter Degraves in 1822.

## BICYCLE

was a 'boneshaker' built by W. A. George at Bathurst, NSW, in 1867 with the help of 'an ingenious Yankee'. This was over a year before bicycles appeared in England. Progress thereafter was slow, and even by 1883, when the first Sydney cycle dealers opened, there were less than 100 bicycles in New South Wales. In May of the following year one A. Edwards demonstrated how practical a form of locomotion it was by riding from Sydney to Melbourne. It was only in 1892 though, when the safety bicycle began to catch on in Australia, that cycling either as sport or as transport began to make an impact on Australian life. It was reported in 1896 that about a thousand riders passed in and out of Sydney daily — 'barristers, doctors, lawyers, merchants, clerks, canvassers, workmen, Chinamen, women in society, women out of society, women of the world, women of the half-world, one or two in divided skirts, and two or three in "bloomers"'.

See also Cycle Race.

## BIKINI

was worn by Miss Pat Riley on Bondi Beach in 1946 and consisted of a two piece bathing costume made of blue netting. She was ordered by police to leave the beach. The first bikini in the world had been designed by couturier Louis Reard and unveiled at a Paris fashion show on 5 July 1946, just four days after the Americans had detonated an atomic bomb at Bikini Atoll in the Pacific. The word 'bikini' was used by M. Reard to signify 'the ultimate'. Evidently the Sydney police thought it was too.

## BILLIARDS

had been introduced to Australia by 1809, emancipist D. D. Mann recording that 'the officers of the colony have . . . built a private billiard-room, by subscription, for their own use'.

## BILLIARD TABLES

were manufactured by Henry Upton Alcock, not himself a billiards player, at Fitzroy, Melbourne in 1853. Alcock found great difficulty in obtaining suitable slate for the beds of his tables, but the problem was overcome when he discovered an unusual source of supply. Prefabricated houses made entirely of slate had been imported from England and erected at Collingwood. By buying up a number of these houses, Alcock was able to keep his factory going.

## BIONIC EAR

in the world, a speech processor which sends nerve impulses directly to the brain of deaf people, was developed by Prof. Graeme Clark of the University of Melbourne and implanted in the mastoid bone of a patient's inner ear for the first time in 1979. The sound of talking as heard by a bionic ear has been described as like hearing Donald Duck on a transistor radio; it is nevertheless an enormous advance for the totally deaf. The device was produced commercially by Nucleus Ltd of Sydney, the first implant of a standard fitment being made on 14 September 1982.

University of Sydney

*William Grant Broughton, the first Anglican Bishop in Australia.*

## BISCUIT FACTORY

was opened in Adelaide by W. Menz & Co. in 1850.

## BISHOP, ANGLICAN

was William Grant Broughton (1788-1853), installed at St. James' Church, Sydney, as Bishop of Australia on 5 June 1836. Broughton had first come to Australia from England as Archdeacon of NSW in 1829 and is remembered as the founder of the King's School at Parramatta in 1832. He became Bishop of Sydney in 1847 when bishops were appointed for Melbourne, Adelaide and Newcastle. Tasmania had been made a separate diocese in 1842.

**The first Archbishop** was William Saumarez Smith (1836-1909), who became Archbishop of Sydney in 1897.

## BISHOP, ROMAN CATHOLIC

was John Bede Polding (1794-1877), who was already Bishop of Hiero-Caesarea when he arrived at Sydney as Vicar-Apostolic of the Australian Colonies on 13 September 1835. He was elevated to Archbishop of Sydney on 9 April 1842.

**The first bishop consecrated in Australia** was Francis Murphy as Bishop of Adelaide on 8 September 1844.

## BOYS' BRIGADE

was established in Melbourne by Prof. Henry Drummond, professor of Natural History at Free Church College, Glasgow, probably in May 1890. The first company, known now as the 1st Melbourne, was connected with the North Esk Church of Scotland. The movement had been founded in Glasgow in 1883 and eventually spread to over 60 countries worldwide.

## BREATHALYSER TESTS

were introduced in Victoria in November 1961. Random breath tests came into force in Victoria on 1 July 1976.

## BLACK BOX FLIGHT RECORDER

in the world was conceived and produced in prototype form by David Warren of the Aeronautical Research Laboratories, Melbourne, in 1958. Based on the Minifon, the first miniature tape recorder, Warren's 'Black Box' could record a flight crew's conversation, as well as aircraft speed, height, pitch and roll, for up to four hours on a very fine stainless steel wire impervious to fire damage. Instead of exploiting Australia's lead in this vital area of aeronautical safety, the Department of Civil Aviation and the RAAF ignored its importance and offered no support. After a judge inquiring into the mysterious crash of a Fokker Friendship in Queensland in 1960 had ordered all Australian airlines to carry flight crash recorders, the Department of Civil Aviation placed an order with an American firm, United Data Corporation. They decided to use magnetic tape instead of wire, with the result that the black box was useless in any crash involving fire or explosion. In the end it was left to the British firm of Darall to exploit, and spread worldwide, an Australian invention that could have been manufactured in Australia.

## BLOOD TRANSFUSION SERVICE

was the Red Cross Blood Transfusion Service, founded by Dr Lucy Boyce in 1926. Until 1938 donors were paid for their blood, a boon to many of the unemployed during the depression years. After a group of donors had held a meeting at the YMCA in Melbourne, and roundly condemned 'the acceptance of blood money', the unpaid voluntary principle was accepted.

## BOAT

built in Australia was a 12-ton launch of native timber, which was laid down by Mr Reid, carpenter of HMS *Supply*, in May 1789. She was used for transporting provisions from the stores at Sydney to the settlement at Rosehill (later called Parramatta). Launched on 5 October 1789, the vessel was officially called the *Prince of Wales*, but known to the convicts as the *Rose Hill Packet* or, more irreverently, as the *Lump* — an allusion to its squat appearance.

See also Ship.

## BOOK

was *New South Wales General Standing Orders: Selected from the General Orders ssued by Former Governors*, printed by the Government Printer, George Howe, at Sydney in 1802.

**The first book to be published as a commercial venture** was the *Colonial Pocket Almanac*, published at one dollar or 5s by George Howe of Sydney on 1 January 1806. The contents included a 'Monthly Kalendar, with Rising and Setting of the Sun and Moon', a chronology of all the important events since

# The first . . .

the discovery of Australia, a register of all vessels arriving and departing since the First Fleet, 'the Gardener, Farmer and Grazier's Kalendar' and 'A Compendium of General Orders', including all regulations affecting the citizenry of NSW.

**The first school book** published in Australia was an adaptation of Lindley Murray's *An English Spelling Book*, printed and published at Sydney in January 1810 by George Howe. The book was produced to the order of the Orphan School, but additional copies were also distributed to the Parramatta Public School and Mr Cook's Academy at Parramatta, while a number were made available for sale to the public.

None of the early school books survive. The earliest Australian school book extant is *Tables for the Use of Schools; intended as an Introduction to Arithmetic . . .*, Sydney, 1831. The single surviving copy was reported in 1955 to be in the collection of Dr. Mackaness of Sydney.

**The first illustrated book** published in Australia was *Birds of New South Wales*, published at Sydney by George Howe in 1813. The 18 engraved plates were by John William Lewin. Six copies of this rare work are known to survive.

**The first work of literature** published in book form and the **first biography** was *Michael Howe, the last and worst of the Bush Rangers of Van Diemens Land*, by Thomas E. Wells, issued by Andrew Bent at Hobart in 1818. Reviewing the slender 40 page work, the English *Quarterly Review* advised readers to get hold of 'this genuine Caxton item of Australian literature'. Few did so, for only three copies survive.

The first full-length work of literature published in Australia was *A Treatise on the Culture of the Vine, and the Art of Making Wine*, by James Busby, Sydney, 1825. According to an article in the *New South Wales Magazine* for September 1833, Busby's copious treatise — it ran to 270 pages — 'fell dead from the press'. At the time of its publication, 'few persons had thought of the vine as anything better than an ornament to their gardens, or an addition to their dessert'. Undeterred by this failure, Busby tried again in 1830 with a rather more slender volume of 100 pages titled *A Manual of Plain Directions for Planting and Cultivating Vineyards, and for Making Wine, in New South Wales* and this work was said 'to have led to

the cultivation of the vine by many colonists'. At the time of the publication of his first book, the 24 year old Busby was employed as an instructor in viticulture at the Male Orphan Asylum at Liverpool — perhaps the only school in the world to offer instruction in such a recondite subject. In 1832 he was appointed British Resident in New Zealand, the first official appointment in that country.

**The first book by an Australian-born author** was William Charles Wentworth's *A Statistical, Historical and Political Description of the Colony of New South Wales*, London, 1819.

**The first children's book** was *A Mother's Offering to her Children: by a Lady, long resident in New South Wales*, published at the *Sydney Gazette* office in 1841. The authoress is believed to have been Lady Gordon Bremer, as the book is dedicated to Master Reginald Gipps, with whose parents, Governor Sir George and Lady Gipps, she was staying at the time. The book contained stories of shipwrecks around Australia, a piece about the founding of Port Essington, anecdotes about Aborigines, natural history and some verse.

The first illustrated Children's book was *The Australian Picture Pleasure Book*, by W. G. Mason, published by bookseller J. R. Clarke of Sydney in 1857. It contained 200 engravings illustrative of Colonial Scenery, Architecture, Natural History, Portraits of distinguished or popular characters, Shipping, Public Events, Theatrical and Operative Notabilia, Etc Etc'. The artist and engraver, Walter Mason, had worked for *Punch* and the *Illustrated London News* before coming to Sydney in 1853. The first children's book with coloured illustrations was Cyrus Mason's *The Australian Christmas Story Book*, published by George Robertson, Melbourne, 1871.

**The first collection of short stories** was *Tales for the Bush* by Mrs Francis Vidal, published in eight parts (each a separate story) by D. L. Welch, Sydney, in 1845. The stories were subsequently published in London as a single volume, running to three editions in 1846.

See also: Atlas; Diary; Gazeteer; Law Book; Medical Treatise; Novel; Paperbacks; Poetry; Publisher; Song Book.

## BOOK REVIEWS

were published in the *Australian Quarterly Journal* in 1828. The first issue, published in Sydney in January of that year, contained reviews of Phillip Parker King's *Narrative of a Survey of the Intertropical and Western Coasts of Australia*, London 1826; and Lancelot

Threlkeld's *Specimens of a Dialect of the Aborigines of New South Wales*, Sydney, 1827. They were probably written by the editor, the Rev. Charles P. N. Wilson, Master of the King's Female Orphan Institution at Parramatta.

## BOOKER PRIZE

The first Australian winner of the booker Prize was Thomas Keneally for *Schindler's Ark* on 19 October 1982. The Booker Prize is the UK's most prestigious literary award.

## BOOKMAKER

to operate on-course in Australia was Bob Sutton at Morphettville race-track, SA, in June 1882.

## BOOKMATCHES

were produced by Bryant & May of Richmond, Vic, in 1926.

## BOOKSHOP

was the Australian Stationery Warehouse, Lower George Street, Sydney, founded in 1829 by 19 year old Glasgow immigrant William McGarvie.

The oldest bookshop in Australia is Birchalls of Launceston, Tas, founded in 1844.

## BOTANIC GARDENS

were formally established by Governor Macquarie in Sydney in 1816 with the appointment of Charles Fraser as 'Colonial Botanist'. The Gardens already at that date contained plants cultivated from seed brought by the First Fleet from Rio de Janeiro and Cape Town and planted at what was originally the Government Farm. The oldest plants in the Gardens today are the Sydney Red Forest Gums, which were in situ when the First Fleet arrived in 1788. Although Sydney Botanic Gardens are among the most extensive and justly celebrated in the world, the land on which it was established consisted of poor quality sandy soil of very little depth. The topsoil had to be brought from elsewhere and made fertile with the addition of humus and compost. Sydney Botanic Gardens became a public park on 30 April 1838.

## BOWLS

The first game was played between T. Burgess and F. Lipscombe for a small stake at Lipscombe's Beach Tavern, Sandy Bay, near Hobart on 1 January 1844. Burgess won by 'the odd game out of 25'. Subsequently Australia's **first bowling green** was laid out at the Beach Tavern and this is known to have been in use by 26 November 1844.

*The first bowls club* was established by John Robinson with the opening of his bowling green at the Boundary Stone Inn, Surry Hills, Sydney, on 10 November 1845. Members met to play on Saturday afternoons.

*The first bowls made in Australia* were turned by Thomas Eades of Parramatta in 1867 for the local tailor, Alexander Johnstone, who practised with them by himself in a paddock at Elizabeth Farm until the neighbours began to doubt his sanity. The **first plastic bowls** in the world were produced from phenolformaldehyde in April 1931 by Hanselite of Melbourne.

*The first interstate match* was held at Annandale, NSW, on 14 April 1880, when Victoria defeated New South Wales 112 to 91.

*Bowls was first played by women* in Australia at Stawell, Vic, in October 1881. **The first club for women** was the Rainsford Bowling Club, founded at the residence of J. Rainsford Needham, which had a private green, at Glenferrie, Melbourne on 16 December 1898.

## BOX KITE

in the world was constructed by aeronautical pioneer Lawrence Hargrave of Sydney and flown at Stanwell Park, near Bulli, NSW, on 16 February 1893. On 12 November 1894 a string of four kites lifted him 16 ft above the surface of the beach at Stanwell Park. Only one of Hargrave's box-kites survives in Australia, preserved at Sydney's Museum of Applied Arts and Sciences. The remainder are at the Deutsches Museum in Munich.

## BOXING

The first recorded boxing match took place in the third week of April 1803 between two unnamed assailants, a butcher and a blacksmith. The blacksmith, it was recorded in the *Sydney Gazette*, eventually called a halt to the contest 'from motives of compassion' in order to spare his opponent further injury.

*The first recorded match under regular prize-fight rules* was fought on Sydney racecourse at Hyde Park on 7 January 1814, when John Berringer defeated Charles Lifton in a bare knuckle contest which lasted for 56 rounds. Both contestants were required to run half a mile before the fight.

# The first . . .

The first Australian-born fighter to defeat a boxer from overseas was 'Young' Kable of Windsor, NSW, who knocked out a visiting English pugilist called Clark in under ten minutes on 20 February 1824.

The first heavyweight champion of Australia was Bill Farnan of Victoria, who won his title at Melbourne against Peter Jackson of Sydney on 26 July 1884 with a knock-out in the third round.

The contest was also the first championship fought with gloves. Bare-knuckle boxing was ruled illegal the same year after the death of Alex Edgar at Randwick, NSW.

The first women's boxing tournament was held at King Island, Tasmania, in 1978. Contestants wore breast shields.

## BRICKS

were the first items of manufacture undertaken in Australia, Charles Worgan, the Surgeon aboard the Sirius, reporting on 27 February 1788 that '8 or 10 convicts of the trade are now employed in the business'. They were used in the construction of two storehouses and of Government House, the first permanent structures in New South Wales.

Until the 1870s, most bricks produced in Australia conformed to the standard English dimensions. At that time the Hoffmann Brick Co of Melbourne became pre-eminent in the trade and Australian bricks have since adhered to the German standard of 9 x 4½ x 3 ins.

## BRICK VENEER

was used for the first time in the world on a house called Tyntynder, near Swan Hill, Vic, in 1850. Built by Peter Beveridge, the walls of the house were tied with hoop-iron straps running lengthways with the bricks. Beveridge also burnt lime for mortar and made the bricks on the site.

The first brick veneer cladding (i.e. half-depth bricks) in the world was used on a Melbourne house by architect John Gawler in 1915. This enabled a timber frame house to assume the dignity of brick at half the cost, though it was not until 1930 that the system was considered sound enough for a bank loan. By the 1960s brick veneer was being used on on some 50% of the houses built in Victoria.

## BRIDGE

was a rude construction of logs built over the Tank Stream at Sydney soon after the arrival of the First Fleet in January 1788. In 1803 it collapsed under the weight of a bullock wagon and was replaced by the first stone bridge in Australia, which was opened on the 27 March 1804. This structure served until the Tank Stream was covered over in the 1840s. The track which led to and from it later became Bridge Street, so named after the Tank Stream Bridge.

The first road bridge was the Duck River Bridge on the Sydney-Parramatta road, built in 1796.

The first bridge built of reinforced concrete was built in 1905 to span the Hawkesbury River at Richmond, NSW, and consisted of thirteen arch spans of 50 ft each.

The oldest bridge in Australia is a 210 ft masonry arch built by convicts over the Coal River at Richmond, Tas, in 1825.

## BRITISH PRIME MINISTER TO VISIT AUSTRALIA

while in office was the Rt Hon. Harold Macmillan, who arrived at Sydney on 28 January 1958.

## BROTHELS, LEGALISED

were first permitted under Victoria's Planning (Brothels) Act which became law on 22 May 1984.To obtain a permit, Madames had to publish a notice of declaration in a newspaper and fix a notice of intent on the premises. No brothel keeper was allowed to have an interest in any other brothels. One immediate effect of the measure was to take the girls off the streets, a transformation in certain areas of Melbourne.

## BUILDINGS (permanent)

were two public storehouses, for which work began on 26 January 1788 with the clearing of the ground. This was the day the first batch of convicts landed at Port Jackson. The buildings, which were made of timber thatched with reeds, were completed in May.

The first permanent dwelling was a stone-built house for the Lieutenant-Governor, construction of which began on the west side of Sydney Cove in April 1788. The first brick-built dwelling was Government House, started on 15 May at the corner of what were to become Phillip and Bridge

Streets. It had two storeys and was surrounded with a verandah supported by columns, the accommodation consisting of a large reception room, 50 ft by 18½ ft, a salon, a dining room, a parlour, and kitchen on the ground floor and bedrooms on the upper floor. Although intended to be temporary, Old Government House, which Macquarie said was 'in point of Size Altogether inadequate to the Residence and Accommodation of even a private Gentleman's Family and much less that of the Governor in Chief', did service as the official residence of numerous dissatisfied Governors until 1843 and was not finally pulled down until 1868.

Other buildings erected during the first year of settlement, with months they were started, included: a bakehouse (March), hospital (March), barracks (March), huts for women convicts and for officers (April), a spirits store (June), an observatory (July), a cottage for Major Ross, Commandant of the Royal Marines (July), a boat-house (December), and a small dwelling for a captured Aboriginal (December).

## BUILDING REGULATIONS
were introduced by an Act effective from 1 January 1838. This applied to Sydney only and prohibited buildings of timber. Already by 1842 the authors of *Sydney Illustrated* were able to report that the weatherboard huts of early Sydney were disappearing and being replaced by 'the stately structures of polished freestone, that are rapidly rising in every part of town'. The provisions of the Act helped to create a colonial metropolis of substantial but elegant late Georgian buildings that was, in its full flowering, a masterpiece of harmonious and pleasing architecture. Save for a few houses in Macquarie Street and Lower Fort Street, little of this golden age of Sydney's development survives. The destruction of the latter is reported to be imminent.

## BUS
was imported in 1836 from London, where the first buses had started running seven years earlier. The *Sydney Gazette* of 12 April reported: 'Mr. Grose, the merchant of George Street, has in his store a splendid omnibus, the first ever brought to these shores. From its capaciousness it is well adapted to carry passengers from one end of Sydney to the other, at set hours, in wet or hot weather'. What happened to this bus is a mystery, as there is no record of it ever going into service. Nothing further is heard of buses in Sydney until 1842. On 16 April of that year the *Sydney Morning Herald* reported that the first licensed omnibus was now running. This

*One of the earliest motor buses, possibly.*

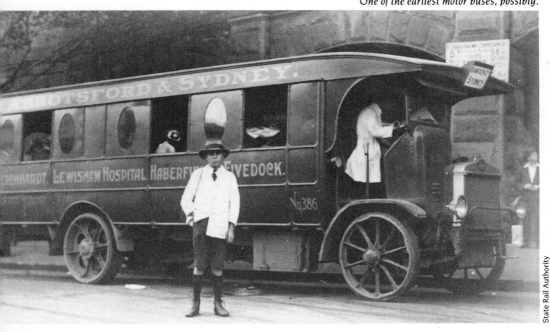

# The first ...

consisted, however, of a small open vehicle which the paper described as being like an Irish jaunting car — a far cry from Mr. Grose's elegant equipage. From the evidence of a drawing of George Street executed by John Rae about this time it would appear that the jaunting car may have been only a stop-gap, because this shows a conventional omnibus of the London pattern. Certainly by 1848 Sydney had a public transport system, since B.C. Peck, who left for England that year, states in his *Recollections of Sydney* that buses ran the length of George Street at half-hourly intervals, fare 6d, with branch services from the George Street terminus to Paddington and Surry Hills.

*The first motor buses* in Australia were the *Pioneer* and the *Progress*, built at the Vulcan Foundry, Geelong, Vic, in 1903 by Humble and Sons for the Albion Magnet Co of Melbourne. It was not until two years later, though, that motor buses went into public service. First in the field was Hobart, where the Electric Tramway Co began running two British-built petrol-driven Milnes-Daimlers to and from Moonah, Glenorchy and Berriedale on 25 March 1905. They remained in service for six months and were then withdrawn because their solid rubber tyres were found to be doing so much damage to the surface of the roads. On 4 December 1905 a small fleet of steam buses, two 18-seat single deckers and two 34-seat double deckers, started to ply between Potts Point and Darlinghurst in Sydney and during the same month the Melbourne Railway Department also introduced steam buses on the route from Prahran station to Malvern.

See also Motor Coach

## BUSH NURSE

was Melbourne-trained Mary Thompson, who took up her post at the remote township of Beech Forest, Vic, on 18 February 1911. She was appointed by the Australian Order of District Nursing, an organization founded the previous year by the Countess of Dudley, wife of the Governor-General, who was concerned that Australia had no organized district nursing system of the kind existing in Britain and Canada. Subscribers paid from 15s — 30s p.a. for nursing services for themselves and their families.

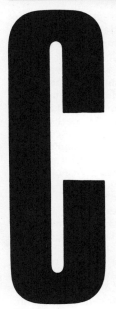

## CAB

to ply for hire was a hackney coach put into service in Sydney by a Mr Hart on 15 November 1830. In 1833 Governor Bourke noted that there were already several hackneys plying for hire in the capital of the colony.

## CALL GIRLS

in the literal sense, meaning ladies of easy virtue whose services could be ordered by telephone, were operating in Melbourne as early as 1891. The leading city brothels established a telephone network to enable tired businessmen to book the girl of their choice without the need of a personal visit. This may be an Australian world first, no earlier instance having been recorded.

## CAMEL

in Australia was landed at Port Adelaide in October 1840. It was employed by John Horrocks on an expedition he made in 1846 to look for sheep runs west of Lake Torrens, but an unfortunate accident occurred when the camel, which was kneeling with Horrocks on its back, lurched sideways and caused its passenger's gun to go off. Horrocks was so badly wounded that he died a month later; the camel was shot in retribution.

Camels first proved their worth in the desert areas of Australia when 24 were brought over from Karachi for the Burke and Wills Expedition in 1860. Having succeeded in traversing Australia from South to North with the aid of these camels, the explorers, before they perished on the return journey, slaughtered them for food.

## CANNED BEER
the first beers sold in cans were Fosters Lager and Victoria Bitter by Carlton and United Breweries Ltd of Melbourne in January 1958. The inaugural 'tinnies' were made of steel and held 13⅓ fluid ounces.

## CANNED FOODS
consisted of preserved beef, mackerel and carrots, which were awarded a second-class prize at an 'exhibition of articles of commerce' held in Sydney on 30 September 1846. The canner was Sizar Elliott and he subsequently established a small plant producing canned goods for visiting American ships.

*The first full-scale canning factory* was inaugurated by the grazier brothers Henry and William Dangar at Honeysuckle Point, Newcastle, NSW, in 1847. The meat they canned consisted of beef, mutton, tongues and bouillon. By the year 1867, canned Australian meat had become a fairly significant element of English working class diet. This was before canned meat began to be imported into Britain from America.

*Fruit canning* was begun by H. Jones and Co. in Hobart in 1891. The same firm pioneered fish canning on a commercial scale in 1905.

## CANOES
were 'Rob Roy' Canadian-style kayaks used by Elia F. D'Arrob and a Mr Essex to paddle the Goulburn River and the Murray River from Seymour to Echuca, Vic, in April 1873. The 220 mile trip took them two weeks.

*The first canoe club* was the Victorian Canoe Club, founded in 1912.

## CAPITAL PUNISHMENT, ABOLITION OF
was first enacted by Queensland in 1922. Offences formerly carrying the death penalty became punishable by life imprisonment and the law did not allow for any reduction in sentence. Such was the resort to hanging in the early days of Australia's development that it was not until 1824 that a criminal session was held at Sydney at which there were no capital convictions. Public hanging had been abolished in NSW in 1853 and in Victoria in 1854. The last person to be hanged

in Australia was Ronald Ryan at Melbourne's Pentridge Prison on 9 January 1967. Ryan had been found guilty of murdering a warder during a gaol break.

## CAR RADIO
was fitted to a Summit, an Australian built car made by Kelly's Motors of Alexandria, NSW, in 1924. Passengers listened in through headphones and the aerial was attached to the waterproof hood. The 1925 model was offered for sale with radio as an optional extra, the first car in the world to be so equipped.

## CARDINAL
was Irish-born Patrick Francis Moran (1830-1911), Archbishop of Sydney, who was created a Cardinal by Pope Leo XIII on 27 July 1885.

*The first Australian-born cardinal* was His Eminence Cardinal Norman Gilroy (1896-1977) of Sydney, a former GPO messenger boy and telegraph operator, who was elevated to the purple at the early age of 49 on 24 December 1945.

## CARRIAGE
was brought to Australia by John and Elizabeth Macarthur, probably in 1795. In a letter to her friend Miss Kingdom, Mrs Macarthur wrote from Elizabeth Farm, Parramatta, on 1 September of that year: 'We use our horses both for pleasure and profit; they alternately run in the chaise or cart'. A chaise was a light two-wheeled passenger vehicle drawn by a single horse. The 'very good carriage road' linking Sydney and Parramatta had only been built in 1794, so it is unlikely the Macarthurs would have found any use for a carriage before that.

*The first self-propelled road vehicle* in Australia was a three-wheeler, nine seat steam carriage with a 5hp engine built in 1879 by a Swiss called Gilgen who lived near Adelaide. There was a charcoal fired boiler under the seat, and the vehicle had a top speed of 20 mph. Prince Alfred and Prince Edward met Gilgen and saw his steam carriage during their tour of Australia in 1880. It is not recorded whether they rode in it. Eventually the Swiss was told to take his contraption off the road because it frightened the horses.

## CARTOON
of the joke rather than the political kind appeared in the first issue of *Melbourne Punch* on

# The first . . .

2 August 1856. Drawn by *Punch's* Russian-born resident staff artist Nicholas Chevalier, it showed an over decorated drawing room with a music teacher supervising the efforts of a disagreeable looking child at the piano while the indulgent mother looks on. The caption, like those below the cartoons in the London *Punch* of the day, was lengthy:

'*Charming and Astute Professor.* — I assure you, Mrs Lukydygar, your delightful little daughter is a perfect prodigy.

'*Mrs Lukydygar.* — I dunno what you mean by a "prodigy", Mr Gamut. The only one as I ever see, was kep in a bottle o'sperrits at a show. But she do play beautiful to be sure.'

The name was a play on 'lucky digger', indicating that the family was a nouveau riche one who had made their pile in the gold rush.

See also Newspaper cartoon.

## CASINO

was the Wrest Point Casino at Hobart, opened on 10 February 1973.

## CASTOR

The modern castor with an inclined domed wheel, of the type used on most of the mobile equipment used in hospitals and on office furniture, was invented by Melbourne oil engineer George Shepherd. A bridge enthusiast, Shepherd felt that the game would be much enhanced by properly designed furniture and in the 1930s he proceeded to design a special card table whose height could be adjusted and chairs which were comfortable for people sitting upright. The one drawback to the chairs was the castors — if you tried to move your chair when you were sitting in it, the castors embedded themselves into the carpet, often in different directions. He set about designing a castor that would not sink into the carpet, aligned properly, had strong bearings to eliminate wobble, was self lubricating and did not jam through an accumulation of dirt. His design, which had the pivot housed inside an inclined wheel, incorporated all these features, including an oil trap for lubrication and a domed cover to keep the moving parts free from lint and dust. The first 60 experimental models he fitted to his own furniture in 1939. The war halted com-

*The Wrest Point Casino, Hobart.*

Federal Hotels

mercial development, but the first production models were manufactured by Consolidated Castors in 1946. they are now used throughout the world.

## CATHEDRAL

was St Mary's Cathedral, Sydney, of which the foundation stone was laid by Governor Macquarie on 20 October 1821. The cost of the edifice was met by subscriptions, not only from Catholics but from many protestant well-wishers. When private resources began to fail, the Governor undertook to match private subscriptions from the public coffers. The cathedral was consecrated by Archbishop Polding on 29 June 1836.

**The first Anglican cathedral** to be consecrated was St James', Melbourne on 30 December 1853. The foundation stone had been laid in 1839 and the incomplete building opened for worship three years later. The foundation stone of St Andrew's, Sydney, had been laid considerably earlier, in 1819, but the cathedral was not consecrated until 1868 and the building only completed in 1877.

## CATS

were brought to Australia with the First Fleet by the Rev. Richard Johnson. In November 1788 he wrote home to England describing the delinquencies of the two animals, the first pets known to have been kept by anyone in the new land. '...Miss Puss has lately behaved so ill — and made such bad work in my garden, that I was obliged to have a Court Marshal upon her: that after frequent threatenings I was at length resolved she should be transported, and accordingly have shipped her off to New Norfolk...Tom Puss is come to high preferment — tired of such poor fare as I could give him, he took himself to the publick stores where he feeds upon the richest dainties of the country'.

## CATTLE FAIR

was held at Parramatta on 11 March 1813 'for the sale of Horses, Horned Cattle and Sheep and was numerously attended with a great Show of cattle...' It was reported that 'two individuals alone disposed of horned cattle to the value of upwards of £600'. The *Sydney Gazette* said that 'the novelty of the occurance, this having been the first fair ever held in New South Wales, drew a vast concourse of persons of all ranks together, many out of curiosity to view a scene which tended so strongly to remind them of their native Country...'

## CATTLE DRIVE

took place in 1837, when John Gardiner, Joseph Hawdon, John Hepburn and George Hitchcock — the first 'overlanders' — drove a mob of cattle several hundred miles from the Murray River to the Port Phillip district.

## CEMETERY

The earliest known tombstone is that of George Graves, boatswain's yeoman of HMS *Sirius*, who died aged 48 on 12 July 1788 and was buried in the original Sydney cemetery on the ridge west of Lower George Street. It is now preserved at Vaucluse House.

Sydney's second cemetery was on the present site of Clarence Street, and used until 1792 or 3. The third, on the side of Sydney Town Hall, came into use in 1793 and continued until 1820. The oldest existing burial ground is St John's Churchyard, Parramatta, where the earliest grave is that Elizabeth Scott, who died 1 April 1789.

## CENSUS(*official*)

was conducted in New South Wales (which then included Tasmania) in 1828, when the European population was 36, 595, of whom 46.4% were convicts.

Men outnumbered women by 27,611 to 8,987 and Protestants outnumbered Catholics by 25,248 to 11,236. Native born white Australians numbered 8,727 or 24% of the total. The population of Sydney was 10,815, a figure which had nearly doubled to just under 20,000 when the next census was conducted nine years later.

The first official census of South Australia took place in 1844, with a return of 17,366 inhabitants of European stock, and the first of Western Australia in 1848, with a return of 11,976.

The non-Aboriginal population of Australia first topped one million in 1858. This represented 60% increase in population since 1850, the intervening period of such remarkable growth being the Gold Rush years. The population doubled to two million by 1877 and reached 3 million in 1889, 4 million in 1905, 5 million in 1918, 6 million in 1925, 7 million in 1939, 8 million in 1949, 10 million in 1959, 12 million in 1968, 15 million in 1981 and 16 million in 1987.

**The first national census** was held on 3 April 1881, when the combined population of the six Australian colonies was 2¼ million. Only

# The first . . .

2½% were aged over 65, while 40% were 14 and under.

## CHAMBER OF COMMERCE

was founded at Sydney in 1826 with 30 members.

## CHANNEL SWIM BY AN AUSTRALIAN

was achieved by 20-year old Linda McGill of Sydney, who made the crossing in 11 hrs 25 mins on 7 August 1965. The earliest Australian attempt had been made in 1907 by Annette Kellerman, the swimming champion and film star who achieved notoriety as the first woman to appear on screen in the nude.

## CHARITY

was the New South Wales Society for Promoting Christian Knowledge and Benevolence in these Territories and the Neighbouring Islands, founded by a group of seven philanthropists on 8 May 1813. Under gentle pressure from Governor Macquarie, who was not a great believer in missionary endeavour among the heathen, the Society concentrated its efforts on the relief of distress in Sydney. During the first years it operated, the SPCK gave assistance to 618 destitute people at a cost of £981. Most of this was in the form of food, but could extend to other necessities, as in the case of 'Robert Jones — about 60 years of age infirm and helpless and rather deranged in mind — to be relieved with trousers and flannel shirt and jacket. In 1818 the SPCK was merged into the newly established Benevolent Society of NSW.
*The first street collection for charity* took place in Sydney on 28 April 1894 in aid of the hospitals.

## CHESS CLUB

was the Australian Chess Club, founded in Sydney in 1840.

## CHILD BENEFIT

was introduced in February 1927 in NSW at the rate of 5s a week per child for families receiving no more than the basic wage. The first child allowance in the world had been pioneered by New Zealand a year earlier. A national system of child endowment for Australia was inaugurated on 29 July 1941, 5s per week being paid for every child under 16 after the first.

## CHILDREN'S ENTERTAINMENT

was a Galanty Show whose arrival in Sydney from England was reported in the *Sydney Gazette* of 10 June 1804. A type of pantomime in which the shadows of articulated figures were thrown upon a screen, a Galanty Show was like a primative form of cinema. The *Sydney Gazette* said that its introduction to Australia 'will undoubtedly seem a very insignificant article of intelligence', but reflected on the fact that as life was made up of trifles, perhaps a future historian might give it a place in some compendium of odd facts.

## CHORUS GIRLS

were the members of Miss Emily Soldene's Company who came to Australia in 1877 and opened in Adelaide with the musical extravaganza *Geneviève de Brabant*. The young ladies had previously toured America, where they were described as 'beefy Britishers', indicating no doubt that they rejoiced in the ample bosoms, majestic thighs and rounded limbs that were the hallmark of the Victorian showgirl.

## CHRISTIAN SCIENCE

services were conducted in Melbourne in 1898. A Reading Room opened the same year.

## CHRISTENING

was conducted at Botany Bay by the Rev. Richard Johnson on 21 January 1788. The son of Joshua Bentley, sailor, and Mary Bolton, convict, was christened Joshua. He did not survive infancy, his burial being recorded on 14 February 1790.

## CHURCH

was a 'wattle and daub' construction commenced by the Rev. Richard Johnson, chaplain to the colony of NSW, on 10 June 1793. Situated at the corner of what were later Bligh and Hunter Streets, the Church served 500 worshippers and cost £67 12s 11d to build.

The acting Governor, Major Grose, who first promised complete cooperation in the venture, and then did everything in his power to obstruct it, observed that 'his charge for this church is infinitely more than it ought to have cost' and that he considered

Johnson 'a troublesome, discontented character'. Major Grose was noticeably absent when the first service was held in the church on Sunday, 25 August 1793, though Mrs Grose 'and some other Quality' attended.

The name of the Church is not known for certain, but it seems likely it was called St Phillip's, as was the replacement church started in 1798 after the first one had been burned down by convicts. (Probably because they were made to attend it.) The name was spelled with two 'ls' in honour of the first Governor of NSW.

The original St Phillip's stood near the intersection of what are now Castlereagh and Hunter Streets. It was replaced by a new St Phillip's, the **first stone-built church** in Australia, for which the foundation stone was laid on 7 October 1798. It was not completed until August 1809. A curious edifice, looking wholly unlike a conventional church, it had a round castellated tower. A new St Philip's (this time with one 'l') was erected adjacent to the old in the late 1840s and opened in 1856. This still stands.

The oldest church in Australia is the Ebenezer Presbyterian Church (now the Uniting Church), built at Swallow Rock Reach on the banks of the Hawkesbury north of Windsor by pioneer Scotch settlers between 1807-1809. The sturdy little stone-built chapel was probably designed by Andrew Johnson, described as 'an eminent settler and a reputed architect'.

The Anglican church in longest use is St Luke's at Liverpool, NSW, where the first service was conducted in 1819. St Matthew's at Windsor, NSW, where services have been held since 1822, was actually begun earlier, the foundation stone having been laid on 11 October 1817, whereas St Luke's was laid on 7 April 1818.

## CHURCH BELLS

arrived in Sydney aboard HMS *Reliance* in September 1795, having been cast by T. Mears of London the year before. They were intended for St Phillip's Church, but the tower still had not been completed when the church burned down in 1798, and the eight bells had to await the building of a new St Phillip's before they could be installed. The first peal was rung, nearly twelve years after the arrival of the bells, on 29 May 1807. They were eventually dispersed, one ending up on a lightship at Port Jackson and another at Bourke jail.

## CHURCH CHOIR

was established at St David's Church, Hobart Town, under the direction of J. Livingstone in 1821. This was only three years after the earliest recorded church choir in England. See also Orchestra.

**The first women choristers** in the world were introduced at St Paul's Pro-Cathedral, Melbourne, in 1887. They were clad in surplices and rounded trenchers. A contemporary journal reported: 'The effect was admirable on the whole, though Church composure was ruffled in some instances.'

## CHURCH SERVICE

was conducted on 3 February 1788 by the Rev. Richard Johnson under a 'great tree', thought by some to have been situated on the site of Macquarie Place in Sydney, by others to have been at George Street North. The convicts were ordered to attend and were 'expected to appear as clean as circumstances will admit'. Holy Communion was celebrated by Johnson on a table in the tent of Lieut. Clark of the Marines on 17 February. Clark wrote in his diary: 'I will keep the table as long as I live, for it is the first table that ever the Lord's supper was taken from in this country.' Services continued to be held under the 'great tree' until it was cut-down; then they were held under cover in a new store-room, but that became filled with stores; and next in an open sided boat-shed. Not until 1793, five years after settlement, was Sydney equipped with a church (see above).

## CIGARETTE CARDS

were issued in 1904 by Sniders and Abrahams of Melbourne, manufacturers of Standard, Peter Pan, King's Own and Milo cigarettes. The inaugural series was of Australian footballers, followed by a set of 31 Australian actresses. Perhaps the most novel Australian cigarette cards were the stereoscopic views, issued with a miniature viewer during World War I.

## CINEMA

was the Salon Cinématographie at 237 Pitt Street, Sydney, opened by Maurice Sestier of the Lumière Co on 27 September 1896. Admission was 1s and the opening programme included a number of actuality films shot locally (see Film). Australia was the fourth country in the world to exhibit movies in an auditorium solely used for that purpose, after

# The first . . .

France (December 1895), the USA (1896) and Germany (July 1896). Elsewhere at this time films formed part of music hall programmes or were shown in tented booths at fairgrounds.

**The first purpose-built cinema** was The King's Theatre in Railway Square, Sydney, which opened in 1910.

**The first cinema in the world to present a double bill** of feature length films was the Glacarium in Melbourne on 15 May 1911. The programme for the week was an Australian melodrama called *The Lost Chord* and an Italian-made historical epic *The Fall of Troy*.

## CIRCUS

was the Australian Olympic Circus, opened by Signor Dalle Case at a tented amphitheatre in Hunter Street, Sydney, on 26 January 1842. The equestrians, according to one who claimed to have been a frequenter of Astley's Amphitheatre in London, were 'far from excellent'. A short-lived venture, it lasted only until the end of June, when the structure was sold for a mere £140.

The oldest circus in the English-speaking world is Ashton's Circus, founded in 1851 at Launceston, Tas.

## CITRUS FRUIT

was oranges, lemons and limes grown from pips obtained by the Rev. Richard Johnson when the First Fleet put in at Rio de Janeiro and planted by him in 1788 in the garden of his residence in what was to become Bridge Street, Sydney. In 1790 he wrote to a friend in England that his fruit trees 'are now some two feet high, and very promising'.

The first to grow citrus fruits on a commercial scale was George Suttor, who planted an orchard near Parramatta in 1800.

## CITY WITH ONE MILLION INHABITANTS

was Sydney, whose population at the end of 1924 was 1,012,070.

## CIVIL COURT

was convened on 1 July 1788 before the Judge-Advocate, the Chaplain and the Surgeon General. Henry Cable and his wife, convicts, sought restitution of a parcel of clothes, books and other articles held by Duncan Sinclair, master of the *Alexander*. After Sinclair's defence had been heard on 5 July, to the effect that the parcel had been moved from one part of the ship to the other and some of the goods lost when it broke open, the court found for the plaintiffs and the defendant ordered to pay £15 in compensation. It is worthy of note that the first civil action in Australia was brought by a convict against a free man and that justice prevailed.

## CLAY TARGET SHOOTING

was begun in 1882 when Frank Albert and Arthur Parker, a dentist of Newport, Vic, acquired an 'Expert' trap from Cleveland, Ohio, and formed the Williamstown and Melbourne Gun Club on a site in Kororoit Creek Road. The original trap is still owned by Parker's descendants.

## CLIPPER

to arrive in Australia was the *Phoenician*, a 478-ton Aberdeen-built vessel which berthed at Sydney on 21 July 1849 after a run of 91 days. The average journey time from England at that time was 140 days. The fastest ever time was 60 days by the *Thermopylae* from London to Melbourne in 1869 and again in 1871.

## CLOCK-MAKER

was James Oatley, convict, who arrived at Sydney on 27 January 1815 and set up a clock manufactory.

## COCA COLA

was first bottled by Long & Barden in North Sydney in 1938. Meanwhile the Coca Cola Co was building its own bottling plant in Dowling Street, Waterloo.

## COAL

was first discovered at Port Stephens, NSW, in May 1796.

**The first coal mine** was opened at Coal River, NSW, under the direction of an experienced miner, John L. Platt, in June 1801. Four shafts were sunk, 34 yards, 31 yards, 27 yards and 10 yards deep, exposing two seams, one three feet thick, and the other 18 inches. The former yielded coal which was, in Platt's opinion, equal to the finest in England. The site was in the region of what is now Hunter Street, Newcastle, NSW. Following a mutiny of the convicts brought in to work the mine, the settlement was abandoned, but active operations were resumed in 1804.

**Coal briquettes** were first manufactured at Yallourn, Vic, in 1925.

## COINS

bearing an Australian inscription were the 'holey dollars' and 'dumps' issued by Gov. Macquarie in 1813. Due to the shortage of coin in New South Wales, the Governor arranged for the import of £10,000 worth of Spanish dollars from Madras. When these arrived aboard the sloop of war *Samarang* on the 26 November 1812, he ordered a convicted forger called William Hershell to start cutting a circular piece from the centre of each coin. These pieces, known as the 'dumps', were then smoothed and stamped with a Crown and 'New South Wales, 1813' on one side and with the value, fifteen pence, on the other. The dollars from which the 'dumps' had been cut were stamped 'New South Wales, 1813' around the rim of the hole on the obverse and 'Five Shillings' on the reverse. Prior to this date all kinds of gold, silver and copper currency, from various nations, circulated in the colony and was valued according to the weight of metal it contained.

**The first coins minted and circulated in Australia** as legal tender were the emergency issue of one pound gold pieces authorised by Act of the South Australian Parliament in November 1852. Known as 'Adelaide Pounds' because they were issued by the Adelaide Assay Office, they were struck from dies made by engraver Joshua Payne. A total of 24,648 sovereigns had been issued by 13 February 1853, when minting ceased as a contravention of the Royal Prerogative. An example was sold in Sydney on 20 November 1980 for US$82,000.

**The first mint** in Australia was the Royal Mint in Sydney, opened 14 May 1855. The first coins were struck on 23 June 1855. At its inception the Sydney Mint produced only sovereigns and half sovereigns. Imperial bronze coinage was first struck in 1868 and Imperial silver coinage in 1879. Issue continued until the closure of the Mint in 1926. The coins were legal tender in Victoria from 1857 and were generally accepted throughout Australia and New Zealand.

**The first Commonwealth of Australia coins** were shilling pieces, struck by the Royal Mint in London, which arrived at Sydney on 1 March 1910. Until the issue of Commonwealth coinage, the coins of Great Britain were legal tender throughout Australia.

A 'Holey dollar' and the 'dump' which was cut from the centre of the coin.              Westpac Bank

# The first . . .

## COMBINE HARVESTER

in the world was invented by Hugh Victor McKay of Raywood, Vic, in 1883 when he was only 17 years of age. He was the fifth of 12 children of a stonemason and miner who became a small farmer in the year of Hugh's birth. The prototype, completed in February 1884, was constructed of odd bits of broken farm machinery and a number of kerosene tins, together with other parts Hugh and his brother forged for themselves. This strange contraption, which nevertheless worked perfectly, was built in a rough bark-roofed hut which the brothers had erected to serve as a workshop. Five machines were made under contract in 1885 and regular manufacture of the 'Sunshine Harvester' begun in Ballarat in 1888.

At the time of McKay's death, the Sunshine plant extended over 28 acres of land and was a township in itself. The little hut with the bark roof in which the world's first combine harvester had been made stood on a lawn in front of the factory.

## COMIC BOOK

originated in Australia was *Jimmy Rodney on Secret Service*, drawn by Tony Rafty and published by the NSW Bookstall Co. Pty of Sydney, price 4d, in late 1940.

## COMIC STRIP

to appear regularly was drawn by Norman Lindsay and started running in *The Lone Hand* magazine in May 1907. It featured two Koalas called Billy Wattlegum and Tommy Topbough.

*The first coloured comic strip* was *Jim and Jam*, drawn by the poet Hugh McCrae, which began in Sydney's *The Comic Australian* on 21 October 1911.

*The first newspaper to carry comic strips* was Perth's *Western Mail*, which introduced the work of May Gibbs in May 1913. These strips did not have regular characters, but appeared under such titles as *The Pommy Imagination and Reality*, *The Animal Ball*, *The Henpecked Husband* and *Do we Resemble Animals?*

*The first Sunday newspaper colour comic section* appeared in the Sydney *Sunday Sun* on 13 November 1921. Among the four strips in the section was one entitled *Us Fellers*, which introduced one of Australia's classic comic strip characters, Ginger Meggs.

*The first daily comic strip* was *Casual Connie*, drawn by Jack Quangle, which began in Sydney's *Daily Telegraph Pictorial* on 19 December 1927. Connie was a typical daffy flapper girl of the period and the story line centred on her relationships with her parents and her two boyfriends, Aub and Porgy.

The oldest comic strip is Stan Cross's *The Potts*, which began as *You and Me* in *Smith's Weekly* on 6 August 1921.

## COMMUNIST PARTY

was formed on 30 October 1920 with the merger of the Victorian Socialist Party and the Sydney-based Australian Socialist Party.

## COMPANY TO OFFER SHARES TO ITS WORKFORCE

anywhere in the world was Mort's Dock and Engineering Co Ltd of Sydney in 1873. The founder of the company, T.S. Mort, offered the shares on particularly favourable terms, explaining that 'I as capitalist, and you as workers, should be bound together by a common tie, with the cords of common interest.' The scheme enabled employees to buy shares on deferment, paying for them gradually by deduction from pay. Nearly all the foremen became shareholders and a considerable number of other workers. Mort's intention was that half the company should be owned by its workforce.

## COMPUTER

was CSIRAC Mark 1, designed by Dr Trevor Pearcey of Sydney for CSIRO and operational in 1951. The fourth all-electronic computer in the world, CSIRAC used 2000 valves to perform its functions and operated one thousand times faster than the most advanced mechanical calculator.

*The first computer for commercial use* was RAMAC (Random Access Method of Accountancy and Control), installed at the Woolworths warehouse at Silverwater, Sydney, in November 1960. It provided a stock control system for all the Woolworths stores in New South Wales and was capable of processing up to 50,000 orders a day. At that date there was a total of 34 computers in Australia, most of them used for scientific work.

## CONCERT

took place in Sydney on 7 June 1826 and was one of ten held during the course of that year.

Little is known about the performers, though it seems that the concerts may have been organized, or at least liberally supported, by the merchant Solomon Levey. Known as the 'Sydney Amateur Concerts', they were of a semi-private nature. A concert was given in Hobart Town late in 1826, followed by another in January 1827, but applicants for tickets had to present themselves to a committee for approval and unless the ticket was countersigned by two members of this self-appointed board of social selection, the holder was not admitted. The first fully public concert was held at Australia's first concert hall, established by Solomon Levey's younger brother Barnett at his *Royal Hotel* in Sydney. The inaugural 'Vocal and Instrumental Concert' took place there on 20 August 1829. This was the first place of public entertainment in Australia since the demise of Sydney's pioneer theatre in 1800. The concert included Cherubini's *Overture to Lodoiska*; a comic song titled 'O no, we never mention him'; O *Lady Fair*, a quartette for flutes and horn; *Ye Banks and Braes*, another overture; and as a finale *The King, God Bless Him*. All seems to have gone well except the quartette, which was interrupted by the audience clinking their glasses — evidently they were allowed to drink as they listened.

## CONCRETE ROAD GUTTERS
were laid at Balmain, Sydney, in 1882.

## CONCRETE, READY-MIXED
was produced by Concrete Construction Ltd of Glebe, Sydney in July 1939. Australia was the second country in the world, after the USA, to introduce the concept of concrete delivered in vehicles with slowly rotating drums. Elsewhere it still had to be prepared on site.

## CONGREGATIONAL SERVICES
were held by William Pascoe Crook in August 1810 at his schoolhouse at the corner of Bligh and Hunter Streets, Sydney.
**The first Congregational Chapel** was opened in Pitt Street, Sydney, on 15 February 1833.

## CONTRACEPTIVE PILL
was announced by Federal Health Department officials in February 1961. The pill had originally been developed by Dr Gregory Pincus of the Worcester Foundation for Experimental Biology at Shrewsbury, Mass., and introduced in the USA for general use in August 1960.

## COOKERY BOOK
was the *English and Australian Cookery Book for the Many as well as the "Upper Ten Thousand"* by 'An Australian Aristologist', London, 1864. This nom de plume, intended to connote a student of 'the art of dining', cloaked the identity of Edward Abbot, a Tasmanian bon viveur, founder of the *Hobart Town Advertiser* and Member for Clarence in the Tasmanian Legislature. His set menus were agreeably indigenous. A 'colonial banquet' consists of asparagus, turtle soup, trumpeter with butter sauce, lamb à *la poulette*, roast kangaroo, Australian blue cheese and fruit together with a different locally produced wine with each course; while for a 'family meal' Abbot recommended a rabbit curry, rice and strong beer with green apricot pudding to follow. Recipes for kangaroo were many and imaginative — baked and stuffed kangaroo, jugged kangaroo, kangaroo hash, kangaroo pastry, kangaroo ham, and such exotic dishes as 'Pan Jam', a fry of jointed kangaroo tail, and 'Skipping Bob', which was kangaroo brain patties fried in emu fat.

## COPPER
was first discovered at Macquarie Harbour, Tas, on 20 April 1827.
**The first copper mine** was opened at Kapunda, SA, on 8 January 1844 and just two weeks later the first of five drays loaded with ore arrived in Adelaide. Copper had been discovered at Kapunda in 1842 when a grazier called Captain Bagot saw rock coated with 'a beautiful green moss' while looking for lost sheep. His neighbour Francis Dutton made a similar discovery while out picking wildflowers and together they had the area surveyed and bought 80 acres of Crown land at the standard £1 an acre. They not only made their own fortune, but attracted new migrants to the infant colony of South Australia and stimulated Australia's first mineral boom. In 1844 it was reported that 'a score or so of men with picks and shovels' had mined over £7,500 of ore.

## CORN FLAKES
were first manufactured in Australia by Kellogg at Chippendale, Sydney, in 1924. The following year the master bakers denounced what they described as 'a certain proprietary

# The first . . .

commodity belittling bread' — a clear reference to the upstart breakfast cereal.

## CORONER'S COURT

was convened under Augustus Alt, magistrate, at Sydney Cove on 14 December 1788 to enquire into the death of convict Charles Wilson. The body of the deceased had been found lying close to a place where he had been making shingles, the face black, the eyes full of maggots, and the corpse smelling very offensive. Surgeon Balmain, who had conducted the post mortem, deposed that 'want of sustenance with the extreme heat of the sun was the cause of death'. It transpired that Wilson had been accustomed to sell all his rations in the hope of paying his passage back to England when he had served his sentence. At the time of his death he had not eaten for more than a week.

The first coroner appointed as such was the artist J.W. Lewin, who became coroner for Sydney and the County of Cumberland on 6 October 1810.

## CORPORAL PUNISHMENT, ABOLITION IN STATE SCHOOLS

was first enacted in the State of Victoria in 1982. Corporal punishment had been prohibited in Church Schools as early as the 1840s.

## COTTON MILL

was established at Ipswich, Queensland in 1890.

## COUNTRY PARTY

was founded under the leadership of M. J. McWilliams at a meeting of a number of MPs representing rural constituencies held at Melbourne 22-23 January 1920. It became the National Country Party of Australia on 9 March 1974, and the National Party on 16 October 1982.

## COURT OF JUSTICE

was convened before Capt. David Collins, Judge-Advocate, at Port Jackson (Sydney) on 11 February 1788. Three convicts were charged with offences. Thomas Barsby, who was found guilty of abusing the Drum-Major and assaulting John West, drummer, with an adze, was sentenced to 150 lashes. Thomas

Hill was found guilty of stealing bread valued at 2d from a fellow convict and was sentenced to a week's solitary confinement on a bread and water diet on the island later known as Pinchgut (because it was used for keeping recalcitrant convicts on short commons) and now as Fort Denison. William Cole was charged with stealing two deal planks, property of government, value 10d. Despite his contention that he had taken the planks in broad daylight, in front of 20 witnesses, and he would not have done that had he known it was a crime, he was found guilty and sentenced to 50 lashes. He was subsequently pardoned by the Governor.

**The first Circuit Court** was convened by Justice James Dowling at Maitland, NSW, on 17 August 1829.

See also Civil Court; Magistrate's Court.

## COURT HOUSE

was a lath and plaster building erected at Sydney in June 1796. Hitherto trials had been conducted at the private houses of the Judge-Advocate and other magistrates, described as a 'great inconvenience'.

## CRAWL

was introduced by 10 year old Alick Wickham, a Solomon Islander working as a houseboy in Sydney, in 1898. Wickham covered a distance of 66 yds in 44 secs during a handicap race at the Bronte Baths in Sydney, whereupon swimming coach George Farmer exclaimed 'Look at that kid *crawling!*' Ten years later Wickham introduced the surf board (q.v.) to Australia and he became a champion swimmer and diver.

## CREDIT CARDS

were introduced to Australia in 1956 by Diners Club. The first credit cards in the world had been pioneered by Diners Club in the USA in 1950.

## CREMATION

was first legalised under South Australia's Cremation Act which became law on 19 December 1891.

**The first crematorium** was opened in West Terrace Cemetery, Adelaide in 1903.

## CRICKET

The first game is generally believed to have been got up by the officers of the *Calcutta*, which arrived at Port Jackson in December

1803. It was recorded in the *Sydney Gazette* for 8 January 1804 that the 'late intense weather' was 'very favourable to the amateurs of cricket'.

**The first cricket clubs** were founded at Sydney in 1826, the Military Club for the garrison and the Australian Club for the native-born cricketers of the colony. The latter did not meet the approbation of the *Monitor*, which reported early in 1827: 'A few mechanics of Sydney got together on New Year's Day, and attempted to play a few games at Cricket, but their mode of handling their bats and balls was most unskilful, and worse playing was never witnessed either in England or the Colony.' Among these despised mechanics was one Edward William Gregory, two of whose sons played in the first Test Match in 1877, one of them, David Gregory, captaining Australia.

**The first cricketers to bowl overarm** in Australia were the brothers John Richard Hardy and William Hardy, who arrived in Sydney in late 1832.

**The earliest recorded match between schools** — also the first known sporting contest between schools in Australia — took place in the Domain, Hobart in May 1835, when Mr Gibbin's School at New Town beat Mr Thomson's School of Melville Street by 75 runs to 46.

**The earliest recorded century** was scored by John Tunks with 112 not out in a match played between the Currency Club and the Victorian Club on 1 January 1845. The Currency Club, which was Tunks' side, was for native-born Australians.

**The first representative inter-State match** was held in Melbourne on 26-27 March 1856 between Victoria and New South Wales. The scores were: Victoria — 68 and 28; NSW — 76 and 7 wickets for 16. It is recorded that the pitch was unadorned by a single blade of grass and that some of the cricketers played with no boots.

**The first visiting team from overseas** was the All England Eleven which arrived under the sponsorship of Melbourne caterers Spiers and Pond in 1861, the players receiving £180 and all expenses. Among the XI, which was captained by H.H. Stephenson, was one G. Wells, who was the father of the celebrated novelist H.G. Wells. The tourists played 15 matches, winning all but two. In order to level up their chances, the Australians fielded teams of up to 22 men. The first match in the series, played at Melbourne Cricket Ground on 1 January 1862, was attended by 25,000 spectators — claimed at the time as a record for the largest crowd ever to have assembled in one place anywhere in the world.

**The first Australian team to tour overseas** was composed of 13 aborigines who played 47 matches in England during 1868, winning 14, losing 14 and drawing 19. The names of the team were; Johnny Mullagh (the highest scorer, with an aggregate of 1,700 runs), Johnny Cuzens, Bolocky, Red Cap, Twopenny, King Cole (who died on tour), Tiger, Dick-Dick, Peter, Charley, Mosquito, Jim Crow and Sundown.

**The first Test Match** was played between England and a combined NSW-Victoria Team at Melbourne Cricket Ground over four days, 15-19 March 1877, and was won by the home team under the captaincy of Dave Gregory with scores of 245 and 104 against 196 and 108. Highest scorer was Australia's Charles Bannerman, who retired hurt at 165.

**The first overseas Test Match** was played against England at the Oval on 6 September 1880, resulting in an English victory by 5 wickets.

**The Six-Ball Over** was first introduced in Australia in 1887, England following suit in 1900.

## CROQUET

was introduced to Australia from Britain with the founding of a club at Kapunda, SA, in 1868.

## CROSS-COUNTRY RUNNING

began with a race organised by Richard Coombes of the Sydney Harriers in 1889.

## CUSTODY ORDER

was made by the Sydney Bench of Magistrates on 15 December 1798, when Charles Seaton was ordered to surrender custody of his infant child Martha to her mother Eleanor Davis.

## CYCLE RACE

took place at Melbourne Cricket Ground on 10 July 1869 and was won by James Finlay of Fitzroy before a crowd of 12,000.

**The first women's race** was held for lady tricyclists by the South Australian Bicycle Club at Adelaide in 1885. The winner was Miss Wills in a time of 9 mins 43 secs for the three mile distance. She was presented with a trophy worth 4 gns. The first on bicycles was

# The first...

won by Miss Dot Morrell at Ashfield, NSW, in 1888.

The 163-mile Warrnambool road race, held annually since 1895 from Warrnambool to Melbourne or vice versa, is the oldest cycle race in the world.

## DAM

was built by Thomas Rose, stage coach proprietor, at Mount Gilstead, NSW in 1825. The *New South Wales Calendar and General Post Office Directory* for 1834 observed that he was 'the first to construct a tank sufficiently capacious to secure him from the want of water in dry seasons'.

**The first masonry dam** and the first built to create a public reservoir was the Yan Yean dam, built near Melbourne to supply the city with water and opened on 31 December 1857. It created what was then the largest artificial reservoir in the world.

## DANCING SCHOOL

was opened in Macquarie Street, Sydney, 1833 by Cavendish de Castell of the Paris Conservatoire. Colonists could acquaint themselves with niceties of the minuet, gavotte, bolero and the 'circassian circle' for two guineas a term.

See also Ballet School.

## DEATH DUTIES

were imposed by Victoria on 16 December 1870. Estates of less than £1,000 were taxed at 1%, rising to 5% on estates of £20,000 and more. First to abolish death duties was Queensland in 1977, followed by NSW in 1982.

## DECIMAL CURRENCY

was introduced on 14 February 1966. Dollars became legal tender for the first time since the abolition of the 'holey dollar' in 1842. It was reported that 'the smoothness of the change, the efficiency of business people and the good humour of the public delighted Decimal Currency Board officials'. There were only isolated instances of confusion, such as the bus proprietor who refused to take his bus out because he did not think he would be able to cope with decimal fares. Among the beneficiaries of decimalisation were Tasmanian children who found out on the very first day that 1c coins could be used instead of 5c coins for rides on mechanical animals, boats and planes in stores.

The original note denominations were $1, $2, $10 and $20. The first $5 notes were introduced on 29 May 1967, followed by $50 notes on 9 October 1973 and $100 notes on 26 March 1984. The first dollar coins minted in Australia were issued on 14 May 1984.

## DECORATION OR HONOUR

instituted by the Australian government was the Order of Australia on 14 June 1975. It originally had three levels of membership — Companion (AC), Officer (AO) and Member (AM). The following year the level of Knight or Dame (AK or AD) was added and also a medal for the Order (OAM). First to receive a Knighthood of the Order of Australia was Sir John Kerr, AK, GCMG, GCVO on 24 May 1976.

## DENTAL OPERATION

was performed on Lt Ralph Clark, who had a tooth drawn by Assistant Surgeon D. Considen at Sydney Hospital on 18 February 1788. Clark's account of the ordeal vividly captures the horrors of even minor surgery in the days before anaesthesia: 'Oh, my God what pain it was. It was so fast in, and the jaw bone very fast to one of the prongs, the tooth would not come out without breaking the jaw bone, which he did. I thought that half my head would have come off, there is a piece of the jaw bone remaining to the tooth. The pain was great, my dear wife, that fainted away and was very ill the remainder of the day, but I would not let Consident report to Major Ross that I was ill but would go on picket; my gum kept bleeding all the day.'

**The first dentists** to practice in Australia were Simon Lear, who combined this avocation with that of 'Corn Operator', and George White, both of Sydney, who each advertised his services in the *Sydney Gazette* during 1818.

## DENTAL SCHOOL

was the Australian School of Dentistry, founded privately in Melbourne by a group of dentists in 1898. It was later affiliated with Melbourne University.

## DETECTIVE FICTION

The first book-length work of detective fiction by an Australian was *The Detective's Album: Recollections of an Australian Police officer* by W. W., published in Melbourne in 1871. Some of these stories had appeared earlier in the *Australian Journal* 'W. W.' cloaked the identity of a certain Mrs Fortune, a widow obliged to support herself by writing. She was the world's first woman writer of detective fiction, since the authoress most commonly accorded this accolade, the American novelist Anna Katherine Green, did not produce her first detective story, *The Leavenworth Case*, until 1878.

The first detective novel published in Australia was Fergus Hume's 'The Mystery of a Hansom Cab', Melbourne 1886. Set in Melbourne, it is notable as one of the earliest 'urban' Australian novels. Hume wrote 140 novels altogether, of which this was the first and most successful, remaining in print to this day and selling more than 500,000 copies.

## DIABETIC TREATED WITH INSULIN

was returned soldier J. F. Loveday at Royal Melbourne Hospital in March 1923. Looking like an old man on his admission, the 43-year old patient had been cured by December. Insulin had first been isolated two years earlier by Dr Frederick Banting of the University of Toronto Medical School.

## DIAMOND DRILL

was introduced for deep lead-mining by George Lansell in 1876.

## DIAMOND MINE

was established at Two Mile Flat on the Cudgegong River, north of Mudgee, NSW, in 1867.

## DIARY

was the *Australian Diary and Almanac, or Daily Memorandum Book for the year* 1837, published by William Moffitt at 23 Pitt Street, Sydney in 1836. Moffitt was one of Sydney's first three booksellers. The octavo diary, which continued to be published for at least ten years, was based on the famous *Lett's Diary* published in London.

## DICTIONARY OF AUSTRALIAN ENGLISH

was Cornelius Crowe's *The Australian Slang Dictionary*, published in Melbourne in 1895. As early as 1812, a convict called James Hardy Vaux had compiled, during what he described as his 'solitary hours of cessation from hard labour', a *Vocabulary of the Flash Language*. This meant thieves' argot, but it may have contained some newly minted convict colloquialisms.

## DIFFERENTIAL GEAR

on a motor vehicle anywhere in the world was applied to a steam car built by David Shearer of Mannum, SA, in 1897. On several occasions Shearer drove the vehicle to Adelaide and back, a return trip of 100 miles, but was required to obtain the permission of the Mayor of Adelaide before he was allowed to enter the city and the car had to be preceded by a man carrying a red flag.

## DIGGER HAT

or slouch hat with one side turned up was designed by Colonel Tom Price for the volunteer regiment he raised, the Victorian Mounted Rifles, on 3 December 1885. These hats were turned up on the right side, according to Price, so that when troops were marching by on ceremonial parades, they could 'look the Inspecting Officer in the eye'. In December 1890, at a meeting in Melbourne of the military commandants of each of the Australian Colonies, it was agreed 'that the whole of the Australian Forces should wear a looped-up felt hat, and that the pattern should be made universal'. The various regiments wore the side up on left or right according to inclination, the left side becoming standard when the Commonwealth Army was created in 1901.

# The first...

## DIPLOMAT

to represent Australia overseas was Sir George Reid, who took office as the first Australian High Commissioner in the UK on 22 January 1910.

*The first Australian diplomatic representative* in a foreign country was F. K. Officer, who became Australian Counsellor at the British Embassy in Washington in 1937.

*The first Australian legation* was established at Washington on 8 January 1940, with the appointment of R. G. Casey as Minister and F. K. Officer as Counsellor. Another followed the same year in Tokyo and further legations were opened in China and Singapore in 1941, in the USSR in 1943, in New Zealand in 1944, and Paris in 1945. The first High Commissioner to India was appointed in January 1944.

*The first Australian Embassy* was established in Washington in 1946, followed by Moscow, Nanking and Paris in 1948 and The Hague and Djakarta in 1950.

*The first overseas diplomatic representative in Australia* was the UK High Commissioner, appointed in 1936. Canada followed suit in 1939, and the first Minister of a non-commonwealth country was appointed by the USA in 1940.

The first woman of Ambassadorial rank was Dame Annabelle Rankin, appointed High Commissioner to New Zealand on 18 March 1971.

## DIRT-TRACK RACING

is generally claimed to have begun at the West Maitland showground, where a cinder track was laid down in November 1923. It would be more correct to say that the revival of dirt-track in Australia dates from this time, since there had been motorcycle racing on a dirt track at Sydney Showground as early as 1911, at Claremont Showground, Perth, in 1914, and dirt tracks had been laid at Penrith, NSW, and Northfield, SA, in 1920. Nor is dirt track a sport invented in Australia — South Africa was racing motor cycles on cinders in 1907 and there may have been events in the USA even earlier.

*The first Australian to become world champion* was Lionel Van Praag of Sydney at Wembley on 11 September 1936.

## DISTILLERY

was established at Parramatta by Joseph Webb in December 1793. From each bushel of wheat he distilled nearly five quarts of spirit, which he sold at 5s a quart.

After this distilling was made illegal and remained so until 1822. The first distillery to be established as a full-scale commercial undertaking was founded in July 1824 by ex-convict James Underwood, who had been a member of the First Fleet. The plant was erected in George Street, Sydney, at a cost of £30,000, making it the most extensive manufacturing concern in Australia at that time. Underwood eventually retired to England a wealthy man, the only veteran of the First Fleet to return to his native land with a fortune.

## DISTRICT NURSE (*trained*)

was Mrs L. Smith, a graduate of the Florence Nightingale Training School, who was appointed by the Melbourne District Nursing Society in 1892.

## DIVORCE

was first legalised by South Australia under the Matrimonial Causes Act 1858, which came into effect on 1 January the following year. The first petitioner was Gottllebe Nelson of Lyndock Valley, SA, who was granted a divorce from her husband William in the Supreme Court at Adelaide on 1 September 1859. The only grounds for divorce in SA were non-consummation and adultery, but the law made it easier for men to sever the marital knot than women. A man could sue on the basis of any philandering by his wife. The wife could only sue for divorce on grounds of incestuous adultery, bigamy, rape, sodomy, bestiality and, in certain circumstances, adultery combined with severe cruelty or adultery combined with desertion. Not suprisingly the incidence of divorce was low, with only 25 dissolutions of marriage in the first five years of the working act; eight of the petitioners were women. Not until 1890 was desertion on its own admitted as grounds for divorce in Australia, when Victoria amended its divorce laws.

*Divorce by mutual consent* conditional only on 12 months separation, and not dependant on evidence of fault on either side, was introduced on 5 January 1976 under the Family Law Act. 'Divorce-by-mail', by which consenting partners were not required to attend court hearings, followed in October 1983.

## DOCTOR

to settle in Australia was John Irving, who was also the first convict to be emancipated. On his sentence being remitted by Governor Phillip on 16 December 1791, he elected to remain in the colony and continue to work as an assistant to the surgeons at the hospital in Sydney. He had practised as a surgeon prior to his sentence to transportation in 1785.

**The first medical practitioner to qualify in Australia** was William Redfern, who was granted a certificate of competence at Sydney in 1801 following examination by a board of three surgeons.

**The first general practitioner** was Dr William Bland, who established a private practice in Sydney in 1815. He had been transported to Australia the previous year for fighting a duel and killing his opponent.

**The first native-born Australian doctor** was William Sherwin, who qualified as a Member of the Royal College of Physicians, London, in 1823. He served his apprenticeship with Dr William Bland of Sydney.

See also Surgeon; Woman Doctor.

## DOLLS

were manufactured by Adelaide draper Sydney H. Hook, who learned the technique of making dolls' heads from a book titled *Henley's* 1001 *Recipes and Formulas* and opened a factory in an old gymnasium in East Street, Brompton in 1916. The painting of the dolls' features was undertaken by Syd's wife Elsie and Elsie's mother was in charge of the girls who stuffed the bodies with kapok. Production of 'Hook's Unbreakable Dolls' ceased when the factory burned down in 1920.

## DRAG ARTISTE

was Sydney actor Joseph Simmons, who played the role of the Italian diva in *The Mock Catalini in Little Puddleton*, presented at the Royal Victoria Theatre, Sydney, on 4 May 1842.

## DRIVING ON THE LEFT

became enforceable by law in New South Wales on 15 August 1820.

## DRIVING LICENCE

was issued to Dr W. A. Hargreaves of Woodville, SA, on 10 September 1906. South Australian licences cost 10s for cars and 2s 6d for motorcycles.

## DRIVING TESTS

were introduced on 1 January 1910 under the Motor Traffic Acts of New South Wales and Victoria. New South Wales asked the Automobile Club of Australia to arrange the tests and two examiners, Harry Skinner and C. O. Sherwood, were appointed for the purpose. Victoria relied on the police, the first examiners being Constables Mooney and Peverill. One veteran motor cyclist recalled that the test he took in 1911 consisted of riding round the yard of the Russell Street police depot, out into the street to do a turn and back again. 'Constable Mooney', he wrote 'stood at the gateway, watched the performance, said "You'll do", and made out the licence forwith'.

## DRUG TRAFFICKING CONVICTION

was secured at Melbourne in April 1923, when Henry McEwan was found guilty of dealing in opium.

## DRYING-OUT CLINIC

was the Retreat for Inebriates opened near Melbourne in October 1873. During its first full year of operation, 21 males and 2 females were admitted, of whom 14 had delirium tremens. All were smokers. The youngest was 23. Of the 19 discharged, it was reported that '5 left with great hopes of permanent cure' and '7 were much improved'.

## DUEL

was fought with pistols on 12 August 1788 between John White, Surgeon-General, and William Balmain, Assistant Surgeon, who had quarrelled during a banquet to celebrate the Prince of Wales's birthday over some dispute about their work. Each fired five shots at the other, the only injury sustained being a slight flesh wound in Balmain's right thigh. At that point the Governor intervened, and stopped them from going on taking pot shots at each other, which they seemed bent on doing, with the observation that it was much better to draw the blood from the arms of their patients with a lance than from one another with pistol balls.

# The first ...

## EARL, AUSTRALIAN-BORN
was Capel Henry Berkely Moreton, 5th Earl of Ducis, a dairy and fruit farmer at Tootgoom, Queensland, who succeeded his father to the title on 7 August 1924.

## EDUCATION, COMPULSORY
was introduced by Victoria under the Education Act which took effect on 1 January 1873. Children between 6 and 15 were required to attend school for at least 120 days a year unless they had already reached a certain educational standard. All state schooling became free under the Act. Before the Act came into force, there were 135,952 children attending public schools; immediately afterwards the figure rose to 207,826, an increase of 53%. The Education Department took over 453 common schools and entered into negotiations for the 590 school houses belonging to the religious denominations.

## EDUCATION, FREE
in all public schools as a right was first introduced in Queensland by Mr Justice Charles Lilley, Colonial Secretary, under an Act which took effect on 1 January 1870. The average cost per pupil was a little over £5 per head. The other Australian colonies followed suit over the next five years.

## EIGHT HOUR DAY
was achieved by Sydney stonemasons, who went on strike while working on two churches and won a reduction from a 10-hour day in September 1855. Other stonemasons in Sydney secured the 8 hour day the following February, with a decrease in wages proportionate to the fewer hours. Melbourne stonemasons were next to win the shorter day in April 1856, followed by Sydney plasterers in 1857 and Queensland stonemasons in 1859. Building Trade workers and government coach builders were the first employees in South Australia with the 8-hour day in 1873, the same year as NSW engineering workers. At this time coal mines in NSW had only just secured a reduction of hours from 12½ to 10, but by 1877 they too were working 8 hour shifts. The 48 hour week had become the average for all workers by 1900.

## EISTEDDFOD
was held by Welsh miners at Ballarat, Vic, in 1855. There were no further eisteddfods until 1875, when one was celebrated at Newcastle, NSW.

## ELECTIONS
were held for the appointment of constables and watchmen in all the districts of New South Wales under an Order of Governor Hunter of 5 December 1798; polling took place on various dates the same month. Voters were enjoined to select their favoured candidates with care, as the number of recent escapes from gaol suggested either inefficiency or corruption. The question of whether women were entitled to vote was resolved by the Judge-Advocate on 22 December; they were not.

## ELECTION, MUNICIPAL
was held at Adelaide on 31 October 1840 for the election of aldermen to the newly established corporation. Sydney had its first municipal elections on 1 November 1842, lagging two years behind the South Australian capital in becoming a legally incorporated City.

## ELECTION, PARLIAMENTARY
was held for the Legislative Council of New South Wales on 15 June 1843 and was attended by riots in Sydney. There were 24 elected members to the new Legislative Council, which first met on 2 August, in addition to 12 nominee members. Formerly the

Council had consisted solely of nominated and ex-officio members.

The first Legislative Assembly elections — the first parliamentary elections following the proclamation of self government — were held in New South Wales on 30 April, 1856, followed by Victoria on 21 November and Tasmania on 2 December.

The first Federal elections were held on 29 and 30 March 1901. There was a 56.6% turnout of the electorate and the inaugural Federal Parliament consisted of 75 Members of the House of Representatives and 36 Senators.

## ELECTRIC DRILL
in the world was patented on 20 August 1889 by Arthur James Arnot of the Union Electric Company, Melbourne, and later Melbourne City Council's first chief electrical engineer. It was designed as a rock drill, coal digger or earth cutter. Electric drills were not introduced in Britain until 1892 and Germany until 1895.

## ELECTRIC LIGHTING
was first used in celebration of the marriage of the Prince and Princess of Wales on 11 June 1863. An arc light mounted on top of Sydney's Observatory tower was described as 'the most conspicuous object in the city' and at the Post Office Prince Albert Edward's name was honoured with a gigantic 'A' made up of vacuum tubes powered from a 100 cell battery and Rumkorff coil.

The first permanent installation of electric light was made, most incongruously, at a candle factory. A Gramme generator was installed at the Apollo Stearine Candle Co. at Footscray, Victoria, in 1877 to power arc lamps used to illuminate the factory for night work.

**The first incandescent electric lights** were Edison Lamps imported from the USA in 1881 and installed at the GPO, Sydney, at Circular Quay and in the interior of South Head Lighthouse. Among the first privately owned buildings to be lit with incandescent bulbs was the Hotel Australia, Sydney, where 1,200 were installed the same year. Also in 1881 was the first incandescent electric lighting in a shop, Fry & Gibson's of Smith Street, Collingwood, Vic.

**The first incandescent electric street lamps** were installed in Tamworth, NSW, on 9 November 1888. There were 78 lamp standards each holding two or three bulbs. Some old timers in the town declared that it was all wrong and people should go to bed at sundown.

**The first municipal power supply** for domestic consumers of electricity was provided by the corporation of Young, NSW, on 15 April, 1889. There was a fixed charge of £1 10s per light per annum regardless of the amount of electricity used.

See also Neon Lighting.

## ELECTRIC TELEGRAPH
was installed between Melbourne and Williamstown on 3 March 1854 by S. McGowan, who had studied telegraphy under Samuel Morse in America. The line was opened for the transmission of telegrams by the general public on 13 March 1854. Rates were 2s 6d for 10 words or less, exclusive of the name and address and signature, for which no charge was made; and 3d for each additional word. A line to Geelong was completed on 5 December 1854 and to Queenscliff on 30 January 1855. By the end of 1857 all the main centres of Victoria had been connected and there was a total of 2000 miles of telegraph line in the Australian colonies as a whole, including the first line in NSW, from Sydney to Liverpool, opened in December, and the Hobart-Launceston line, which had been inaugurated in August. Thereafter progress was extremely rapid and Sydney, Melbourne and Adelaide were linked for the first time on 29 October 1858, Sydney with Brisbane in 1861 and, to complete the coast-to-coast link, Adelaide with Perth in 1877.

**The first submarine telegraph cable** was laid across Bass Strait to link Melbourne and Tasmania and was opened for traffic on 1 May 1868.

**The first overseas telegram** sent to Australia was received via the recently completed Java-Port Darwin telegraph on 20 November 1871. This cable had been opened by the British-Australian Telegraph Company as a link in the line to England.

**The first electric telegraph line between Britain and Australia** was opened with the arrival of the first telegram from London, a despatch from Reuter's, on 1 July 1872. The route was via Gibraltar, Suez, Madras, Singapore, Batavia and Darwin to Adelaide. The 2,000 mile long Australian land line, which had been laid by the South Australian government, had one gap of 60 miles and a horseman had to gallop between the two points. The price of the cable service was

# The first...

The first escalators were installed at Milson Point Station in 1924.

£9.7.6. for 20 words. With this notable innovation, Australia was brought into same-day communication with nearly all parts of the civilised world.

The last of the state capitals to be linked to London and the rest of the world by wire was Perth with the completion of the Transcontinental Overland Telegraph on 9 December 1877. From this date none of the Australian colonies was isolated from international affairs.

The extent to which Australia was cut off from the rest of the world before the advent of the electric telegraph is exemplified by the fact that news of the outbreak of the Austro-Prussian War of 1866 did not reach these shores until after the war was over.

**The Pacific cable** linking Australia with N. America via a 7,320 mile submarine cable between Vancouver Island, British Columbia and Southport, Queensland, was used for telegraphy for the first time on 31 October 1902. Previously communication with the Americas was via London.

## EMPLOYMENT EXCHANGE

(state run) was the Labour Bureau opened in Sydney on 18 February 1892, followed by one in Adelaide on the 26 of the same month.

## ENCYCLOPEDIA

was the Australian Encyclopedia, a two volume work published by Angus & Robertson of Sydney under the editorship of Arthur Jose in 1925.

## ENGRAVINGS

executed in Australia were the work of the artist naturalist John William Lewin and published in the *Natural History of the Lepidopterous Insects in New South Wales*, London, 1805. The 18 plates for the book were drawn, engraved and coloured in the colony during the course of 1803-04.

**The first engravings published in Australia** were a group of views of Sydney and surrounding country, executed by W. Presston and P. Slaeger from drawings by convict artist John Eyre and issued for sale by the brewer-cum-art publisher Absalom West in January 1813 at £3 the set of 12. Later the same month he offered additional views of the 'Seat of Ultimo' and the 'Seat of Woolloomoola' at 2gns the pair.

## ESCALATORS

were installed at Milson Point Station, North Sydney in 1924.

## EUCALYPTUS OIL

was first distilled commercially from *Eucalyptus amygdalina* in 1852 by Joseph Bosisto, chemist, at Dandenong, Vic. Marketed as Parrot Eucalyptus Oil, it was the first branded product in Australia to be exported.

## EVENING CLASSES

were inaugurated by George Howe, the Government printer and publisher of the *Sydney Gazette*, on 17 November 1806. Classes were offered in Arithmetic, Writing and English grammar and lasted from 5.30 to 8.30 each night.

## EVEREST, ASCENT BY AUSTRALIANS

was achieved on 30 October 1984 by Tim Macartney-Snape and Greg Mortimer, who were also the first mountaineers from anywhere in the world to climb the north face without oxygen.

## EXECUTION

took place at Sydney Cove at 6.30 pm on 27

February 1788, when Thomas Barrett was hanged for stealing butter, pease and pork. The executioner, a volunteer convict, found that his nerve had failed him and, refusing to perform his grim office, was threatened with being shot down by the Marines. In the event it fell to the Provost-Marshal, Midshipman Henry Brewer, to fix the noose around Barrett's neck. Arthur Bowes, Surgeon aboard the *Lady Penrhyn*, recorded: 'Just before Barrett was turned off, he confessed the justice of his sentence, and that he had led a very wicked life. He requested leave to speak to one of the convict men ( a very bad kind of man) one Seddiway, which was granted him and he also expressed a wish to speak to one of the women convicts, but was refused. He then exhorted all of them to take warning by his unhappy fate and so launched into Eternity. The body hung an hour and was then buried in a grave, dug very near the gallows.'

## EXHIBITION, INTERNATIONAL

was opened at the Garden Palace in Sydney's Botanic Gardens on 17 September 1879. there were well over 13,000 exhibits and during the six months of the exhibition it was visited by over a million people, at a time when the colony of NSW had a total population of only 751,000. The Garden Palace was destroyed by fire in 1882.

## EXPORTS

The first cargo for export consisted of sixty large cedar logs from the Hawkesbury and a quantity of mahogany, which Edward MacLellan, master of the *Experiment*, purchased as a speculative venture and shipped to India on 23 March 1795.

**The first export cargo of coal** was a load from the Hunter River, shipped to Bengal aboard the *Hunter* in August 1799. One hundred and eighty years later coal had become Australia's biggest export earner at some $20,000 million a year.

**The first consignment of wool** was 534 lbs from NSW to England in 1807. The trade had become established by 1819, when 71,299 lbs were exported. Only ten years later the figure passed 1 million lbs for the first time; and by 1835 was nearly 4 million lbs.

**The first cargo of mixed goods** to be exported left Sydney aboard the *Minstral*, 350 tons, in July 1813. She sailed with 20 tons of colonial wool, a quantity of raw hides, 50-60 tons of pearl shell, and a quantity of sperm oil, seal skins, timber, flour, tallow and blue gum. Freight charges were £12 a ton for oil, £10 a ton for skins.

**The first shipment of metal ore** was 10 tons of silver lead, mined at Glen Osmond, near Adelaide, which was exported to England in 1841.

**The first consignment of cotton** consisting of 70 bales, arrived at Liverpool from Brisbane in February 1854.

**The first Australian wine to be exported** was sold in Calcutta in March 1846.

**The first shipment of oranges** was a consignment from NSW and South Australia aboard the *Garonne* in 1880.

**The first commercial shipment of apples and pears** was made from Tasmania to England aboard the *Warwick* in 1884. (The 1828 shipment had been strictly experimental).

**Exports exceeded imports** for the first time in 1844.

**The first exports to Japan** now Australia's leading export market, were made in 1865 with a shipment of £550 worth of coal. Wool was exported to Japan for the first time in 1874. Not until 1912 did trade with Japan top the £1 million mark, but by 1966 Australia's far eastern trading partner had overtaken the US and UK to become her major overseas customer. Main exports are coal and iron ore.

See also Frozen Meat.

# The first . . .

## FAIR

was held at the Cricket Ground, Sydney, otherwise known as St George's Fields, starting on Easter Monday, 23 April 1810. The Sydney Gazette reported: 'The recreative pastimes . . . were carried on with much decorum and with no less festivity for three days, during which the "merry dance" was kept alive in every booth, and other fair customs of the mother country closely imitated.'

## FAMILY ALLOWANCE

: see Child Benefit

## FARM

Clearance of land for a government farm began at the head of Farm Cove, Port Jackson, on 1 February 1788. By July of that year there were '9 acres of corn'. The area is now the Botanic Gardens and the oblong beds of the Middle Garden are preserved as following the first furrows ever ploughed in Australia.

**The first privately owned farm** was established on a grant of land at Rosehill (the then name of Parramatta) made to James Ruse, time expired convict, who took possession on 21 November 1789. It was recorded that Governor Phillip was 'desirous of trying . . . in what time an industrious active man, with certain assistance, would be enabled to support himself in this country as a settler'. Ruse had been a 'husbandman' at Launceston, Cornwall, before receiving a sentence of 7 years at Bodmin Assizes in 1782. There were no boundaries to Experiment Farm, as it was named in the title deed. He himself explained: 'The exact limit of what ground I am to have, I do not yet know; but a certain direction has been pointed out to me, in which I may proceed as far as I can cultivate.' Ruse grew wheat, maize and vegetables; by February 1791 his crops were sufficiently abundant for him to be able to support himself, though his wife continued to draw her own food supplies from the public store. He also maintained (Dec 1791) four breeding sows and 30 fowls. The farmhouse was a comfortable abode of brick. Ruse sold the 30 acre property to John Harries in October 1793 for £40.

## FASHIONS

The female inhabitants of early New South Wales were dependant on the clothes they brought with them, or such copies of outmoded fashions as could be rendered by local needlewomen. The first occasion on which it was possible for the ladies of the colony to indulge in clothes shopping occurred with the arrival of the East-India packet Swallow at Sydney Cove on 3 January 1800. Former Judge Advocate David Collins recorded: 'She had on board a great variety of articles for sale, which were intended for the China market; but the master thought and actually found it worth his while to gratify the inhabitants, particularly the females, with a display of many elegant articles of dress from Bond Street, and other fashionable repositories of the metropolis.' Since there were less than a dozen 'ladies of quality' in the colony at this time, it would seem that Bond Street fashions were also in demand among those other ladies who had made their home in Australia involuntarily. Their menfolk were less fortunate. Since they were clad in rags, and there being no men's clothing available, Governor Hunter purchased 'a thousand bed rugs' which arrived from Spanish California in February 1800 and had them made up into suits for the male convicts.

**The first full-time dressmaker** known by name was Mrs Martha Matthews, who announced in the Sydney Gazette in 1809 that she was separating from her husband, who ill-treated her, and was opening a dress-making establishment 'adjoining Mr Cuff's School, in Upper Pitt's Row.' In that same year the emancipist D.D. Mann observed: 'The shops are particularly respectable and decorated with much taste. Articles of female apparel and ornament are greedily purchased; for the European women in the settlement spare no expense in ornamenting their persons, and in dress, each seems to vie with the other in extravagance.'

By the 1830s Sydney could boast 'fashionable emporiums' comparable with the best shops in a large English provincial city; indeed, some claimed they were comparable to those of London itself.

## FERRY SERVICE

was inaugurated on a regular basis between Sydney and Parramatta in 1793, the year before Australia's first highway was completed between the two towns. This was the first form of public transport in Australia. The fare was 1s. Ferries continued to run on the Parramatta River until 1928.

*The first regular ferry service to the north shore of Sydney Harbour* was established in 1817 by a 6 ft Jamaican ex-convict called Billy Blue, formerly Governor Macquarie's water bailiff and unofficial court jester. Billy plied between Dawes Point and Blues Point, which was named after him. When he became too old to row himself, his passengers were obliged to propel themselves, but such was Billy Blue's ability to make them laugh that they willingly paid for the privilege. Starting with but a single boat, he soon had 11 plying on the harbour, prompting his old mentor Governor Macquarie to exclaim 'Why, Billy, you have a regular fleet. I'll have to name you Commodore'. From then until his death in 1834, Billy was always known to Sydneysiders as 'The Old Commodore'.

*The first vehicular ferry* was a double-ended paddle punt called the *Princess*, which began carrying carts and carriages between Dawes Point and Blues Point in August 1842. Fares were 3d per person, 1s per horse, and 2s 6d per carriage or cart.

*The first Manly Ferry* in regular service was operated by a man called Kerrina in 1853.

## FICTION

The first work of fiction published in Australia was an untitled serial story which began in the *Sydney Gazette* on 16 July 1809. A melodramatic tale about the disappearance of an ancestral seal, and the consequent vendetta between two brothers, the story was published anonymously and it is not known whether it was written in Australia or copied from an English publication. Added to the other uncertainties about Australia's inaugural work of fiction is how the story ended; it was supposed to be in four parts, but only three were published. The denouement, which should have been published in the *Gazette* of 6 August, never appeared in print.

*The first short stories* known to have been written in Australia were the work of Thomas Richards, journalist and medical practitioner, who contributed to the *Hobart Town Monthly Magazine* from its inception in March 1833 until it closed in August 1834.

See also Novel.

## FIELD MARSHAL

in the Australian Forces was Sir Thomas Blamey (1884-1951), promoted on 8 June 1950.

## FIGURINE

The earliest known pottery figure is a small, glazed earthenware bust of George Washington, signed by Anson Moreton and dated July 1822. Moreton was only 11 years old at this date. He was the son of a Staffordshire potter, John Moreton, who had arrived in Sydney as a convict in May 1822. Father and son established the Surry Hills Pottery, which continued in production until about 1847.

## FILMS

screened before the paying public were presented at the Opera House, Melbourne, by Carl Hertz on 22 August 1896 as part of a variety bill. The films shown included an Italian skirt dance, a boxing match, traffic crossing London Bridge, *Rough Seas at Dover* and a scene from *Trilby* showing the death of Svengali. Most of these had been made by the pioneer British film producer R.W. Paul.

*The first films made in Australia* were taken by Marius Sestier, who arrived in Sydney from Paris with a Lumière camera during the third week of September 1896. Using Falk's Photographic Studio as a base, he proceeded to make a number of 60 ft scenes of the harbour, including one of the crowds disembarking from the ferry at Manly, and others of the NSW Horse Artillery at Victoria Barracks, Government Printing Office employees leaving work and Sunday strollers in

# The first . . .

the Domain. Sestier spent about six months in Australia, his most successful motion picture venture being a film of the 1896 Melbourne Cup in November. The negative is now in the Cinémathèque Française, whose assistant director said in the 1950s that 'It is as fragile as very old lace and more precious than gold'.

**The first dramatic (i.e. acted) films** were made by Joseph Perry of the Limelight Department of the Salvation Army, Melbourne, beginning with a 75ft story of a man convicted for stealing bread who is aided by the Army's 'prison-gate' brigade on his release. This untitled film, made probably in 1897, was followed two years later by a series of 13 short subjects, known collectively as the *Passion Films* which told the story of Jesus Christ. Another series of longer films were made by Perry in 1900 under the title of *Soldiers of the Cross*. Shot mainly at the Salvation Army's girls' home at Murrumbeena, outside Melbourne, with the girls playing the female roles, these biblical stories ran for some 50 minutes playing time and formed part of a 2¼ hour lecture on the early Christians which included 200 magic lantern slides and a full musical score. It was premiered before an audience of 4,000 at Melbourne Town Hall on 13 September 1900.

**The first feature length film** in the world was Charles Tait's *The Story of the Kelly Gang* a 1906 production with a running time of a little over an hour. In other countries at this date few films ever ran more than ten minutes, most of them less.

A biopic of Victoria's notorious bushranger Ned Kelly (1855-80), the film was produced by the theatrical company J & N Tait of Melbourne, Victoria, and shot on location over a period of about six months at Whitehorse Road, Mitcham (Glenrowan Hotel scenes, including the last stand of the Kelly Gang); at Rosanna (railway scenes); and on Charles Tait's property at Heidelberg, Vic (all other scenes). The actual armour which had belonged to Ned Kelly — a bullet-proof helmet and jerkin fashioned from ploughshares — was borrowed from the Victorian Museum and worn by the actor playing the role, an unidentified Canadian from the Bland Holt touring company who disappeared before the film was finished. It had to be completed with an extra standing in as Ned, all these scenes being taken in long shot. Elizabeth Veitch played Kate Kelly, and others in the cast included Ollie Wilson, Frank Mills, Bella Cole and Vera Linden.

Made on a budget of £450, *The Story of the Kelly Gang* was premiered at the Athenaeum Hall, Melbourne, on 24 December 1906 and recovered its cost within a week, eventually grossing some £25,000, including receipts from the English release. No complete print survives but stills from the film were issued as picture postcards and give the impression of a vigorous all-action drama made with imaginative use of outdoor locations — a significant advance on the studio-bound one-reelers being turned out in Europe and America at this period. It was long believed that the film had been totally lost, but recently a 210 ft long fragment was discovered in Melbourne.

The Kellys were portrayed in the film as romantic heroes, the police as oppressors. A review in the *Bulletin* for 24 January 1907 observed: 'These splendid bushrangers never came within a hundred yards of a woman without taking off their hats, and on occasion they remove their hats as many as nine times to a woman. This is held to be a glorious characteristic, and justifies all Ned Kelly's viciousness and villanies.'

The film was also the first to be censored. It was banned by the Chief Secretary of Victoria for showing in Ned Kelly's home territory around Benalla and Wangaratta, lest it invite public disorder. In 1912 a revised version was banned throughout Victoria.

It was shown on tour with a complete range of sound effects, small boys being employed to provide these from behind the scenes. The *Bulletin* reviewer complained; '. . . there is a deal too much racket in connection with the show — sometimes you can't see the picture for the noise of horses, trains, gunshots and wild cries!'

In 1911 a number of European countries began making features, but Australia still easily led the world in production output, with 16 full-length pictures against 3 from Poland, 2 from Italy and one each from Germany, Russia, Denmark and Serbia. Neither the USA or Britain made a feature film until 1912.

**The first feature directed by a woman** was *Those who Love*, by Paulette McDonagh, who also produced and scripted the film. A romantic melodrama, the interiors were shot at the historic Drummoyne House in Sydney, the home of Paulette and her sisters Phyllis, who art directed, and Isobel, who starred under her stage name Marie Lorraine. It was premiered at Newcastle, NSW, on 22 November 1926, though it had been shown earlier to the Governor of NSW, who was reduced to tears by the pathos of the story. There were at this time not more than half a dozen film directors in the world.

**The first talking film** was a news reel of the Duke of York (later King George VI) opening Parliament House, Canberra, taken by De Forest Phonofilms (Australia) Ltd on 9 May 1927. Prof. Lee De Forest was an American physicist who had produced the first commercially made sound-on-film shorts in the USA in 1923. He sold his patents to Fox, who made the first sound-on-film features using an adaptation of De Forest's technique.

**The first feature length talkie** released in Australia was Warner Bros. *The Jazz Singer* which opened at the Lyceum Theatre, Sydney, on 29 December 1928.

**The first Australian feature film with sound** was a part-talkie thriller titled *Cheaters*, produced and scripted by the Sydney film-maker Paulette McDonagh and starring her sister Marie Lorraine. Completed as a silent early in 1929, additional scenes were shot in Melbourne in March 1930 using the sound-on-disc system and the film premiered at the Roxy Theatre, Parramatta on 1 June 1930. It had little commercial exposure, owing to the poor quality of the sound.

**The first all-talkie features** were A.R. Harwood's *Spur of the Moment* and *Isle of Intrigue*, shot 'back-to-back' with the same crew in a converted factory at West Melbourne with a crude sound-on-disc system and premiered as a double bill at the Palace Theatre, Melbourne on 26 September 1931. James Alexander starred in both productions.

**The first Australian musical and the first sound-on-film (as opposed to sound-on-disc) feature** was Norman Dawn's *Showgirl's Luck*, starring his wife Katherine under her stage name of Susan Denis. Premiered at the Lawson Theatre, Redfern, Sydney, early in December 1931, the film was not unlike typical Hollywood musicals of the period, except that instead of making her name on Broadway, the showgirl Lennie achieves stardom in 'Australia's first talkie'.

**The first colour film** was a travelogue on Melbourne made by the Cinema Branch of the Department of Commerce in the Multicolour bi-pack process in 1932. No copy is known to survive.

**The first foreign language film to be dubbed into Australian** was the Russian feature *Memory's Harvest*, released in 1946 by McCreadie Brothers Embassy Pictures.

**The first feature in colour and the first Cinemascope production** was Byron Haskin's *Long John Silver*, a sequel to *Treasure Island* (which Haskin had directed in Hollywood for Disney in 1950), starring Robert Newton in an overblown eye-rolling performance and premiered at the Plaza Theatre, Sydney, on 16 December 1954.

**The first feature film based on a TV series** was *Funny Things Happen Down Under*, derived from the 1965 *Terrible Ten* children's TV comedy, which had its Australian premiere at the Princess Theatre, Melbourne, in December 1966. It was chiefly notable for the first screen appearance of 17 year old Olivia Newton-John.

**The first animated feature film** was Eric Porter's *Marco Polo Jnr. versus the Red Dragon*, the story of an adventurous lad who discovers he is the seventh son of the seventh son of the legendary Marco Polo. Made in Sydney, the 88-min film was released in Australia in December 1972, won two major prizes at the 1973 Australian Film Awards, and was shown on Television in 1976.

## FILM CLUB

for amateur film makers was the Australian A.F.C. of Sydney, whose first production was *Caste*, a war film made in 1928 with Australian troops as extras. It was directed by Victor A. Bindley and six cameras were used.

## FILM CORPORATION, STATE

was the South Australian Film Corporation, established by the Dunstan government to provide information and facilities for feature films and TV series. The first three feature films produced under the auspices of the Corporation were *Sunday Too Far Away* (1975), *Picnic at Hanging Rock* (1975) and *Storm Boy* (1976).

## FILM MAGAZINE

was *The Photo-Play*, Sydney, first published on 6 January 1912. This was only two months after the appearance of the first fan magazine in Britain (*Pictures*) and less than a year after the first in America (*Motion Picture Story Magazine*).

# The first . . .

## FILM SCHOOL
was the Australian Film and Television School, opened at North Ryde, Sydney in 1973.

## FILM STUDIO
was erected by the Salvation Army's Biorama Co in Inkerman Road, Caulfield, Vic, in 1909. Two major feature films were made there, *The Scottish Covenanters* and *Heroes of the Cross*. The venture was short lived. In 1910 a new and unimaginative Commissioner for the SA closed down the Biorama Company and its studios.

## FINGERPRINTS
were first used for criminal investigation by Police Sergeant Walter Childs, who took the prints of 20 year old clerk John Miller at the Water Police Court in Sydney on 28 December 1902. Miller had been arrested for breaking and entering a dwelling in Mackay Street, Potts Point, five days earlier. Sargeant Childs discovered prints on the top sash of the upper window of the third storey and had the wood cut away as evidence. Ernest Soane of the Department of Prisons, in charge of the finger-print bureau, confirmed that the prints on the sash matched those of the accused. Britain's first conviction on the evidence of fingerprints had taken place three months earlier. The technique had been pioneered by the La Plata police in Argentina in 1892.

## FIRE BRIGADE
was formed in 1837 by the Australian Fire and Life Assurance Co. of Sydney. By 1840 it had two fire stations, with a fire engine at each, and 25 firemen. Various fire brigades were established by insurance companies over the next forty years, providing a service to buildings which carried the company's fire mark. These were united as the Sydney Fire Brigade in 1884.

*A Scene from 'Soldiers of the Cross', one of the first dramatic films made in Australia.*

## FIRE ENGINES

were first used on the occasion of a fire at No 2 Barracks at what is now Wynyard Square, Sydney, in January 1822. The appliances were kept at the barracks and housed in the Ordnance Section.

*The first motor fire engine* was a Merryweather imported from England by the Sydney Fire Brigade in April 1904.

## FIREWORK DISPLAY

took place at Government House, Sydney, on 25 June 1807 as the culmination of a reception given by Governor Bligh in honour of Captain Hagamaester, commander of the visiting Russian sloop-of-war *Neva*.

## FLAG, AUSTRALIAN NATIONAL

was flown for the first time above the Exhibition Building, Melbourne, on 3 September 1901. At the time of Federation, a competition had been announced for the best design for an official flag for the Commonwealth of Australia. There were 30,000 entries, of which five, almost identical to each other, were judged equal winners. These five designs were incorporated into one, represented by the flag flown at Melbourne that 3 September — essentially consisting of the Blue Ensign bearing the five stars of the constellation of the Southern Cross and the large six-pointed star representing the six states of the Commonwealth. The five people who each submitted the design on which the flag was based were Mrs Annie Dorrington of Perth; E. J. Nuttal of Melbourne; Ivor Evans of Melbourne; Leslie J. Hawkins of Sydney; William Stevens of Auckland, N.Z. The last three named were boys in their teens. King Edward VII's approval of the design was promulgated in the *Commonwealth Gazette* on 20 February 1903.

## FLAG, STATE

The first of the Australian States to have its own official flag was Victoria, which adopted a design consisting of 'five white stars, representing the constellation of the Southern Cross' on 4 February 1870. It was raised for the first time aboard HMVS *Nelson*, flagship of the Victorian Navy, at Williamstown on 9 February. The only change to the Victorian flag is that since Federation in 1901 it has borne a St Edward's Crown in addition to the constellation. The oldest unchanged state flag is that of Western Australia, also adopted in 1870, which has preserved the same Black Swan design since that date.

## FLOODLIT FOOTBALL MATCH

was held at Adelaide Oval by electric light on 1 July 1885.

## FLOWER SHOW

was held by the Floral and Horticultural Society at Sydney on 19 September 1838.

## FLUSH LAVATORY

was a Bramah pedestal and cistern installed at Government House, Sydney, during Governor Macquarie's period of office and listed in an inventory of furnishings made by Major Anthill in 1821.

The first private house in Australia definitely known to have contained a water closet was Aberglasslyn, near Maitland, NSW, where John Verge installed this notable sanitary improvement when the house was built in 1840.

## FLYING DOCTOR

service began on 15 May 1928, when Pilot A. Affleck and Dr. K. H. Vincent Welsh began operating a DH50A air ambulance, equipped with two stretchers, out of Cloncurry, Queensland.

## FLYING SCHOOL

was Hart's Aviation School, established by the first licensed pilot in Australia, dentist W. E. Hart, at Penrith, NSW, on 3 January 1912.

*The first military flying school* was the Central Flying School founded at Point Cook, Vic, in 1914, to train military aviators. At the outset the entire staff comprised two pilot instructors, two mechanics, a cook and a caretaker. Training began on 17 August, when four trainees began learning to fly on a pair of Deperdussins and a Bristol Box Kite. These 'planes were the **first Australian military aircraft**. The first pilot to qualify was Lt R. Williams on 12 November 1914.

## FOOD RATIONING

was introduced on 30 March 1942. Tea was limited to half a pound per person for five weeks and sugar to a pound per person a week. Butter rationing started on 7 June 1943 at half a pound per person a week and meat rationing on 17 January 1944 with 2½ lbs per person a week.

# The first . . .

## FOOTBALL

is first recorded in twin reports that appeared in the *Monitor* and the *Sydney Gazette* on 25 July 1829. Said the former: 'The privates in the barracks are in the habit of amusing themselves with a game of football' and added that the ball could be 'daily described repeatedly mounting higher or lower, according to the skill and energy of the bold military kickers thereof'. The *Gazette* identified the players as belonging to the 57th and 39th, both Irish regiments, whose men were said to 'show considerable ability in the practice of one of their national recreations'.

**The first soccer club** was the Wanderers, formed by an English schoolmaster, J. W. Fletcher, at a meeting held at Aaron's Exchange Hotel, Sydney, on 3 August 1880. The first match under Association Rules was held on Parramatta Common before a crowd estimated at over a thousand on 14 August 1880, when the Wanderers beat the King's School 5-0.

**Australian Rules Football** began in a rudimentary form in 1858, though the rules were not properly codified until eight years later. The founders of the game were Tom Wills and his cousin and brother-in-law H. C. A. Harrison. Wills, the grandson of a convict, had been educated at Rugby School, where he was captain of the football team. On returning to his father's station at Lexington, Vic, in 1856, he advised Harrison against taking up the Rugby game, as he thought it 'unsuitable for grown men engaged in making a living'. Instead the cousins determined to found a new form of football, though in what respect it was more suitable for grown men is unclear, except that it is even more violent. **The first club** is believed to have been established at Geelong, while **the first match** was played between Melbourne Church of England Grammar School and Scotch College at Melbourne on 7 August 1858. This was played with 40 a side with goals half a mile apart, and the first team to score two goals was to be the winner. The game started at noon and when darkness fell only one goal had been scored, by Scotch College. It resumed a fortnight later, but by dusk there had been no further score. When another afternoon's play the following week again failed to yield a goal for either side, the match was declared a draw. The rules as codified by Wills and Harris were agreed at a meeting of the various Melbourne clubs on 8 May 1866.

See also Rugby Football.

## 40 HOUR WEEK

became standard on 1 January 1948 under a ruling of the Commonwealth Arbitration Court. Day shift print workers of the Melbourne *Age* and *Argus* newspapers had won a 40 hour week in 1936.

## FOSTER CHILD

to be committed to care by a magistrate's court was Rebekah Allen, daughter of Private John Brown and Susannah Allen. The latter, a convict woman, died in childbirth on 17 October 1789 and on 24 October the infant Rebekah was given into the custody of Frances Davis, who was 'informed that she would be allowed to keep the child for as long as she did justice to it'.

## FOUR DAY WORKING WEEK

was awarded to 200,000 employees in the motor trade by the Arbitration Commission in April 1983.

## FOXES

were introduced to Australia by 'Gentleman' Pyke of Upper Werribee, Victoria, in 1845. Over the next 40 years they became a serious pest on the mainland. There are no foxes in Tasmania.

## FREEPOST

was introduced in May 1975.

## FREEWAY

The first freeway was the Circular Quay by-pass road, Sydney, built at a cost of £2.5 million and opened on 24 March 1958. It was later extended to Woolloomooloo as the Cahill Expressway, completed in March 1962.

## FREIGHT CARRIER

to operate a scheduled service by road was William Highland, who began operating a once-a-week stage-cart between Sydney and Richmond on 1 October 1814.

## FRENCHMAN

to land in Australia was a convict called Peter Paris, who arrived with the First Fleet on 18 January 1788. He was probably also the first convict to escape from Australia, together with a female companion called Ann Smith. It is believed that they stowed away on one of the French ships of the Comte de la Perouse's expedition, which left the shores of NSW in March 1788 after a six week stay.

**The first French settler** was James Larra, who came to New South Wales with the Second Fleet in June 1790 and later became Australia's first restaurateur at Parramatta.

## FRIENDLY SOCIETY

was the Shipwright's United Friendly Society founded in Sydney in 1830 by a group of boatbuilders for the mutual protection and benefit of members of their trade. The oldest friendly society in Australia is the Independent Order of Odd Fellows, whose first lodge was established at Sydney in 1836.

## FRINGE BENEFITS TAX

was announced by Federal Treasurer Paul Keating on 19 September 1985. Two major items covered in the Act were entertainment and substantiation, which came into force on 19 September 1985 and 1 July 1986 respectively.

## FROZEN EMBRYO BABY

in the world was Zoe Leyland, born in Melbourne on 28 March 1984.

## FROZEN FOODS

were Birds Eye Farm Fresh Frosted Foods, launched at two dozen stores in Sydney and Orange, NSW, in January 1950. There was originally a range of 14 locally grown fruits and vegetables and a number of imported lines, including fish fillets. The word 'frosted' was used because it sounded more enticing than 'frozen'. Australia came late to frozen foods, which had been pioneered by Birds Eye in the USA in 1930.

## FROZEN MEAT

The first shipment was of 40 tons of frozen beef and mutton, which left Sydney aboard the *Strathleven* on 28 October 1879 and arrived in London on 2 February 1880. It was sold at 6½d a pound. The meat was frozen by the ammonia process developed by James Harrison and E.M. Nicolle and adopted commercially by T.S. Mort. This was the first cargo of frozen meat to arrive in Britain, though not the first in the world — a shipment of 5,000 carcasses of mutton having been shipped

*A picture of frozen meat being exported to England on the* Strathleven.

from Buenos Aires to Le Havre aboard the SS *Paraguay* in April-May 1878.

## FURNISHED LODGINGS

The earliest reference to the availability of furnished lodgings is an advertisement in the *Sydney Gazette* of 1 February 1807 offering such accommodation at No 10 Sargeant Major's Row, Sydney. The landlord was Owen Cannor.

## FURNITURE

The earliest record of cabinet-making in Australia is contained in the Labour Returns of Work by Convict Artisans at the Lumber Yard in Sydney for 1800, which refer to a dressing table and toilet mirror made for the wife of Lieutenant-Governor King.

The first cabinet maker known to be practising his craft on a regular commercial basis was T. Williams of 26 Chapel Row, Sydney, whose advertisement in the *Sydney Gazette* early in 1804 'Respectfully acquaints Gentlemen and the Public in general that he Manufactures for sale all kinds of folding Desks, Tea Chests and Caddies, Writing, Card, Pembroke and oblong Dining Tables, Sea and Clothes Chests, Quadrant Cases richly ornamented in the native woods and a variety of other Articles peculiar to his profession, in a handsome style and at moderate prices.' No known examples of his work survive.

The earliest surviving piece of Australian furniture whose origins are documented is a specimen cabinet on a stand of she-oak veneered on to cedar and pine, made in 1815 by James Packer, the Australian-born apprentice of Irish cabinetmaker Lawrence Butler, a convict who had come to Sydney in 1802.

# The first ...

## GAOL TO INSTITUTE FILM SHOWS

in the world was Goulburn Gaol, Sydney, commencing on 3 January 1911 with a programme presented by the Methodist chaplain, the Rev J. H. Lewin. The *Melbourne Argus* reported: 'Some of the long-sentence prisoners had never previously seen moving pictures and they more especially enjoyed the entertainment. The pictures were of course of an elevating character, including *Waterways of Holland, Dogs of Various Countries* and *The Visit of the American Fleet*.'

## GARDEN

was dug on the east side of Sydney Cove, starting on 29 January 1788, at the site prepared for the erection of the first Government House. Trees, shrubs and other plants brought from the Cape of Good Hope and Rio de Janeiro were planted. At about the same time as the Governor's garden was planted a kitchen garden was dug next to the temporary hospital, in order to provide fresh vegetables for the sick.

Charles Worgan, Surgeon aboard the *Sirius*, recorded at the end of the first week of February that 'A few beans, peas, small sallad, that were sown on our arrival here have come up and appear at present very luxuriant'. Fruit was also cultivated,

Governor Phillip writing in September that his oranges, figs and vines, apples, pears and strawberries were all 'in fine order'.

## GARDENING BOOK

was A *Manual of Practical Gardening, adapted to the Climate of Van Diemen's Land*, Hobart, 1838.

## GAS FIRES

were marketed by the Metropolitan Gas Co of Melbourne in 1886.

## GAS LIGHTING

The first gas-lit building was the home of J. T. Wilson at 24 Upper Pitt Street, Sydney, illuminated on 19 July 1826. Wilson also hung a gas-lamp over the entrance to his place of business, which he renamed 'The Gas Light Brewery'.

*Public gas supply* was inaugurated by the Australian Gas Light Company on 24 May 1841, a day deliberately chosen to coincide with Queen Victoria's birthday. Nearly 200 private houses and offices and a number of hotels were illuminated with what the *Sydney Herald* described as 'a brilliancy almost too dazzling to look upon'. Street lighting was rather less dazzling. There were only 23 street lamps, a parsimonious government having decided only to erect them in front of its own buildings. As a further economy they were left unlit for the first two nights following each first full moon.

The gas was supplied from Australia's first gasometer, built at Darling Harbour at a cost of £8,000. The entrepreneur who brought the first gas lighting to Australian streets and buildings was Ralph Mansfield, a former Methodist missionary who had abandoned his spiritual calling in favour of more earthy pursuits. He was also the editor of the *Sydney Herald*, which not surprisingly extolled the venture as a credit to 'Sydney's taste and public spirit'.

*The first municipal gas supply* was established at Bega, NSW, in 1885.

## GAS STOVE

was manufactured by R. A. Walker of Melbourne in 1872. Walker was one of five gas stove manufacturers to exhibit at the Intercolonial Exhibition in September 1875 and he claimed to have already sold some 2,000 units. To demonstrate the capacity of a £4 Walker Stove, the chef of the Athenaeum

A.G.L. Collection

The first showroom of Australian Gas Light Company

Club, Alfred J. Wilkinson, used one to prepare a banquet for 20 which was 'pronounced excellent by all present'.

## GAZETTEER

was A *Geographical Dictionary; or Gazateer of the Australian Colonies*, by William Henry Wells, Sydney, 1848.

## GENERAL

The first Australian soldier to obtain the rank of General was John Soame Richardson (1836–96), the commandant of the New South Wales Contingent which fought in the Sudan in 1885, who was promoted to the rank of Major-General on 15 August 1885, two months' after returning from active service.

## GEOLOGICAL MAP

was of the Wellington Valley, published by T. L. Mitchell of Sydney in 1838. The first of the Australian continent was prepared by J. B. Jukes in 1850.

## GIFT TAX

was introduced by Queensland under the Gift Duty Act which became operational on 1 July 1926. This form of taxation had been

# The first...

pioneered by New Zealand as part of their Death Duties Act 1909.

## GIN

was produced by Robert Cooper, an ex-convict who had been transported for smuggling French brandy into England, at the Glenmore Distillery he established at Frog's Hollow, Paddington, in 1824. Cooper made a substantial fortune from his 'juniper juice' and built himself a mansion which he named Juniper Hall in celebration of the fact.

## GIRL GUIDES

The earliest troops are believed to have been formed in Powelltown, Tas, and at Hawthorn and Richmond, Vic, shortly after the movement was established by Sir Robert Baden-Powell and his sister Agnes in England in 1910.

## GLASS

was manufactured by convict Thomas Hutchinson on behalf of Messrs Lord and Williams at Simeon Lord's Macquarie Street premises in May 1812. The first articles produced were half-pint flint glass tumblers, said to be 'by no means inferior in appearance to any of the kind imported.'
**The first glass bottles** made in Australia were medicine and soft drink bottles produced by an English glass manufacturer called Ross who set up a glassworks in Liverpool Street, Sydney, in 1867.

See also Milk Bottles.

## GLIDER

flight was made by G. A. Taylor of the Army Intelligence Corps at Narrabeen Heads, near Sydney, on 5 December 1909. Taylor's glider, which he designed himself, was a biplane 28ft long and weighing 102 lbs. It had an 18ft wingspan and was built on the Voisin principle with a Hargrave box-kite tail. Exceptionally stable for an aircraft of this period, the machine could be turned and flown into the wind.

On the same day Taylor's wife Florence made the world's **first glider flight by a woman**, covering a distance of about 90 yards.
**The first gliding club** was established at Granville, NSW, in 1926.

## GOLD

was discovered by Assistant Surveyor James M. Brian on the Fish River, about 15 miles east of Bathurst, on 15 February 1823. His Field Book records: "At 8 chains 50 links to river and marked gum-tree, found numerous particles of gold in the sand and in the hills convenient to the river'.

The first sale of gold was made by a boy called Thomas Chapman, who sold a 16 ounce nugget he had found at Daisy Hill, Victoria, to Mrs Brentani of Collins Street, Melbourne, at the end of 1849. Fearful of the authorities, he then fled to Sydney aboard the *Sea-Horse*.

The place of Edward Hargraves in the chronicle of Australia's gold discoveries is an important one, since he stimulated the first gold rush, but he was by no means the first to find gold either in New South Wales or Victoria. He was, however, the first to successfully *pan* for gold, a technique he had learned in California, making his initial strike washing the gravel at the junction of Summer Hill and Lewis Pond creeks, at Ophir on 12 Feb 1851.

Numerous other discoveries were made in New South Wales and Victoria during that year and the first prospector's license was issued to Richard Roe on 24 May 1851 authorising him to dig for gold at Bathurst.

## GOLF

was introduced to Australia by the Hon. James Graham of Fife, Scotland, who joined with others in having a course laid out at Flagstaff Hill, Melbourne, in 1847.
**The first golf caddies** were employed by the Royal Melbourne Golf Club when the Caulfield course was opened on 4 July 1891.
**The first professional golfer** was Richard Taylor of Hoylake, who was appointed to Royal Melbourne Golf Club in 1891 at the age of 20.
**The first championship match** was the Ladies' Championship of Victoria played at Geelong on 29–30 August 1894 and won by Miss C. B. Mackenzie, who also won in the following two years and again in 1898. Ladies having shown the way, the gentlemen followed with their own Australian Amateur Championship at Caulfield in November 1894.
**The first Australian Open** golf title was won by the Hon. Michael Scott on 3 September 1904.
**The first Australian to win the US Open Golf Championship** was David Graham on 21 June 1981.

## GOLF BALLS

manufactured in Australia were produced in 1932 by the Dunlop Rubber Co. of Melbourne.

## GOVERNMENT ADVISER ON WOMEN'S AFFAIRS

in the world was former Adelaide solicitor Elizabeth Reid, appointed in July 1973.

## GOVERNOR-GENERAL

was the former Governor of Victoria, John Adrian Louis Hope, seventh Earl of Hopetoun, who assumed his new office on 1 January 1901.

**The first Australian-born Governor-General** was Sir Isaac Isaacs, former Attorney-General and Chief Justice of the High Court, who took office on 22 January 1931.

**The first Governor-General of working class origins** was Sir William John McKell, appointed on 11 March 1947. McKell left school at 13 and worked as a boilermaker before entering politics.

## GREEK ORTHODOX PRIEST

was Archimandrite Dorotheos, who arrived from Samos in 1896 and began ministering to the Greek communities in Sydney and Melbourne.

**The first Greek Orthodox church** was Holy Trinity in Bourke Street, Surry Hills, Sydney, whose foundation stone was laid on 29 May 1898.

## GREEKS

first arrived in Australia on 28 August 1829 on board the convict ship *Norfolk*. The seven Greeks — Andonis Manolis, Damianos Ninis, Georgios Vasilakis, Ghikas Boulgaris, Konstandinos Strombolis and Nikolaos Papandreas — had been convicted of piracy and transported to New South Wales. In their twenties and unmarried, they came from the Greek island of Hydra.

## GREEN BAN

meaning the refusal of union labour to work on developments reckoned to be damaging to the environment, was imposed on Kelly's Bush at Hunters Hill, Sydney, in 1971. The term 'Green Ban' was coined by Jack Mundey, secretary of the Builders' Labourers Federation. Some 50 Green Bans were de-clared in Sydney over the next three years and nearly 30 in Melbourne.

## GREYHOUND TRACK RACING

was inaugurated by the American 'Judge' Swindell on a specially constructed track within the trotting circuit at Forest Lodge, Epping, NSW, on 28 May 1927.

## GUIDE DOG

was a black labrador called Dreena, who arrived in Perth, WA, with blind economics lecturer Arnold Cook in August 1950. Dreena had been trained at the Exeter Guide Dog Centre in England.

**The first guide dog training centre** in Australia was opened in two disused tram-cars, bought for £90, at Shenton Park, Perth in January 1952. The director of the centre was Miss Betty Bridge, who had formerly been a trainer at the Exeter Centre.

**The first Australian-trained guide dog** was Beau, who graduated in August 1952 and was delivered to its new owner Mrs Elsie Mead. They were together 13 years. On one occasion Beau prevented Mrs Mead from walking into a lift shaft when the doors were open but the lift several floors below.

Department of Defence

*Sidewinder air to air missiles seen on a jet.*

## GUIDED MISSILES

were Bristol Bloodhound MK 1 ground-to-air missiles and Sidewinder air-to-air missiles which went into service with the RAAF in 1960.

## GUIDED MISSILE BASE

was opened at Williamtown, NSW, in 1961.

## GYMNASTICS

were introduced to Australia by M. Cavendish de Castell, late of Paris, and taught at the Academy of Dance he opened in Sydney in 1833.

# The first . . .

## HAIRDRESSER
(known) was W. Rafter of 5 George Street, Parramatta, in 1825.

## HALF-HOLIDAY
on Saturdays was first adopted by Farmer & Co., draper's of Sydney, in 1866. Later the same year James McEwan's, a large hardware store, became the first business house in Melbourne to close at lunchtime on Saturdays.

## HALFTONE ILLUSTRATIONS
or direct reproduction of a photograph in an Australian newspaper was a group portrait of Indian cricketers on a visit to England, which appeared in *The Sydney Mail* in October 1888.

## HANSARD
was *The Victorian Hansard*, published by the proprietors of the *Melbourne Argus* starting in November 1856. It became an official publication of the Government of Victoria some ten years later. South Australia's Hansard began in 1857, Queensland's in 1865, Western Australia's in 1876 and New South Wales' in 1879. Only Tasmania of the Australian colonies failed to produce a Hansard and as late as 1950 its Parliament was reported to be the only one in the British Commonwealth with-

out one. (Tasmania eventually succumbed in 1979.)

## HATS
were first manufactured in a hat factory established by merchant Simeon Lord on his Macquarie Street premises in June 1811 and carried on under the direction of Reuben Uther, an expert hatter. The factory produced both ready-to-wear and made-to-measure 'ladies', gentlemen's and children's fancy brown hats'. The enterprise was still in being in 1820, when prices were quoted at 10s-25s.

## HEALTH FOOD SHOP
was opened in Royal Arcade, Sydney, by the Sydney Sanitarium and Benevolent Association in 1902. It was run by Seventh Day Adventists.

## HEART TRANSPLANT
was performed on 57-year old Richard Pye at St Vincent's Hospital, Sydney, by Dr Harry Windsor on 23 October 1968. This was less than a year after Prof. Christian Barnard's pioneer heart transplant at Cape Town.

## HELICOPTER
was a RAAF Sikorski S 51 test flown at Laverton, Vic on 3 October 1947.
*The first helicopter in regular commercial service* was the Bristol 171 *Yarrana*, which became operational with Australian National Airways on 19 May 1956.
*The first solo Atlantic crossing by helicopter* was made in a Bell 206 Jetranger by Australian pilot Dick Smith, who left Fort Worth, Texas, on 6 August 1982 and arrived at Stornaway in the Hebrides via New York, Canada, Greenland, Iceland and the Faroes 12 days later.

## HELIPORT (*commercial*)
was opened at Melbourne on 20 December 1960.

## HIRE PURCHASE
finance house was established by Western Australian Ian Jacoby in 1925 when he lent £60 to a friend to buy a Studebaker car. Jacoby arranged for the loan and the interest to be paid off in instalments, retaining ownership of the car until the debt was discharged. Aged 25, at that time he was manager of the passenger department of shipowners

MacIllwraith McEacharn, a position he had held since he was only 21. During this period he had saved £1,000 from his salary and, following the initial venture with the Studebaker, went on to finance some 30 other hire purchase agreements over the next three years. In 1928 he joined the newly formed Industrial Acceptance Corporation, taking control the following year from its American founders and building it up into Australia's first hire purchase company.

## HISTORY, COMPLETE WORK OF

was Roderick Flanagan's *History of New South Wales; with an Account of Van Diemen's Land, New Zealand, Port Phillip, Moreton Bay and other Australasian Settlements*, published in two volumes in London in 1862.

## HOCKEY

was first played by Royal Navy teams in the Parklands at Adelaide in 1882.

## HOLIDAYS, PAID ANNUAL

for all members of a particular trade were introduced for typographers in Western Australia in 1914 under an Award made by the State Tribunal. The first Federal Award was made to commercial printers on 31 December 1936.

**The first State to legislate for annual holidays for all employees** was New South Wales, with effect from 1 January 1945.

## HOME MOVIES

began in Australia early in 1897 with the introduction of the 35mm Motorgraph, an English-made combined projector and camera, by Messrs Watson and Sons of Swanston Street, Melbourne, suppliers of scientific instruments. Watson's offered a selection of about 100 films for home viewing. Originally marketed in London at 12 gns the previous November, the tiny 6ins x 5½ins Motorgraph was the world's first cinematograph apparatus specially for amateurs, making its appearance less than a year after the Lumière brothers had pioneered motion pictures as a commercial entertainment.

## HOMOSEXUAL DISCO

was Capriccio's Disco in Oxford Street, Sydney, opened in June 1968.

## HOMOSEXUAL HOTEL

was the *Cricketers' Arms*, Surry Hills, Sydney in December 1972.

## HOMOSEXUAL SAUNA

was the Bondi Junction Steambaths opened in February 1966.

## HOSPITAL

was established in a tent on the west side of Sydney Cove and is first mentioned in Orders for the Day on 30 January 1788. Construction

Department of Defence

*The first Australian-built helicopter, the Sikorsky S51.*

# The first ...

of a permanent building, known as Sydney General Hospital, began in March 1788. Capt. David Collins of the Royal Marines wrote: 'A building for the reception of the sick was now absolutely necessary, and one, eighty-four feet by twenty-three, was put in hand, to be divided into a dispensary, (all the hospital-stores being at that time under tents), a ward for the troops, and another for the convicts. It was to be built of wood, and the roof to be covered in with shingles, made from a species of fir found here.' This hospital, which was staffed by Surgeon John White and his four assistants, stood between what are now Argyle Street and Globe Street. Conditions for the sick were far from ideal — besides the shortage of medicines, Surgeon White reported in July 1788 that there were no sheets or blankets to cover the beds.

**The first military hospital** was built at Sydney in 1798 for the rank and file of the New South Wales Corps.

**The first maternity hospital** was the Melbourne Lying-in Hospital, which was established at Eastern Hill at the instigation of Mrs Edward Barker and received its first patients on 19 August 1856. It became the Hospital for Women in 1886.

**The first children's hospital** was the Melbourne Hospital for Sick Children, which was opened with six beds in a small house in Stephen Street (now Exhibition Street) in September 1870. It is now the Royal Children's Hospital.

## HOSPITAL ALMONER

was Anges McIntyre, formerly of St Thomas's Hospital in London, who was appointed to Royal Melbourne Hospital in 1929.

## HOTEL

offering residential accommodation of a high standard was the *Freemason's Arms*, a substantial brick building erected in 1800 by French settler James Larra at Parramatta on the site now occupied by the Court House. Larra had opened a pub with the same name in 1796, but this was a crude wattle and daub edifice with few pretensions to gentility. Visiting French naturalist Francois Peron, who stayed

*Sydney's first Hospital set up for convicts in 1788.*

at the new *Freemason's Arms* in July 1802, re-counted: 'During the six days we remained at Parramatta, we were served with an elegance and even a luxury, which we could not suppose obtainable on these shores. The best wines, such as Madeira, Port, Xeres, Cape, and Bordeaux, always covered our tables; we were served on plate, and the decanters and glasses were for purest flint; nor were the eatables inferior to the liquors. Always anxious to anticipate the taste or wishes of his guests, Mr. Larra caused us to be served in the French style; and this act of politeness was the more easy to him, because among the convicts who acted as his domestics, was an excellent French cook, a native of Paris, as well as two others of our countrymen.'

Peron paid £14 6s 0d for six nights, rather more than a first class hotel in London would have charged at the time — indicative of the luxurious accommodation offered by the only true hotel in the rude penal colony.

Sydney was well behind Parramatta in offering anything comparable. The capital's first hotel, and the first in Australia so designated, was the *Sydney Hotel* in George Street, opened by postmaster Isaac Nichols on the occasion of the Bachelors' Ball on 26 June 1811. The name was selected by Governor Macquarie, who was guest of honour at the ball.

For the first pubs see *Licensed Premises*.

## HUNT

on record was organized by officers of the 73rd Regiment and took place in November 1811. The *Sydney Gazette* reported that it began with an unsuccessful draw for a dingo near the Nepean and culminated with a kangaroo 'kill' in the bush.

**The first regularly established hunt** was the Sydney Subscription Hunt, founded at a meeting held at the Pulteney Hotel on 17 February 1835. The subscription was £5 p.a.

## HYDRO-ELECTRIC STATION

was established at Thargomindah in the dry south-west of Queensland, where a water-wheel was harnessed to an artesian bore in 1893 to supply the community with electricity.

**The first municipal hydro-electric station** and the first to be generated by a river, was the Duck Reach plant built by Launceston City Council on the South Esk River in Tasmania and brought into operation in 1895.

*Hydrofoils have been operating on Sydney Harbour for over 20 years.*

## HYDROFOIL

in regular service began plying between Circular Quay, Sydney and Manly on 7 January 1965.

## HYMN BOOK

was *An Abridgement of the Wesleyan Hymns, selected from the larger Hymn-book, Published in England, for the use of the people called Methodists* published by Robert Howe at Sydney in 1821. Howe also published the first Church of England hymnal in Australia, *Select Portions of the Psalms of David*, in 1828. The first Roman Catholic hymnal was published the same year by Arthur Hill of Sydney as a supplement to a book titled *Antidote to Misrepresentation and Impiety*.

## INCOME TAX

was imposed by South Australia under its Parliament Act No 323 of 14 November 1884 at the flat rate of 3d in the pound on earned

# The first . . .

income and 6d in the pound on unearned income. New South Wales and Victoria followed suit in 1895, NSW introducing a flat rate of 6d in the pound over £200 and Victoria sliding scale of 4d-8d in the pound for incomes over £200. Tasmania's first income tax was in 1894, Western Australia's in 1899 and Queensland's in 1902.

*Federal income tax* was introduced on 13 September 1915 as a war measure.

**PAYE** was introduced in February 1943.

## INDUSTRIAL FILM

was *The History of a Loaf,* made by Cousens Spencer for the Abel & Co Ltd bakery of Newtown, NSW, and premiered at the *Lyceum Theatre,* Sydney on 14 March 1908. The film followed the progress of a loaf from the harvesting of the wheat to taking the newly baked bread from the oven.

## INHABITANTS OF EUROPEAN STOCK

were 1,024 convicts, Marines, naval personnel, wives and children who made landfall aboard the eleven vessels of the 'First Fleet' at Botany Bay on 18 January 1788. The terrain at Botany Bay being unsuitable for a settlement, one of the vessels, the *Supply,* set sail again for Port Jackson, arriving on the evening of 25 January. Forty convicts having been disembarked the next day, Saturday 26 January, an immediate start was made on clearing the ground to erect storehouses and a hospital, the first buildings in what was to become the city of Sydney. A flagstaff was erected at the landing place and Governor Phillip formally took possession of the new land for His Majesty King George III. The rest of the First Fleet arrived at Port Jackson on the same day. The composition of the first group of arrivals from Europe was as follows:

Governor Arthur Phillip, R. N. and 9 staff; Marines — 209; wives of Marines — 31; children of Marines — 23; convicts — 717: (female 188); children of convicts — 17; servants — 2; others — 15. The last member of the First Fleet remaining in Australia died 75 years later in May 1863. Only 130 of the members of the First Fleet have descendants living today in Australia who are able to prove their lineage.

*The first free settler* was William Smith, the only one to sail with the First Fleet. Governor Phillip was not told of his presence and only found out, much to his displeasure, when they reached the Cape of Good Hope. On arrival at Botany Bay, the Governor refused him permission to land and he remained on board ship when the rest of the First Fleeters disembarked at Port Jackson. A petition to the Governor in his favour by Arthur Bowes, Surgeon on the *Lady Penrhyn,* led to a change of heart and Smith was allocated a tent and made Constable of the infant settlement. He settled on shore at Port Jackson on 21 February 1788, and that day was assigned a negro and a boy called Joseph Harris as servants. Smith remains rather a shadowy character in the annals of early New South Wales. Certainly he does not seem to have been universally liked. Ann Smith, a convict woman who had a dispute with him about some trifling matter a few months after the founding of the settlement, said that he was a busybody, and that 'though on the ship she took him for a gentleman, she now found quite the contrary'. Early in 1789 he was seconded to Parramatta, where he was put in charge of a party of convicts cultivating land. Being advanced in years he found it difficult to keep the convicts under control and was made a storekeeper instead. Nothing is known of his later life.

*The first group of migrants* to Australia were Mr and Mrs Thomas Rose and family, Edward Powell, Joseph Webb, Thomas Webb and Frederick Meredith, who arrived at Sydney aboard the *Bellona* transport on 16 January 1793. They were to be granted lands free of expense and to have 'an assortment of Tools and Implements out of the public stores', in addition to two years' provisions and the service of convicts 'to be assigned free of expense'. Their passage to New South Wales was paid by the government. Each was given a farm at Liberty Plains, two miles from what is now Circular Quay, the district being so named because they were free men and not convicts.

## INSTANT COFFEE

was Nescafé, imported in 1939. It had been first manufactured the previous year by Nestlé at Vevey, Switzerland. This followed eight years of research after the Brazilian Institute of Coffee had asked the company to find a way of reducing coffee beans to a soluble powder. Nescafé was first produced in Australia in 1947.

## INSURANCE

was underwritten in Sydney by Alexander Riley and Richard Jones, who announced their appointment as representatives of Lloyd's of London in October 1816.

*Life assurance* was first offered in Australia by Robert Howe, Sydney agent of the London-based Eagle Assurance Office, on 10 February 1827. The premiums for whole life ranged from 3.72% at aged 21 to 6.03% at age 50. Native born Australians were offered cheaper rates as they were considered more likely to withstand the rigours of colonial life. The Eagle made a special point of the fact that, unlike other insurance companies, it was prepared to accept policies from people who suffered from gout, hernia and 'emotion or mental derangements'.

*The first Australian insurance company* was the Australian Marine Insurance Co, founded at Sydney on 31 January 1831.

*Fire insurance* was first offered by the Sydney and Hobart agents of the Alliance British and Foreign Life and Fire Insurance Co of London on 26 July 1833.

*The first Australian fire and life insurance company* was the Australian Fire and General and Life Company, which made its initial announcement in the *Sydney Gazette* of 5 January 1836.

*The first insurance salesman* was Benjamin Short, who became a full-time agent for the Australian Mutual Provident Society of Sydney in June 1860.

## IRON

was first produced in a Catalan furnace at Ironstone Bridge, Mittagong, NSW in 1848. The first products made from the iron were a cast iron stove and a number of spades. One of the spades was used for turning the first sod of the railway line between Sydney and Parramatta and it still exists today. The Ironstone Bridge smelter was renamed the Fitz Roy Ironworks after a visit from Governor Fitz Roy in 1850 and iron continued to be mined and smelted there until 1877.

## IRON RAILS

were laid down at Newcastle, NSW, by the Australian Agricultural Co in 1827 to form a tramway running from the head of a coal mine to the wharf. Coal could be tipped directly from the wagons on to the collier. The Australian Agricultural Co. held a monopoly on coal mining in the Newcastle district.

## IRON FOUNDRY

was established by James Blanch in 1823 next to the *Royal Hotel* in George Street. Blanch produced a wide variety of metalwork, ranging from 'handsome dish covers, equal to any made in London' to a complete beam steam engine which was still in existence at an old flour mill in Dapto as late as 1900.

## JAM MANUFACTURE

on a factory scale was established by George Peacock at Hobart in 1861.

## JEHOVAH'S WITNESSES

formed a branch of the Watchtower Bible and Tract Society in Melbourne in 1904. The sect was declared illegal in January 1941 because of its neutrality in the War, but kept going as an underground movement and was rehabilitated by an order of the Supreme Court in 1943.

## JEWELLERY

The earliest recorded piece of Australian-made jewellery is referred to in a letter from the Irish political convict, W. Maum, to Viscount Castlereagh in May 1806. ' Governor King having, at the intervention of Mrs King (his lady) granted an unconditional pardon to Austin and Meurant, the two notorious forgers on the Irish Bank in 1798 and whose lives were saved on the express conditions of their being transported for life, incurred much censure for his conduct as these men were never in the employ of govern-

# The first . . .

ment since their arrival nor were they in any degree instrumental in contributing to the welfare of the colony and were solely employed in making jewellery and trinkets for Mrs King, Meurant in particular, having made her a present of a necklace to the value of £66. 5s.'

Meurant and Austin, both lifers, arrived in Sydney on 11 January 1800, while Philip Gidley King became Governor of NSW on 28 September of the same year. It is possible therefore that jewellery was being manufactured in Australia from the first year of the 19th Century.

**The first jeweller and watchmaker** to set up a regular business enterprise was W. Moreton of Pitt's Row, Sydney, who advertised in the *Sydney Gazette* of 15 May 1803 a range of goods and services including 'Miniatures mounted, Devices in Hair for Rings, Pins and Lockets: — Gold Chains, Seals, Fancy Rings, Pins, Ear-Rings, Necklaces, Etc. Etc.'

## JEWISH IMMIGRANT

to come to Australia as a free settler was Barnett Levey, who arrived in Sydney at the age of 23 in December 1821. As proprietor of the *Royal Hotel* he had a somewhat chequered career in the 1820s, though he was the instigator during this period of regular public concerts and also the first regular theatrical performances since the 1790s. In 1833 he established the *Theatre Royal*, an event which marks the start of the continuous history of drama in Australia. He died only four years later, largely unappreciated by the colonists he sought to entertain and amuse — only a few weeks before his demise he had been vilified in the *Sydney Gazette* as 'a slight unmeritable man, one so little capable of distinguishing between his real friends and his pretended ones, and so injudicious as to raise a storm which it is not in his power to allay'.

When the first census in New South Wales was conducted in 1828, there were 95 inhabitants (including convicts) professing the Jewish religion.

## JEWISH WORSHIP

was conducted by German-Jewish convict Joseph Marcus at Sydney in 1820. He continued to hold services until his death in 1828.

**The first Jewish marriages** were performed by Phillip Joseph Cohen at his house in George Street, Sydney, in 1828. He had a licence from the Chief Rabbi in London enabling him to undertake this office.

**The first Rabbi to visit Australia** was Aaron Levy, who arrived at Sydney in 1830 to arrange a religious divorce.

**The first synagogue** was established in a small rented building on the north side of Bridge Street, Sydney, in 1831. There were at that time 345 Jews resident in Sydney.

**The first purpose-built synagogue** was 'an elegant piece of architecture in the Egyptian style . . . seventy-two feet long by thirty-eight wide', erected in York Street, Sydney, and consecrated on 2 April 1844.

## JEWISH PERIODICAL

was *The Voice of Jacob* of *The Hebrew's Monthly Miscellany*, Sydney, first published on 27 May 1842. It ran for three issues.

## JUNIOR FARMER'S CLUB

was founded at Glen Innes, NSW, in 1928.

## JUVENILE COURT

in the world was established in April 1890 in a room of the State Children's Department, Flinders Street, Adelaide, SA. It was instigated by social reformer Miss Caroline Clark. The Police Magistrate or two Justices of the Peace attended to try cases and only the parents and witnesses were allowed to be present. Under an Act of 1896 it became mandatory to try offenders under 18 at the Children's Court in the City and suburbs and in the Magistrate's room in the country. According to a report a few years later, a large proportion of the misdemeanours tried were 'breaking windows, obstructing or endangering the streets by playing games in the public thoroughfares, and so on. Offences like these against city by-laws of course, have to be repressed, but they do not necessarily indicate the beginning of a criminal record. Hence the danger that this should be the case is minimised by the operation of a Court which does not have any criminal taint behind it'.

America had its first children's court at Chicago in 1899 and Britain did not follow Australia's lead until 1910.

# KIDNAPPING

for ransom took place on 7 July 1960 when 8½ year old schoolboy Graeme Thorne was snatched after his father had won £100,000 in the Sydney Opera House Lottery. The kidnapper, Stephen Bradley, killed the boy and was later apprehended, receiving a sentence of life imprisonment.

# KNIGHTHOOD

to be conferred on a native of Australia was granted on 12 March 1856 to Sir William Macarthur, born at Parramatta in 1800 the son of John and Elizabeth Macarthur, in recognition of his services as Commissioner for New South Wales at the Paris Exhibition of 1855.

# KENTUCKY FRIED CHICKEN

was opened at Guildford, NSW, on 27 April 1968. According to *Newsweek*, the Colonel's recipe consists of 'one part food, one part packaging, and one part mythology'. Within ten years there were 168 of the red and white striped chicken parlours throughout Australia.

# KOALA, SIGHTING OF

by white inhabitants of Australia took place near Mittagong, NSW, in 1798 when ex-convict John Wilson and a youth called John Price saw what the latter described as 'an animal which the natives call cullawine, which much resembles the sloths in America'.

*The earliest known illustration of a koala.*

Mitchell Library

71

# The first . . .

## LABOR POLITICIAN TO BECOME A STATE GOVERNOR

was Sir James O'Grady (1866–1934), who was born at Bristol, the son of a dock labourer and started work at the age of 9. A Labor MP in the British House of Commons for 18 years, he took up office as Governor of Tasmania on 23 December 1924. He was subsequently Governor of the Falkland Islands.

## LABOR REPRESENTATION

The first political party dedicated to the purpose of securing Parliamentary representation of the working class was the Political Labor League of Victoria, which was founded at Melbourne under the chairmanship of Ben Douglas, a plasterer, on 22 March 1859. It marked a completely new departure in working class politics, for it was intended as a Labor party that would seek the election of nominated Labor candidates, not simply as a pressure group supporting the candidate most likely to reflect its own interests. The party's platform included the payment of MPs, the 'immediate repeal of the Master and Servants Act and all class laws', the legal enforcement of an 8 hour day, and as a guiding principle, 'equality of all citizens'. In fact the Labor League had little effect on mainstream Victorian politics; after an existence of little over a year, it was merged with the Land Convention, having enjoyed a single triumph at the polls.

**The first Labor MP** was Charles Jardine Don, a stonemason and former Chartist, who had emigrated to Victoria from Glasgow in 1853. He stood as Political Labor League candidate for Collingwood and was elected to the Legislative Assembly on 26 August 1859, continuing to sit, after the Labor League had been merged with the Land Convention, until 1864. According to a letter addressed to Sir Henry Barkly by the Duke of Newcastle, 24 December 1861, Don's maiden speech in the Legislature was made amid 'the stares and stillness of intense curiosity. The incarnation of our democracy was before our statesmen, and that was no joke . . . He introduced himself as a new fact in the British Empire — an actual working artisan in a Legislative Assembly to speak and vote for his class.' Don accorded to the description of 'working artisan' in a fullest sense, for he used to work at his trade of stonemason by day and attend Parliament only at night. At one time he was actually one of the workmen employed on repairs to the Parliament Building, leaving the scaffolding at the end of the day to go down and sit in the Chamber.

**The first Labor Party** to be so called was the Queensland Labor Party, founded at a meeting convened by the Queensland Provincial Council of the Australian Labor Federation at Blackall in September 1890. The first two members elected under the auspices of the new party were T. J. Ryan for Barcoo and G. J. Hall for Bundaberg in 1892, though there were already two sitting members who had been elected in the Labor interest before its founding. Labor won 16 seats out of 72 in the first General Election it contested, held in April–May 1893. The South Australian Labor Party had also contested its first General Election in April 1893, winning 10 seats.

**The Federal Parliamentary Labor Party** was founded on 8 May 1901 under the chairmanship of 34 year old newspaper compositor Chris Watson. The Labor leader had been born at Valparaiso, Chile, when his Scottish father and English mother were en route to New Zealand. In 1904 he became the first Labor Prime Minister of a sovereign nation (see below).

**The first Labor Government** in the world came to power in Queensland on 1 December 1899 under the leadership of Anderson Dawson, Member for Charters Towers, who had become the world's first Labor Prime Minister three days earlier. It was a short-lived government, lasting but a single day in Parliament — when the House refused to adjourn on Dawson's motion on 5 December, his Ministry resigned forthwith. Born at Rockhampton the child of poor Scottish parents, Anderson Dawson was a mining amalgamator by trade and though possessed of little formal education, was a gifted orator and able administrator.

**The first Labor Government of the Commonwealth of Australia** was formed by J. C. Watson with a minority in Parliament on 27 April 1904, following the resignation of Alfred Deakin over a Labor amendment to the Conciliation and Arbitration Bill. Among the members of his Ministry was Anderson Dawson, the world's first Labor premier (see above). Less than four months later Watson resigned and Deakin resumed the reigns of office.

**The first majority Labor Government and the first to be elected** was formed under Andrew Fisher on 13 April 1910.

## LACROSSE

was introduced in 1874 by visiting Canadian L. L. Mount, who showed some Lacrosse sticks to a group of boys playing in a Melbourne park and taught them the rudiments of the game. Some of these boys were founder members of the first Lacrosse club in 1879.

## LAND REGISTRATION

was introduced in South Australia under the Real Property Act which became law on 27 January 1858. The measure was introduced by [Sir] Robert Torrens, a colourful individual who attracted both adulation and opprobrium for his efforts to reform the law on the conveyancing of property. His interest in the matter had originally been stimulated by a brush with authority in 1844 when he had acted for his sister on a matter concerned with the ownership of property. Although he dealt with her land for her benefit, he acted as though he had power of attorney, which he did not, and was reprimanded for his conduct. The fundamental principle of the Torrens system of registered conveyancing was that land ownership is recorded in a public Register which secures indefeasability of title. This meant that, fraud apart, the title of a registered proprietor could not be upset. No such system existed in Britain, nor anywhere else except certain parts of Germany and Austria–Hungary. The Torrens system subsequently spread not only to the other Australian colonies, but also to New Zealand, Ireland, Western Canada, the USA, a number of African and Asian countries and Israel.

## LAW BOOK

was the *Australian Magistrate; or, a Guide to the Duties of a Justice of the Peace for the Colony of NSW*, by John Hubert Plunkett, Sydney, 1835. At 428 pages, it was the largest volume to have been published in Australia.

## LAWN TENNIS

was first played on an asphalt court laid at Warehousemen's Cricket Ground in St Kilda Road, Melbourne in 1878. This proved sufficiently popular for a grass court to be added the following year.

**The first tennis club** was the Association Ground Lawn Tennis Club, Sydney, founded in 1878.

**The first tennis tournament** was the Victorian Championships, held under the auspices of the Melbourne Cricket Club in 1880.

Australia, or more correctly Australasia, competed in the **Davis Cup** for the first time 17–19 July 1905, when Norman E. Brookes, Anthony Wilding (NZ) and Alfred Dunlop were eliminated by the USA in the second round. Brookes and Wilding won the Cup for Australasia for the first time on 23 July 1907, defeating Britain in the final, and won again in 1908 and 1909, defeating the USA in the final on both occasions.

**The first Australian to win the Wimbledon Championships** was Norman Brookes, who took not only the men's single title on 4 July 1907 but also shared the doubles and mixed doubles titles. This was the first occasion on which a non-Briton had triumphed at Wimbledon.

**The first Australian to win the Wimbledon women's singles** was Margaret Court of Western Australia, who defeated Billy Jean King of the USA 6–3, 6–4 on 8 July 1963.

## LAWYER

(with legal training) was Richard Dore, who arrived at Sydney in the *Barwell* on 18 May 1798 to take up the office of Judge–Advocate. A harsh and disputatious man, he earned a fair degree of opprobrium during his short career in New South Wales before his death in December 1800. Among the reasons for his unpopularity was that he demanded fees from litigants, whereas before his arrival the inhabitants could, in the words of Governor Hunter 'receive justice in all their concerns without expense'.
(NB: Earlier Judge-Advocates were military men and not lawyers by training.)

# The first...

The first solicitor to practice in Australia was the convict George Crossley (1749–1823), who was transported for perjury and arrived at Sydney in 1800. He had been admitted as a solicitor in London in 1771 and soon acquired a reputation for sharp practice. On one occasion he is reputed to have put a fly in the mouth of a dead person whose will he had forged and then swore that there was life in the testator at the time the will was witnessed. From 1803 to 1808 he practised as a solicitor in Sydney, becoming one of the wealthiest men in the colony — his earnings for 1807 were said to be over £4,000 or double the salary of the Governor.

The rebels who overthrew Governor Bligh, whose supporter Crossley was, had him charged with practising as an attorney while still a convict and he was sentenced to two years in gaol. After his release he resumed practice, handling about nine-tenths of the cases that came before the courts until he was disbarred by Judge Bent on account of being an emancipist. He then went into a secret partnership with a newly arrived lawyer, T. S. Amos, pretending to be his managing clerk but in fact conducting most of the business of the firm. Crossley was again convicted of perjury at the age of 72 in 1821 — apparently a shady lawyer to the end.

The first solicitor to qualify and to be admitted to the profession in Australia was George Allen (1800–77) who came to Sydney at the age of 15 in 1816, was articled first to W. H. Moore, then to Frederick Gatling, successive Crown Solicitors, and enrolled as a solicitor by the Supreme Court of New South Wales on 22 July 1822. The law firm he founded is still in practice. Allen's diaries, a fascinating insight into early Sydney life, were published by Angus & Robertson in 1958.

The first barristers to be admitted to the Supreme Court were William Wentworth and Dr Robert Wardell on 10 September 1824. Hitherto the only barristers in Australia were the judges and the chief law-officer, so all advocacy was performed by solicitors. The latter were permitted to continue practising as advocates until 1829, when it was decreed that only barristers should perform this function, as in England.

## LEGACY CLUB
was founded in Hobart by Major–General Sir John Gellibrand in 1922.

## LEGAL AID
was introduced under the Queensland Poor Prisoners' Defence Act 1907 and the New South Wales Poor Prisoners' Defence Act 1907.

## LETTER BOX
was erected in Sydney at Simeon Lord's warehouse and manufactory in September 1804 for the receipt of letters to Great Britain.

The first post office letter boxes were erected on the sides of buildings in several parts of Sydney with the inauguration of the 2d post in 1831. They were cleared twice a day and were for payment-on-receipt letters only. People wanting to prepay postage — there were no stamps at this date — had to go to the main post office.

The first roadside letter boxes were 12 in number and cast by Bubb and Son of the Victoria Foundry, Sydney, following an invitation to tender published in the NSW *Government Gazette* of 2 November 1855. This was the same year that letter boxes were introduced in London. Based on the style of cylindrical pillar box adopted in Brussels, the first city with roadside letter receivers, the pioneer Sydney boxes looked like an upended canon and had three vertical apertures facing in different directions. This was to enable horsemen to post letters without dismounting. The first of the 12 original models was erected near the Customs House at Circular Quay. Three Bubb letter boxes remain in service — one near the Grand Central Hotel, Clarence Street, one near St James Railway Station, Hyde Park, and another in Harley Street, Alexandria.

## LIBERAL PARTY
The present Parliamentary Liberal Party was formed by Robert Menzies at a conference of anti-Labor State and Federal MPs and representatives of sympathetic organizations held at Albury, NSW, 14–16 December 1944.

## LIBRARY
earliest reference to, is contained in a notice published by the Secretary's Office on 24th February 1810 requiring anyone who had removed books from the Government Library

'either on the arrest of Governor Bligh or at any other time' to return them. As Governor Bligh was arrested in January 1808, it is apparent the Government Library was in existence before that date.

**The first library open to the public** was the Australian Subscription Library and Reading Room, opened in Sydney on 7 March 1826. It was founded by a group of gentlemen who, some five years earlier, had made a joint catalogue of all the books in their private libraries so that they could borrow from each other. The Australian Subscription Library retained the exclusiveness of these origins. The entrance fee was 5 guineas, annual subscription 2 guineas, and election to membership was by ballot. The library was taken over by the Government of NSW in 1869, becoming the Sydney Free Library, which was renamed the Public Library of New South Wales in 1895. The lending branch, which dated from 1877, was separated from its parent in 1909 to become the Sydney Municipal Library.

**The first public library** was the Public Library of Victoria, opened under the librarianship of A. H. Tulk at Melbourne on 11 February 1856. There were originally 3,846 books, including a set of Gould's *Birds of Australia* acquired for £140.

**The first children's library** was established as part of Sydney Municipal Library in 1912.

## LICENSED PREMISES

The first licences for the sale of alcoholic beverages were issued under the direction of Governor Phillip in October 1792, the steamship *Royal Admiral* having brought a quantity of porter to the colony. Capt. David Collins, RM, recorded that, in defiance of the regulations, spirits were also sold at these taverns, 'where rioting and drunkenness prevailed as long as the means remained'. The price of porter at this time was from 1s to 1s 3d per quart. The arrival of the *Philadelphia* with a cargo of American spirits the following month turned these 'porterhouses' into unashamed grog shops. The penalty for selling liquor without a licence was somewhat drastic — not only was the liquor seized, but the offender's house was pulled down.

**The first real public houses** of a permanent character were licensed in 1796. The records having been lost, it is not known how many of these there were and the only one whose name has come down to us was the *Mason's Arms* in Parramatta. This was rebuilt as the *Freemason's Arms* in 1800, when it became a proper hotel (qv) with residential accommodation and a trained chef. In 1821 it became the *Woolpack*, reverting to its former pub status, and still exists today, though in premises across the street from its original site. The *Woolpack* can therefore boast the oldest continuous licence in Australia and the only one first issued in the 18th century. The earliest Sydney pub known by name was the *Three Jolly Settlers* established in 1797.

**The first bush pubs** were the *Malting Shovel* at Eastern Boundary on the Parramatta River, licensed in the name of emancipist James Squires on 19 September 1798; and the *Rose and Crown* at East Plain, licensed in the name of John Prosser on the same date.

The oldest pub still occupying its original building is the *Macquarie Arms* in Windsor, NSW, which was licensed in 1814. Between 1840 and 1870 it was a private house. The oldest continuously licensed pub building in Australia is the premises of the *Alexandra Hotel*, Hobart, built as the *Hope and Anchor* some time prior to 1818.

## LICENSING HOURS

restricting the opening times of public houses were introduced by an Order of the Governor of 27 October 1800. Pubs were to close after the sounding of Taptoo (9pm) and not reopen until noon the following day. They were also to close during the hours of divine service.

The 'six o'clock swill' originated with new licensing laws in South Australia which came into effect on 26 March 1916. New South Wales followed suit in July, as a direct result of 15,000 disaffected troops from Casula army camp going on a drunken rampage in Liverpool and Sydney, and Victoria in October. First to restore evening drinking was New South Wales in 1955, Victoria relaxing its hours in 1966 and South Australia in 1967.

## LIFE SAVING CLUBS

were branches of the Life Saving Society founded in 1894 and based on the beaches at Bronte and Waverley, NSW.

**The first surf life saving club,** dedicated to life saving in the conditions peculiar to the Australian surf, was the Bondi Surf Bathers Life Saving Club, founded in 1906.

First to pass the surf life saving exam and become a qualified instructor was L. B. Nott on 20 March 1913.

# The first . . .

**The first laser beam lighthouse** in the world began operating at Point Danger, NSW, in 1970.

## LIFE SAVING REEL

in the world was demonstrated at Bondi Beach on 23 December 1906 by its designer Lester Ormsby, captain of the Bondi Surf Bathers Life Saving Club. It was based on a model he made out of hairpins and a cotton reel. The first rescue took place on 31 December, when a lad called Charlie Smith, of Yates Street, Sydney, was hauled out of the water to safety. He was to achieve greater fame in an altogether more elevated sphere as pioneer aviator Sir Charles Kingsford Smith.

## LIFT

was a freight elevator installed at Allan's Music Warehouse in Collins Street, Melbourne, in 1877.

**The first passenger lifts** made their appearance in both Melbourne and Sydney in the same year, 1884. In Melbourne contractor F. W. Fell installed Otis elevators in four blocks of apartments, varying from six to nine storeys high, at the river end of Queens Street. Meanwhile in Sydney, photographer William Tuttle was having a lift put into the building he occupied in Pitt Street, where the studio and processing rooms were up eight flights of stairs. Two young men, Sam Hood and Arthur Aitken, were trained to operate the lift and tend the machinery. They were much given to stopping the lift between floors to flirt with the girls from the retouching department. The formidable lady who ruled over the girls, a Miss Douglas, had the two boys sacked. When it occurred to the management that they were the only two people in Sydney who could operate a lift, they were sent for, admonished and reinstated.

## LIGHTHOUSE

was Macquarie Tower, a 76-ft high stone edifice at South Head, Port Jackson, designed by the convict architect Francis Greenway and formally commissioned by Governor Lachlan Macquarie on 16 December 1817. The Governor showed his approbation of his master architect's work by granting him his emancipation the same day. The oil light at the top of the tower, 353 ft above sea level, was visible 24 miles out to sea. The original lighthouse was replaced in 1883.

**The first lighthouse with a fully-automatic electric flashing light** was built at

## LITHOGRAPHY

was introduced to Australia in 1821 when two lithographic presses, said to have been invented by a man called Morrison and to be 'of improved construction', were set up at Parramatta Observatory for the use of Government Astronomer Christian Rümker. One of these presses was later used for the production of the first published lithographs, Augustus Earl's 'Views of Australia' of 1826, which were printed in five colours. The other press was consigned to the Surveyor-General in 1828 and used to produce Australia's first printed maps.

## LOCOMOTIVE FOUNDRY

was the Phoenix Foundry at Ballarat, Vic, which began producing British-designed engines in 1873 for the use of Victorian Railways.

## LONG SERVICE LEAVE

in the world was introduced by New South Wales under an amendment to the Industrial Arbitration Act made on 1 July 1951. Three months leave was allowed after 20 years of service.

## LOTTERY

was drawn in Sydney in January 1849. Tickets cost £4 each and the winners received title to lands held by the Bank of Australia, then in liquidation. Following this, lotteries were held to be illegal in NSW.

**The first regular lottery** was Tattersall's Sweepstake, organized by George Adams, proprietor of Tattersall's Hotel in Sydney, on the Sydney Cup of 1881. The total subscribed was £2,000, of which £1,700 was returned in prize money: first prize £900, second prize £600, third prize £200. When the New South Wales government made sweeps illegal in 1892, Adams removed his to Queensland. That colony outlawed sweeps in its turn in 1895, and Adams then took Tatts to Tasmania. There the sweeps remained until 1953, when another move was made to Victoria.

**The first government-run lottery** was Queensland's 'Golden Casket', started in 1916 by a voluntary committee to raise 'patriotic funds' for the war effort. It came under the control of the Department of Health in March 1920 when permission was given for the draws, now in aid of hospitals, to continue. The New South Wales State Lottery held its inaugural draw in August 1931.

**Lotto** was inaugurated in New South Wales on 5 November 1979.

## LUTHERAN SERVICE

was held in a store room at Port Adelaide, SA, on 25 November 1838, being attended by the first of many congregations of Lutheran refugees from Prussia who were seeking a new life and freedom of worship in South Australia.

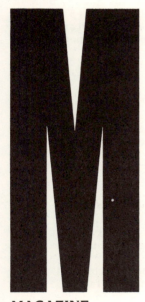

## MAGAZINE

was the *Australian Magazine: or Compendium of Religious Literary and Miscellaneous Intelligence*, a 32pp crown octavo monthly first issued in May 1821, price 1s 3d. It was published by Robert Howe, the Government Printer, and edited by two Methodist ministers, Walter Lawry and the 22 year old Ralph Mansfield, and a Cornish evangelist by the name of Benjamin Carvasso. Its thirteen issues contained a variety of somewhat ponderous articles on such subjects as 'The Superiority of the Spade over the Hoe in Cultivation' and 'Essay on Literary Precautions in the Study of Technology'; some poetry culled from overseas publications, and a two-part work of fiction *A Tale of Varaoo* about a native feud on a South Seas island.

**The first magazine to contain illustrations** was the *Hobart Town Monthly*, which ran from March 1833 to August 1834 and several of whose issues were embellished with a lithographed frontispiece.

The first with illustrations interspersed in the text was *Heads of the People*, a humorous and general interest weekly founded by William Baker in 1847. First to contain illustrations of topical events were the *Melbourne Illustrated News* and the *Illustrated Sydney News*, both in 1853. The first colour illustration was a double page spread of Giffinnan's painting of Cook taking possession of Australia, reproduced in line from photographs of the original and issued with the *Illustrated Sydney News* in 1865.

**The first Women's Magazine** was *The Muff or Punch's Telescopic Review of New South Wales*, which began in June 1844. No copies survive but a prospectus makes it clear that it was intended for 'the fair sex'. Surprisingly there were no other general interest women's papers until as late as 1882, when the *Australian Woman's Magazine and Domestic Journal* began publication in Melbourne. Only nine of the 450 general interest magazines published in Australia during the 19th century were devoted to women's interests.

**The first children's magazine** (other than missionary tracts) was *The Young Idea*, of which No 1 was published at Sydney on 20 October 1891.

**The first successful boy's paper** was *Pals*, modelled on the popular English weeklies *Chums* and *Boy's Own Paper*, which was founded in Melbourne in 1920.

**The first fashion magazine** was *Weigel's Journal of Fashions*, published monthly at Richmond, Vic, price 7d a copy, from 1 February 1880.

Magazines represented one of the most prolific areas of Australian publishing before 1850, albeit most were short-lived. There were at least 79 magazine launches, 8 of them in the 1820s, 28 in the 1830s and 43 in the 1850s. Even as early as 1828 there were four magazines running simultaneously (two from Sydney and two from Hobart) and in 1835 there were no less than eight new magazine starts. Most of these publications suffered from a paucity of material — they were often written entirely by the editor — as well as difficulties in distribution and competition from imported English magazines. Nevertheless they represented the genesis of

# The first ...

Australia's literary endeavour and the beginning of a tradition of quantity and breadth of choice that persists to this day.

## MAGISTRATE

was Augustus Alt, first Surveyor-General of NSW, who was sworn in as JP on or about 28 January 1788, shortly after the arrival of the First Fleet at Port Jackson. Together with the Judge-Advocate, he was 'to examine all offences committed by the convicts and determine on and punish such as were not of sufficient importance for trial by the criminal court'. Alt presided together with the Judge-Advocate at the first magistrates' court convened on 19 February, when Mary Jackson was charged with detaining a shirt, a pair of trousers, a new frock and a pair of stockings, the property of Edward Deane, a seaman from the *Lady Penrhyn*. Mary was discharged when it was revealed that she and Deane had cohabited on the voyage out, and that her lover had only demanded the clothes back when she refused him her favours. Since she was to be married the following day, to another convict called John Leary, it was as well that Alt saw fit to set her at liberty.

## MAN-MADE FABRIC

to be produced from Australian-made yarn was rayon by Prestige Ltd, who opened a rayon yarn factory in Brunswick, Vic, in 1935 to supply their own knitting mills.

## MANUFACTURED GOODS

were plates, jars and tobacco pipes produced from local clay by convict Elijah Leeks, who established a small one-man pottery at the bottom of what is now Wentworth Avenue, Sydney, in 1788.

**The first factory** set up to produce consumer goods was the Earthenware Manufactory, established in Pitt's Row, Sydney, by Samuel Skinner in 1801. The range of goods manufactured was extensive: Flower pots (1s 6d per pair); tea pots (1s 6d - 2s 6d); cups and saucers (6d - 10d); slop basins (6d - 1s 2d); wash-hand basins (1s 6d - 2s); cream jugs (4d - 6d); mugs (6d - 2s); water jugs (9d - 2s 6d); butter tubs with covers (1s 6d - 3s); porringers (6d); children's tea sets (4s - 6s); cruet sets (1s), etc. Mr Skinner assured purchasers that his wares were 'by no means inferior to the Workmanship of the most eminent Potteries of the Mother Country'. Prices were well below the costs of imported goods: English cups and saucers were selling for 1s at this time, the Colonial made article being available for half the price.

By 1891 Australia was producing half the manufactured goods required for domestic consumption.

## MARATHON

was organized by Sydney Y M C A and run at Sydney Cricket Ground on Easter Monday, 12 April 1909. None of the contestants had run a marathon before and each was given a medical examination prior to the race to ensure they were fit to run over such a gruelling distance. The winner was Andrew Sime of South Sydney in a time of 3 hrs 5 mins 30.2 secs. Other marathons were run at Brisbane and Melbourne the same year, both of them won by Sime.

## MARKET

was established at Parramatta in April 1792, principally as a measure to discourage the selling or exchanging of stolen goods among the convict population. The prices prevailing at the outset of the venture were recorded by Capt. David Collins of the Royal Marines, as follows:

Flour, 1s per lb.
Maize per bushel from 11s to 13s.
Laying hens from 7s 6d to 10s each.
Cocks for killing from 4s 6d to 5s each.
Chickens two months old 3s each.
Eggs per dozen 3s.
Fresh pork per lb from 1s 1d to 1s 3d.
Salt pork per lb from 10d to 1s.
Potatoes per lb from 3d to 4d.
A lot of cabbages, per hundred 10s.
Tea per lb from 16s to £1 1s.
Coffee per lb from 2s to 3s.
Moist sugar from 2s to 2s 6d per lb.
Tobacco grown in the country from 1s 6d to 2s per lb.
Virginia or Brazil from 4s. to 6s.
Soap from 1s. 6d. to 2s 6d per lb.
Cheese from 1s 6d to 2s per lb.

The Sydney market was established in June 1792.

## MARRIAGE GUIDANCE COUNCIL

was founded in Sydney at the instigation of the Christian Social Order Movement in April

1948. Others followed in Melbourne, Brisbane and Hobart the following year.

## MARTIAL ARTS CLUB
was the Brisbane Club, founded in 1928 by Dr A. J. Ross following a visit by Japanese judo exponent Shinzo Takagaki.

## MASONIC LODGE
was St John No 1, Norfolk Island, which was in existence in 1800.

The first person to be admitted a Freemason on the Australian mainland was Anthony Fenn Kemp at a gathering of the 'Knights of the Rose Croix, Master Masons and Companions of the same order in lodge not regularly constituted, but properly assembled', at Sydney on 17 September 1802.

The first Masonic Lodge on the mainland was 'Social and Military Virtues No 227', founded by officers of the 48th Regiment at Sydney in 1814.

## MATERNITY BENEFIT
known as the 'baby bonus', was introduced by the Federal Government on 9 October 1912 at the rate of £5 for every woman brought to childbirth.

## MATERNITY LEAVE
was first offered to expectant mothers by the Reserve Bank of Australia in January 1966.

Unpaid maternity leave of up to 12 months was awarded by the Commonwealth Arbitration Commission on 9 March 1979.

## McDONALD'S
was opened in the Sydney suburb of Yagoona on 30 December 1971 under the management of Peter Ritchie, the present chairman of McDonald's Australia. Unlike the American outlets, the menu included chicken as well as hamburgers — considered essential to the Aussie diet.

## MEDAL, MILITARY
was the Victoria Volunteer Long and Efficient Service Medal, instituted by the Victorian government in 1880.

**The first medals for gallantry** were instituted on 14 June 1975 and consisted of the Cross of Valour, the Star of Courage, the Bravery Medal and the Commendation of Brave Conduct. Formerly Australian servicemen were awarded Imperial medals.

## MEDICAL INSURANCE
was introduced at Hobart by Dr E. S. P. Bedford in 1847. Premiums varied, but an 18-year old joining for life was entitled to treatment at St Mary's Hospital and free medicines for a subscription of 1s 6d a month.

## MEDICAL RESEARCH INSTITUTE
was the Australian Institute of Tropical Medicine, founded at Townsville, Queensland, in 1909.

## MEDICAL SCHOOL
was established in 1863 at Melbourne University with three students under Dr George Halford, Professor of Anatomy, Physiology and Pathology. The first premises of this august institution consisted of a shed at the back of Halford's home in Madeline Street, now part of Swanston Street. In 1891 it became the first medical school in the British colonies to secure recognition of its degrees in Britain.

**The first teaching hospital** was Prince Alfred Hospital, opened in the grounds of Sydney University in 1882. Instruction began the following year with the opening of Sydney University Medical School.

**The first female medical student** in Australia was G. Dagmar Berne, who entered the medical faculty of Sydney University in 1885. She did not complete the course, but graduated from Edinburgh University in 1893.

See also Woman Doctor.

## MEDICAL TREATISE
was *General Observations of the Smallpox*, by Principal Surgeon Thomas Jamison, which was published in the Sydney Gazette of 14 October 1804.

**The first treatise on dentistry** was *Hints for the Preservation of the Teeth*, by Sydney dentist Dr Henry Jeanneret, London, 1830.

**The first medical text book** published in Australia was Robert Porter Welch's *A Familiar Treatise on the Diseases of the Eye*, Sydney, 1840.

## MEDICARE
was introduced on 1 February 1984. Doctors who resigned from public hospitals in protest were to be banned for seven years under legislation passed by the NSW Government in June, but this was repealed in August.

# The first . . .

## MERINO SHEEP

were brought from Cape Town in 1797 by Captain Waterhouse, who had purchased them from a Mrs Gordon for £4 each, and sold to Captain John Macarthur of the New South Wales Corps, the Rev. Samuel Marsden, William Cox and Alexander Riley. Macarthur, who more than any other man is regarded as the father of Australia's wool industry, purchased 4 ewes and 2 rams. In 1801 he took samples of wool with him to England and when he returned to Sydney in 1805, brought with him five Merino rams and one ewe from the Royal flock at Kew. Two years later he dispatched his first consignment of wool to England, a single bale, but of sufficient quality to obtain 10s 6d a pound. In the meantime the Rev. Samuel Marsden had begun cross-breeding merino with English breeds such as the Southdown and he arrived in England in 1807 with a suit made from the wool which he wore at an audience with King George III. It was he who made the first commercial shipment of wool to England, some 4,000 - 5,000 lbs aboard the *Admiral Gambier* which left Sydney on 2 December 1811. The wool sold well at auction, fetching an average price of 5s a pound. Macarthur and Alexander Riley started exporting their wool in July 1813 and from this time it may be said that grazing was established as a significant element in the commercial life of the young colony.

## METHODIST CHAPEL

was a rough slab building erected at Castlereagh, NSW, by John Lees, an ex-private of the New South Wales Corps, and opened by the Rev. Samuel Leigh (see below) on 7 October 1817.

## METHODIST MINISTER

was Samuel Leigh, who arrived in Sydney on 15 August 1815 and immediately began his task of ministering to the Godless — of whom there appear to have been plenty. Having made a personal visit to every house in the city, he reported that there was but an average of one bible to every ten families. His first convert, a convict, later achieved the distinction of becoming the first stage coach proprietor in Australia. Leigh had difficulty in establishing a congregation, due to the opposition of the Governor, but having won the support of the Rev. Samuel Marsden, Colonial Chaplain, he conducted his first service in Sydney on 16 March 1816. It was attended by 44 people.

## MIGRANT SHIP

carrying assisted passage immigrants was the *Palamban* which arrived at Sydney on 31 July 1831 after a voyage of four months and one week from Cork, Ireland. Those being brought out as free settlers were 50 girls from the Foundling Hospital at Cork, together with two matrons, their husbands and seven children. The orphan girls were brought out to help redress the severe male imbalance of the population of NSW.

## MILITARY COLLEGE

was the Royal Military College of Australia, Duntroon, ACT, opened on 27 June 1911 with 32 Australian and 10 New Zealand cadets. The first intake was graduated prematurely in August 1914 to officer the 1st AIF and the NZEF.

*The opening of the Royal Military College, Duntroon.*

## MILK BAR

in the world was opened in Martin Place, Sydney by Clarence and Norman Burt in 1933. There was an electric cow in the window to attract passers-by. Milk shakes were 4d (with an egg yolk was extra), ice cream sodas were 6d and sundaes were 9d. Milkbars were introduced into Britain by Australian entrepreneur and fight promoter Hugh D. McIntosh in 1935.

## MILK BOTTLES

The first milk to be sold in bottles was Camden Vale milk, which was also the first from herds certified free of tuberculosis. First marketed in 1922, it was sold in bottles sealed with golden aluminium foil tops and soon became known as 'Gold Top'. Because of its purity, and the fact that it was the highest grade of milk authorised under the New South Wales Milk Act, it was considered especially beneficial for invalids and babies.

Camden Vale milk was produced at Camden Park, the vast dairy farm first established by John Macarthur in 1820.

## MILKING MACHINE
was imported from Scotland by the Bodalla Company in 1892 and installed at their dairy station at Bodalla on the South Coast of New South Wales. The machine was capable of milking 50 cows an hour, the station manager reporting that it was 'very simple and any ordinary farm labourer can thoroughly understand it'.

## MONASTERY
was St Mary's, founded by Archbishop Polding at his residence in Sydney on 24 August 1843, when five priests were inducted into the Benedictine Order under Prior Henry Gregory. There were also eight postulants.

The oldest existing monastery in Australia was established by Benedictine monks Dom Salvado and Dom Serra at New Norcia, some 80 miles north of Perth, WA, in April 1847. Norcia is the place in Italy where St Benedict was born. The main function of the monastery then, as now, was to minister to the local Aboriginal inhabitants.

*The first and only Anglican monastery* in Australia was the House of the Kelham Fathers, established near Adelaide in 1947.

## MONEY ORDERS
were introduced in Tasmania by the Post Office on 25 September 1852.

## MONORAIL
public transport system was the TNT Harbour-Link, planned on a 3.6 km route linking the Darling Harbour complex with Sydney's city centre. There are eight stations and the silent, rubber tyred trains, designed by von Roll-Habegger of Switzerland, were scheduled to traverse the circuit in 12 minutes at an average speed of 33 kmh. The monorail is carried above the city streets on 'I' beam support columns spaced some 30 metres apart.

## MORMONS
to arrive in Australia were American missionaries Charles Wandell and John Murdoch, who landed at Sydney on 30 October 1851 and conducted their first baptisms of Australians into the Church of Jesus Christ of Latter-day Saints on 3 December of that year.

## MOTEL
was the A.A. Motel, opened by Accommodation Australia Ltd at the corner of Northbourne Avenue and Yass Road, Canberra, in May 1956. Built at a cost of £120,000, it contained 46 sleeping-units around a large landscaped quadrangle.

## MOTORBUS
See Bus.

## MOTOR CAR
was a three-wheeled vehicle powered by a Daimler petrol engine, built by Charles Highland of Annandale, Sydney, in 1894. It was not an outstanding success, never progressing further than the length of a single street and reportedly displaying an inclination to burst into flames at inauspicious moments. This was because the ignition burner was too close to the primitive carburettor. A second three-wheeler built by Highland in 1896, this time with a De Dion engine, was much more workable and may be regarded as the first practical petrol-driven car built in Australia. In May of the same year Herbert Thomson built a steam-driven car at his workshop in New Street, Armadale, Vic.

*The first imported car* was a German-built 4½ hp Benz acquired by the Tarrant Motor Co of Melbourne in late 1896. It was purchased by Mr A. D. Terry, whose son drove it in a contest against the Australian-built Thomson steamer. The native product won.

*The first four-wheel petrol-driven car built in Australia* was the Pioneer, a chain-driven vehicle with a single-cylinder horizontal engine, which was constructed to the order of the Australasian Horseless Carriage Syndicate by William Grayson at Fitzroy, Melbourne and exhibited in public at the Melbourne Exhibition on 16 February 1897. Described by the *Australian Cyclist* as 'a stylish double-seated dog cart', it took the Governor of Victoria, Lord Brassey, for a spin around the cycle track of the Exhibition at speeds reported to be over 10 mph.

*The first car manufacturers* in Australia were the Thomson Motor Car Syndicate of Melbourne and the Tarrant Motor Car Co., also of Melbourne, both of which began production in 1901. Thomson's first model was the Royal Steam Buggy, of which ten were sold. The company later manufactured oil and electric as well as steam cars, remaining in production until 1908. The inaugural production model of the Tarrant, launched by

# The first...

Harley Tarrant and champion cyclist Howard Lewis, was powered by a rear-mounted 6 hp MMC-De Dion engine. It was delivered to Mr W. Chandler of 295 Napier Street, Fitzroy on 23 September 1901. This was followed by a 10 hp two-cylinder model, of which five were turned out. First to be sold was bought for £275 by Mr Maurice Smith, who kept it until the mid-1960s. He then presented it to two of Harley Tarrant's grandsons, Kenneth and Peter Holmes, who undertook its restoration. In 1903 Tarrant's manufactured the first car specially designed for use in the outback, with a high wheelbase and outsize mudguards.

Another pioneering venture, in 1906, was the **first fully enclosed car** assembled in Australia, a 'one off' on a De Dion chassis with bodywork by J.W. Flood. Tarrant continued manufacturing cars until 1909, when Harley Tarrant acquired the Ford agency for Victoria.

The first car with a self-starter imported into Australia was the Italian S.C.A.T. in 1912.

**The first Japanese car to be imported to Australia** was a Datsun, the sole representative of the Rising Sun among the 825,228 motor vehicles on the road in 1939.

**The first mass produced all-Australian car** was the Holden, which began coming off the production line at the General Motors-Holden's plant at Fisherman's Bend, Vic, on 29 November 1948. A total of 120,402 units of the original model were produced.

**The first Australian-made station wagon** was the FE Holden of 1957.

## MOTOR CAR JOURNEYS

**The first car journey from Sydney to Melbourne** was undertaken by Mr J.W.C. Elliott in December 1900 driving a De Dion Voiturette. The trip took 38 hours.

**The first transcontinental motor car journey** from south to north was achieved by H.H. Dutton and Murray Aunger who left Adelaide in a Talbot on 30 June 1908 and completed the 2,100 miles to Darwin in 42 travelling days on 20 August.

**The first transcontinental motor car journey from west to east** was made by cycle dealer Francis Birtles and Sydney car salesman S.R. Ferguson, who drove a 10 hp Brush car the 2,600 miles from Fremantle to Sydney in 28 days, an average of 92 miles a day, between 16 March and 13 April 1912. The intrepid automobilists were obliged to keep to the route of the overland telegraph line, so that every time they got bogged down in sand they could wind a rope round the nearest telegraph pole and haul themselves out.

**The first man to drive round Australia** was Seventh Day Adventist evangelist Noel Westwood, who left Perth in a 7 hp Baby Citroen on 4 August 1925 and arrived back at his starting point on 30 December.

## MOTOR COACH

was a 12-seater vehicle built in 1904 by Finlayson Bros & Co Pty Ltd, engineers and machinery merchants of Devonport, Tas, and used for tourist excursions.

*The Holden was the first mass produced all-Australian car.*

## MOTORCYCLE

was built in 1893 by H. Knight-Eaton, manager of the Austral Cycle Agency, Brisbane, who connected a small petrol engine of his own design to the rear wheel of an ordinary safety bicycle. Three years later, having moved to Sydney, he had brought over from Germany the first motor cycle imported into Australia. This was a 2½ hp Hildebrand & Wolfmuller Motorrad with a 760 cc single-cylinder engine, a model originally produced in Munich in 1894 and the first motorcycle in the world in regular series production. Billed as 'The Death-Defying Speed King', Knight-Eaton gave an exhibition of the Motorrad's prowess in December 1896 when he careered through the streets of Sydney at a 'terrific speed approaching 25 mph'.

*The first Australian-made motorcycles* were built at the Beauchamp engineering works in Prahran, Vic, in 1904, including two to the order of the Dunlop Rubber Co. of Melbourne. Production ceased when the engineer-in-charge, Charles Rayman, was killed while practising for a motorcycle race at Eaglehawk on Boxing Day 1904.

## MOTOR CYCLE RACING

began with a contest for motor tricycles held on the concrete cycle track encircling Sydney Cricket Ground on 1 January 1901. The winner was Jack Green at an average speed of 37.7 km/h.

*The first purpose-built motorcycle race-track* was opened at Aspendale, Vic, on 28 January 1906. The mile long circuit had a crushed gravel surface.

See also Dirt Track Racing.

## MOTOR CYCLING CLUBS

were the Pioneer Motor Cycle Club, Sydney, the Victorian Motor Cycle Club and the Perth Motor Cycle Club, all founded in 1904.

## MOTOR RACING

The first organised race meeting for four-wheel cars was held at Maribyrnong, Victoria on 30 April 1904 under the auspices of the Automobile Club of Victoria. It has long been supposed that the first car (as opposed to motor tricycle) racing events in Australia were held at Morphettville, SA in 1903, but it has recently been established by the Historian of the sporting club of South Australia that this actually took place in November 1904, some six months after the Victoria's pioneering venture.

*The first motor racing track* was a clay and cinder circuit 66 ft wide and nine furlongs in circumference which was laid at Victoria Park, Sydney, in 1908.

*The first Australian Grand Prix* was held at Cowes, Phillip Island, Vic, on 31 March 1928 and won by South Australian driver A.C.R. Waite in a 750 cc supercharged Austin 7 at an average speed of 56.25 mph.

*The first Australian to win the world Grand Prix drivers' championship* was Jack Brabham at Sebring, Florida, on 13 December 1959. He had to push his Formula I Cooper the last third of a mile to the finishing line. Brabham won the championship again in 1960 and 1961.

*The first World Championship motor race in Australia* was held at Adelaide on 3 November 1985 and won by Keke Rosberg of Finland in a Williams-Honda at an average speed of 154.032 km/h over a distance of 309.8 km.

## MOTOR RALLY

was organised by the Dunlop Rubber Co. and run over 572 miles of roads between Melbourne and Sydney, commencing on 21 February 1905. There were 42 starters, including 15 motor cycles. The winner of the 'larger car' class was Harley Tarrant in an Argyll, after a 'run-off' between the seven vehicles which had completed the rally without losing a point. Best time was by H. L. Stevens at 23 hrs 42 mins.

## MOTOR TRUCKS

built in Australia were 50 four-cylinder vehicles designed by Adelaide engineer Felix Caldwell and produced by the Caldwell Vale Co of Auburn, NSW, in 1911. Priced at £1250, they were designed to carry 24-ton loads over clay roads at 4¾ mph. The Caldwell Vale had four-wheel drive and was among the first motor lorries in the world with power steering. A number of the trucks were used by contractors to the Federal Government during the building of Canberra. Another was in the service of a travelling circus in South Australia for many years. Two examples survive, and can be seen at Gilltrap's Auto Museum, Coolangatta.

*The first mass produced motor truck* was the International, which began manufacture at a temporary plant in Melbourne in August 1950. Two American-designed models were produced at the rate of 10 trucks a day, output later increasing to 26 a day when Inter-

# The first . . .

national Harvester's new plant at Dandenong was opened. **The first Australiandesigned Army truck,** a 2½ ton vehicle powered by a 6 cylinder 148 hp engine, was manufactured by International Harvester in 1959.

## MOTOR VAN

was put into service by Mark Foy's of Sydney in 1901. Their drivers were instructed not to take the steam-driven parcels van above 6 mph lest they frighten the horses.

*The first Australian-made motor van* was an 8 hp Tarrant supplied to the *Melbourne Herald* in 1907 for newspaper deliveries.

## MOTOR MAIL VAN

was introduced on the Nowra to Ulladulla route in New South Wales by mail contractors J. Schilling and B. McTernan in 1909.

## MOTOR VEHICLE LICENCE PLATES

were introduced in South Australia on 10 September 1906. The first plate bore the designation SA-1 and was issued to Dr W.A. Hargreaves of Woodville for his 6 hp Buston-Humber. He transferred it to all the subsequent vehicles he owned until he gave up motoring in 1955. Dr Hargreaves was also the first holder of an Australian driving licence (q.v.). There was no registration of vehicles in NSW or Victoria until 1910.

## MOTORING ASSOCIATION

was the Automobile Club of Australia, later the Royal Automobile Association, which was founded by Harry Skinner with six members on 20 March 1903. Skinner had been booked by a police constable for parking his car in the street without an attendant. The officer had insisted that the machine might start up of its own volition. It was to combat this petty persecution of motorists that Skinner established his Automobile Club. Another aim was to press for sensible speed limits and one of the club's first successes was in persuading the town council of Parramatta that a 6 mph restriction was unnecessarily low. Two other motoring associations were founded in1903, the Royal Automobile Club of Victoria and the Royal Automobile Association of South Australia; Western Australia and Queensland established theirs two

years later, Tasmania following on in 1907. The Australian Automobile Association was founded in 1925 as an umbrella organisation for the State associations.

## MOTORING OFFENCE

resulting in a conviction was perpetrated in 1897 by Mr George Innes of Sydney, who was fined 10s for driving his de Dion tricycle at a speed of 8 mph.

The first conviction for an offence in a motor car was secured in 1903, when the well-known cyclist Charles Kellow was charged and fined for 'furiously driving' along the Toorak Road in Melbourne.

## MOUNT KOSCIUSKO, ASCENT OF

was achieved by Polish-born Paul de Strzelecki and Parramatta-born James Macarthur, third son of the redoubtable John, on 15 February 1840. This day also marked the discovery of the 2229 m mountain, Australia's highest, and its naming after the Polish patriot Tadeusz Kosciuszko (who unlike the mountain has a 'z' in his name).

## MPs, PAYMENT OF

was formally introduced by Victoria on 14 September 1870, with salaries of £300 a year for members of both the Council and the Assembly. As early as 1859 the working class MPs in the NSW Legislative Assembly, both gold diggers, were being paid regular salaries by their constituents — James Hoskins, member for Northern Goldfields, and Robert Wisdom, member for Western Goldfields.

## MULTISTOREY CAR PARK

was opened at the corner of Russell and Little Collins Streets, Melbourne, in 1939. There was accommodation for 450 cars and it was claimed that a vehicle could be brought down by elevator from its parking place on any of the six storeys in 90 seconds.

## MUNICIPALITY

was Perth, which formed a Town Trust of justices of the peace and proprietors of over 1,000 acres in 1838. Not until 20 years later did Perth have an elected municipal council.

Adelaide became the **first legally incorporated city** on 19 August 1840, Sydney and Melbourne assuming city status in 1842.

*The first mayor* was James Hurtle Fisher, one of the founders of the colony of South Australia in 1836, who was elected to office of

Mayor of Adelaide on 31 October 1840. He was five times re-elected, the last time in 1853.

See also Election, Municipal; Town Hall.

## MURDER
was committed by persons unknown on 5 January 1794, when an elderly convict called John Lewis was stabbed and his throat cut in some woods near Parramatta. He was known to carry his money about his person, presumably the motive for the crime. The body was found in a ravine, concealed beneath logs and grass, with both hands eaten off by native dogs and the flesh of one arm wholly consumed.

## MUSEUM
was the Colonial Museum, Sydney, a collection of botanical and geological specimens brought together in a room in the Judge-Advocate's office in 1830. It moved to Parliament House in 1836 under its new name of the Australian Museum and to the present premises at the corner of College and William Streets in 1849.

The first science museum was the Industrial and Technological Museum of Victoria, opened on 7 September 1870.

**The first children's museum** was formed as part of the South Australian Museum, Adelaide, in 1937.

## MUSIC
composed in Australia, of which there is record, was the work of the two regimental band masters, both of whom produced their first known Antipodean compositions in 1825. Bandmaster Reichenberg of the 40th Regiment offered 'a first set of Quadrilles for Australia, with proper figures adapted to it, for the Pianoforte, Flute or Violin; as also for a full Band'. It was available in manuscript, price 6s. At about the same time Bandmaster Kavanagh of the 3rd Regiment brought out his 'Original Australian Music', which comprised such melodies as 'General Ralph Darling's Australian Slow March', 'Lady Brisbane's Waltz', 'Currency Lasses', 'My Native Distant Home' — this was a 'Scotch Air' — and 'The Trumpet Sounds Australia's Fame'. None of this music survives.

**The first Australian-born composer** was Thomas Stubbs, whose inaugural work, The Minstrel Waltz, was published at Sydney in 1836.

**The first orchestral music** was composed by

Isaac Nathan (1790-1864), formerly musical librarian to George IV and instructor to Princess Caroline, whose The Aboriginal Mother and Long Live Victoria were performed at a concert held in Sydney in October 1841. Nathan also composed the first Australian opera (q.v.)

## MUSIC FESTIVAL
was held at St Mary's Cathedral, Sydney, on 31 January 1838. The principal performers were the Irish musician William Vincent Wallace and his brother and sister.

## MUSIC SCHOOL
was opened in Sydney by the Irish composer and musician William Vincent Wallace in March 1836.

**The first college of music** was the Adelaide Conservatorium, founded by Immanual G. Reimann in 1883.

## MUSIC SHOP
was opened in George Street, Sydney, by Robert Campbell in 1824.

*Kim Ryrie (left) and Peter Vogel with Fairlight CMI music synthesiser.*

## MUSIC SYNTHESISER
produced in Australia was the Fairlight CMI, designed by 20 year old university drop-out Peter Vogel of Sydney and put on the market in 1980 after five years of development at $30,000. The first model was sold to Stevie Wonder and other purchasers included Kate Bush, Bruce Oldfield, Paul McCartney, Elvis Costello, The Bee Gees, Duran Duran, Fleetwood Mac, Oxford University, the BBC and Dr Robert Moog, inventor of the synthesiser. Moog declared that the Australian machine was the only synthesiser in the world which represented a significant advance on his original device.

# The first...

## NATIONAL PARK

was the Sutherland National park (renamed the Royal National Park in 1954), a conservation area of 18,000 acres at Port Hacking which was designated by the NSW Government on 28 April 1879. This was the world's second national park, the first, Yellowstone in Wyoming, having been designated in 1872.

## NATIONAL PARTY

See Country Party.

## NATIONAL TRUST

was the National Trust of New South Wales, founded in 1947 to preserve the State's architectural heritage. The name was borrowed from Britain's National Trust, established 1895.

## NATURAL GAS

was struck at Roma, Southern Queensland in 1900 and used to light the town for 10 days in 1906 until the flow ceased.
*The first natural gas pipeline* was opened between Roma, Queensland, and Brisbane in March 1967, following a further and much more successful strike in the same area as the one made in 1900.

## NATURALISATION

The first foreigner naturalised in Australia was Timothy Goodwin Pitman (1791-1832) of Boston, Mass., who was 'admitted to exercise the privileges of a British subject' on 5 July 1825 under a special Act passed by the Legislative Council of New South Wales. Pitman had arrived in Australia from China the previous year, setting himself up in George Street, Sydney, as a dealer in general merchandise ranging from silk to gunpowder. One of the conditions of naturalisation was the swearing of an oath denying the doctrines of authority of the Church of Rome.
*The first woman to be naturalised* was Josephine de Reuss, a native of French Flanders, who came to Sydney from Batavia in 1826 and swore the oath of allegiance in 1834.

The status of 'Australian Citizen' did not exist until the Citizenship Act came into force on 26 January 1949. Prior to that date all Australians were British subjects.

## NAVAL COLLEGE

was the Royal Australian Naval College, opened in temporary premises at Osborne House, Geelong, Vic, on 1 March 1913. As well as the sterner marine sciences, training included ballroom dancing, etiquette and table-setting. Three of the 18 cadets of the original intake, J. A. Collins, H. B. Farncomb and H. A. Showers, were to become Admirals. The College moved to Jervis Bay in February 1915.

## NAVY

was the Victorian Navy, established with the arrival of HMVS *Victoria* at Williamstown from London on 31 May 1856. *The Times* had observed at the time of her launching that 'this event marks the foundation of a great navy in Southern seas' — a prophetic statement, but one not fully realised until the present century. A 580 ton screw sloop of war, she had been built for the Victorian government — the first warship built to the order of any British colony — at a cost of £38,000 and was armed with one long and two medium 32-pounders. The full complement of the vessel was eight officers and 150 ratings, though she rarely carried a crew of this size. Recruited mainly in Melbourne, most were ex-Royal Navy or Merchant Marine. Under the command of Commander W. Norman, who received £600 p.a. for his services, they were employed on various 'brown water' activities along the coast of Victoria, such as surveying and patrol duties. In 1860, though, HMVS *Victoria* was on active service in New Zealand waters and a detachment of her seamen were the first Australian servicemen to engage an enemy in warfare (see Armed Forces to Serve Overseas). The last survivor of the original crew was Richard Grimwood, whose grandsons served with the Royal Australian Navy in World War II.

Following Victoria's lead, each of the Australian colonies with the exception of WA formed its own modest navy, though most were manned with volunteers. These were amalgamated as the Commonwealth Naval Forces following Federation and eventually merged into the newly formed Royal Australian Navy on 10 July 1911. The first ships to be commissioned in the RAN were the British-built torpedo boat destroyers *Parramatta* and *Yarra*, which entered service in Australian waters with the hoisting of the Blue Ensign at Port Phillip on 15 November 1911.

**The first offensive operation by a vessel of the Royal Australian Navy** took place at Rabaul, New Britain, on 12 August 1914, when the destroyer HMAS *Warrego* landed a raiding party to destroy German communications facilities. **The first encounter between a ship of the RAN and an enemy vessel** occurred off New Britain the same day when HMAS *Australia* seized the small German steamer *Zambesi* as a prize.

**The first shots by an Australian vessel to be fired in anger** were the bombardment of Toma, New Guinea, by the light cruiser HMAS *Encounter* on 14 December 1914.

**The first Australian warship to destroy an enemy vessel** was HMAS *Sydney*, which engaged the German cruiser *Emden* off the Cocos Is on 9 November 1914 and drove her aground, after heavy artillery bombardment, on North Keeling Island. During the 100 minute battle, *Emden* lost 134 killed, 65 wounded and 110 prisoners; *Sydney* 4 killed and 12 wounded.

**The first Australian naval vessel lost in warfare** was HMA Submarine AE1 off New Britain on 14 September 1914. The first surface vessel lost was the auxiliary minesweeper HMAS *Goorangai* in a collision with MV *Duntroon* in Port Phillip on 11 November 1940, and the first lost in enemy action was the destroyer HMAS *Waterhen*, sunk by a German aircraft off the Libyan coast on 30 June 1941.

**The first Australian vessel to sink a sub-** marine was the destroyer HMAS *Stuart*, which destroyed the Italian submarine *Gondar* in the Mediterranean on 30 September 1940. The first Australian vessel sunk by a submarine was HMAS *Parramatta*, with the loss of 139 lives, by a German U-boat off the Libyan coast on 27 November 1941.

The first aircraft carrier of the Royal Australian Navy was HMAS *Sydney*, commissioned on 16 December 1948.

## NEON LIGHTING
was first displayed in the showrooms of the Electricity Supply Department of the Sydney City Council in 1929. A company called Neon Lights Ltd was formed later the same year. Neon lighting had been invented in 1910 in Paris, where the first neon sign was erected two years later.

## NEWSPAPER
was *The Sydney Gazette and New South Wales Advertiser*, first published on 5 March 1803, price 6d. Vol 1, No 1 of the paper contained four pages, leading with 'General Orders' and continuing with ship news, court reports, news from England, accidents and deaths, advice on how to make a vineyard and 'an Account of the Advantage of a Cottager of keeping a Pig.' The news items included a report of two seamen being robbed by doxies in the Rocks area, another that 15 Irishmen variously described as 'depredators', 'desperadoes' and 'banditti' had escaped from the agricultural settlement of Castle Hill and committed rape and 'many acts of violence and atrocity', and an overseas report that wives were being publicly exhibited for sale in Manchester — 'Good ones, being scarce, brought a good price', the paper said. This inaugural issue also contained the first advertisement (q.v.) to appear in a newspaper and also the first recorded Australian joke: 'The Belles Lettres the other evening becoming the topic of conversation, one of the party observed that he had read Chesterfield's letters, but had never seen Bell's.'

Published weekly, the paper was edited, and much of it written, by George Howe, the Government printer, and was subject to close censorship by the Governor's private secretary. Nothing controversial was allowed in its pages — 'We open no channel to political discussion or personal animadversion; information is our only purpose', the editor declared in the opening number.

# The first . . .

Howe was born in 1769 at St Kitts in the West Indies, the son of the Government Printer there. At the age of 30 he was convicted of robbing a mercer's shop at Alcester, Warwickshire, and sentenced to death. The sentence was commuted to transportation and he arrived in New South Wales aboard the *Royal Admiral* on 22 November 1800.

Production of the *Sydney Gazette* was by no means easy. Howe recorded in 1819, referring to himself in the third person: 'He bought the paper at a very dear price, he distributed his type, he invented and obtained new matter, without any auxiliary assistance; he worked the paper off at press; and afterward carried it out, that is to say, delivered it to the Sydney subscribers. His subscribers at one period were under 350.' He could also have mentioned that he even had to make the ink himself.

George Howe died in 1821 and the paper was carried on by his son Robert Howe. It ceased publication in 1842.

**The first country newspaper** was the *Tasmanian and Port Dalrymple Advertiser*, launched at Launceston, Tas, on 5 January 1825 by George Terry Howe, son of the George Howe above. The first on the mainland was the *Geelong Advertiser*, launched on 21 November 1840.

**The first sustained daily newspaper** was the *Sydney Herald*, founded as a weekly in 1831, which became a daily on 1 October 1840. The present title of the *Sydney Morning Herald* was adopted in 1842. (NB: The *Sydney Gazette* was published daily for a brief period in January 1827.)

**The first Aboriginal newspaper** was the *Aboriginal Flinders Island Chronicle*, established on the Bass Strait island in 1836, weekly, price 2d. It was still being published in February 1838, when the editor was an aboriginal youth called Thomas Brune. Only one copy is known to survive. Exactly one hundred years passed before the next venture into aboriginal newspaper publishing, Jack Patten starting *The Australian Abo Call* in Sydney in April 1938.

**The first newspaper avowedly for working men** was the *Star and Working Man's Guardian*, published weekly by Edmund Mason, price 1d, from 2 March 1844 until 23 May 1846. The first issue was published in Sydney, subsequent issues at Parramatta. It was the first penny paper issued in Australia.

**The first evening newspaper** was the *Daily News and Evening Chronicle*, published in Sydney from 2 October until 29 November 1848.

**The first foreign language newspaper** was *Die Deutsche Post fuer die Australischen Kolonien*, which began weekly publication at Adelaide on 6 January 1848.

**The first newspaper to be printed on power presses** was the *Sydney Morning Herald* in August 1853. The plant consisted of a British-made two feeder Cowper printing machine driven by a steam engine. The circulation at that time was 6,000 a day.

**The first Sunday newspaper** was the *Sunday Times* of Sydney, inaugurated by Thomas Revel Johnson on 17 June 1849. Sunday newspapers were illegal in Victoria until 1949.

**The first newspaper in the world with a children's section** was the *Adelaide Deutsche Zeitung* which introduced a supplement titled *Adelaider Blaetter fuer Ernst und Scherz* in 1862.

**The first newspaper set on linotype machines**, thus eliminating the need to compose type by hand, was the *Sydney Daily Telegraph*, which installed 12 machines in April 1894 at a cost of £639 each. This was eight years after their introduction in America. Linotype operators in Australia earned up to £6 pw, about three times the average male wage. Within a few years most of the hand compositors had lost their jobs in the big publishing centres, and were forced to seek work on country newspapers where the pay averaged only 30s pw.

**The first Labor daily newspaper** and **the first union-owned daily** in the English speaking world was the *Barrier Daily Truth*, published by the Barrier District Council of the Australasian Labour Federation at Broken Hill, NSW, from 2 November 1908.

**The first tabloid newspaper** was the Sydney evening paper *The Australian Star*, which changed its format from broadsheet in March 1909. It reverted back the following January.

**The first newspaper to carry news on its front page** rather than advertisements was the Sydney *Sun* from 1 July 1910.

**The first newspaper to introduce photo-typesetting** was the *Melbourne Herald*, which acquired a Fotosetter for photogravure production work in 1954.

**The first national daily newspaper** was the *Australian*, which began publication on 15 July 1964.

**The first newspaper to introduce computer typesetting** was the *Canberra Times* in May 1977.

See also Halftone Illustrations.

## NEWSPAPER CARTOONS

began appearing in the *Cornwall Chronicle* of Launceston, Tas, in 1835. At that time the paper was edited by the bellicose and outspoken ex-sea captain William Lushington Goodwin, a man wont to drive his seamen to their posts with a mallet, who drew and engraved the cartoons himself. Although a meagre draughtsman, Goodwin imbued his crude sketches with biting satire, most of it directed at his hated enemy Governor Arthur.

## NEWSREEL

was West's Pictures *Journal of Daily Events*, inaugurated by New Zealander T. J. West of Sydney on 21 July 1910. The first issue showed scenes at the site of a rail crash which had taken place at Richmond Station, Melbourne the previous Monday. West's great rival showman, Cosens Spencer, responded by founding *Spencer's Gazette*, which was soon joined by *Williams' Weekly* and the *Pathé Australian Animated Gazette*. The **first sound newsreel** was *Movietone*, introduced in Australia from the US on 2 November 1929. The content was American, but sometimes Australian items were tacked on to the end. *Australian Movietone*, which began on 1 January 1931 and continued for 45 years, was the first sound newsreel produced in this country.

Rivals established the same year were the long running *Cinesound Review* and the short-lived *Melbourne Herald Newsreel*.

## NICKEL MINE

was established at Kambalda, WA, by the Western Mining Corporation on 28 January 1966. Nickel ore had first been discovered in the Kambalda area by George Cowcill twelve years earlier, but it was not until he read of the world's nickel shortage in the mid-sixties that he was prompted to take samples to Western Mining at Kalgoorlie for assay. By the late 1970s Australia was the world's fourth largest producer of nickel.

## NOBEL PRIZE WINNER

was Adelaide-born (Sir) Lawrence Bragg, who together with his British-born father, Sir William Bragg, was awarded the Nobel Prize for Physics on 12 November 1915 for research into X-rays. At 25, he was the youngest Nobel prize winner ever, a record which still stands.
**The first Australian winner of the Nobel Prize for Literature** was Patrick White, whose award on 18 October 1973 was in recognition of 'an epic and psychological narrative art which has introduced a new continent into literature'.

*The Nobel prizewinner Sir William Bragg gives a scientific demonstration.*

# The first...

## NONTUPLETS

in the world (authenticated) were the five boys and four girls born to Mrs Geraldine Boodrick at Sydney's Royal Hospital on 13 June 1971. Two were stillborn and one, Richard, only survived six days.

## NOTEPADS

in the world were Silvercity Writing Tablets, marketed by the Tasmanian stationers Birchall's of Launceston c. 1902. Prior to this date all writing papers were sold in folded form, usually with a rough edge. The loose sheets were packed in boxes, 24 making a quire and 20 quires a ream. It was J.A. Birchall who conceived the idea of cutting the paper into smaller sheets, backing them with a piece of cardboard and gumming them together along the top. He asked his regular paper suppliers, the London firm of Wiggins Teape, to supply notepads to this specification. At first the directors of Wiggins Teape were unwilling to comply with this crude colonial notion, but Birchall persisted and eventually they were persuaded to make up a trial shipment at his expense. To begin with sales were slow, Tasmanians being reluctant to depart from accepted English practice, but gradually they found that the tablets were much more convenient than loose sheets, and before long not only Australia, but Britain and then the rest of the world had followed Launceston's lead and adopted the notepads that broke 500 years of tradition in paper manufacture.

## NOVEL

published in Australia was Henry Savery's *Quintus Servinton*. A three volume work published at Hobart, price 18s, in 1830. The story of a well-to-do, public school educated man who is transported for forgery, the fictional tale was based on Savery's own experiences. A well known British sugar broker, he had been transported in 1825 at the age of 31 for fraudulent insolvency and forgery, becoming a clerk in the Colonial Treasurer's Office at Hobart. Later he worked as a journalist under Henry Melville, proprietor of the Colonial Times, who published *Quintus Servinton*.

**The first novel written by a woman** was Mrs M.L. Grimstone's three-volume *Woman's Love*, London, 1832. It is believed that this was written in Hobart before the first Australian novel to be published, *Quintus Servinton*.

**The first novel by a woman writer to be published in Australia** was Anna Maria Bunn's *The Guardian*, Sydney, 1838, a romance set in England and Ireland, which was also the first novel published in New South Wales.

**The first novel by an Australian-born writer** was *The Wetherby's, or Chapters of Indian Experience*, by Sydney-born John Lang (1816-64), which was published in London in 1853. Lang left Australia for India in 1842 and remained there the rest of his life.

**The first novel by an Australian-born woman writer** was Caroline Louisa Atkinson's *Gertrude the Emigrant; A Tale of Colonial Life*, Sydney, 1857.

**The first historical novel about Australia** was Charles De Boos' *Fifty Years Ago*, published in fortnightly parts in Sydney in 1866. De Boos was a reporter on the *Sydney Morning Herald*. The story centred on a vendetta against a group of Aboriginals after they had killed the family of a pioneer settler.

**The first novel by an Aborigine** was Colin Johnson's *Wild Cat Falling*, which was published in 1955.

## NUCLEAR EXPLOSION

took place when the first British atomic bomb was detonated at the Monte Bello Islands, off Western Australia, on 3 October 1952. The test was intended to simulate explosion in a port, the bomb being exploded aboard HMS *Plym*.

The nuclear reactor HIFAR at Lucas Heights, Sydney.

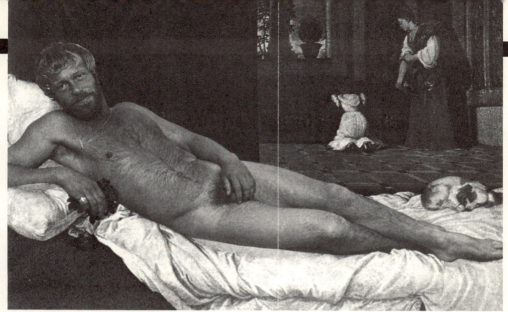

*The magazine* Cleo *was the first to publish a nude male pin-up.*

## NUCLEAR REACTOR

was HIFAR (High Flux Australian Reactor) which became operational at Lucas Heights, Sydney on 18 April 1958. It was used to study the effects of high intensity radiation on materials, provide a source of neutrons and produce radio-isotopes.

## NUDE BATHING

was legalised at Maslin's Beach, south of Adelaide in February 1975.

## NUDE MALE PIN-UPS

were published in *Cleo* magazine, starting with the inaugural issue of November 1972. First to expose his nether charms for the delectation of Australian womanhood, as well as the inhabitants of Kings Cross of both sexes, was macho actor Jack Thompson.

## NUMBERING OF HOUSES

was carried out in Sydney during October 1803 and completed on the 12th of that month, the purpose being to compile a directory of all householders and lodgers for police use. The man whose job it was to paint the numbers on the doors declared that he had found this task particularly difficult in the notorious Rocks area, which was like a shanty town, but claimed that 'no single avenue went unexplored'.

## NUNS

were five Sisters of Charity who arrived at Sydney on 30 December 1838.
**The first convent** was the Convent of the Holy Cross, established by six Sisters of Mercy from Dublin in rented premises in St George's Terrace, Perth on 17 January 1846. Sister Mary Ursula described it as 'a very elegant house, too nice indeed for Sisters of Mercy . . .'
**The first order of nuns founded in Australia** was the Sisters of the Good Samaritan, founded by Bishop Polding in 1857 to maintain schools for Catholic girls.

## NURSES, TRAINED

were two Irish nuns who began work at the sick bay of the women's penitentiary at Parramatta Gaol in 1839. They had received their training in Paris. Meanwhile the hospitals were staffed mainly by elderly untrained convict women, many of them dissolute and drunken, who robbed the patients to buy grog. This unsatisfactory state of affairs continued until March 1868, when five nursing sisters under the direction of Miss Lucy Osborn arrived from England to become the first trained hospital nurses in Australia. They worked at Sydney Hospital, where Miss Osborn established the first training school for nurses. She and the five pioneer hospital nurses had been specially selected by Florence Nightingale, who had introduced trained nursing in England following the Crimean War.
**The first Army nurses** were 26 young ladies who were formed into the Australian Nursing Service of New South Wales on 13 August 1898. Thirteen of their number went to South Africa in 1900 to serve in the Boer War, the first Australian women on active service.

# The first...

## OBSERVATORY

was a wooden building erected at Dawes Point, Sydney, in July 1788. It was under the superintendance of Lieutenant William Dawes of the Royal Marines, who had been sent out by the British Board of Longitude to make astronomical observations. Mrs Macarthur wrote of Dawes that 'he is so much engaged with the stars that to mortal eye he is not always visible'.

*This observatory in Sydney is built on the site of the first windmill.*

BHP

*Offshore oil fields were first discovered in Bass Strait by BHP and ESSO.*

## OIL

was produced from shale by the New South Wales Shale and Oil Co. Ltd, which was established in 1865 to work a lode discovered at Hartley Vale in the Blue Mountains. The company's leading product was Comet kerosene, which was said by the *Australian Yearbook* (1883) to be 'well known in every colony in Australia, and in each it is used in preference to any other discription of oil that is imported'. The company had its own oil refinery, the first in Australia, at Alexandria.

**The first oil wells** to produce oil in commercial quantity were drilled by an Australian-American consortium at Moonie, Queensland, where a strike was made on 3 December 1961. Full-scale production began 8 April 1964 with the completion of the first oil pipeline, laid over 300 km of rough country from Moonie to the Lytton refinery in Brisbane. The search for oil had been going on ever since drilling operations first began in the Coorong area of South Australia nearly seventy years earlier.

**The first offshore oil field** was discovered in the Gippsland Basin area of Bass Strait by BHP and Esso Exploration, production starting on 18 February 1965.

**The first Australian-built offshore oil rig** was *Ocean Digger*, launched at Whyalla, SA, in July 1967.

## OLD AGE PENSIONS

were introduced in Victoria and New South Wales in 1901. Victoria enacted its measure after New South Wales, but managed to make its scheme operative, albeit in a temporary form, ahead of its sister State. Starting on 1 January 1901, anyone of 65 who had lived in Victoria for 20 years, and had insufficient means of support, was eligible for a pension of 1s a day.

The New South Wales provisions, which came into force on 1 July, were more stringent, although the pension could be higher. The age qualification was also 65, but applicants had to have been resident in New South Wales for at least 25 years and were required to be of good conduct. Moreover the Upper House of the Legislature, anxious lest the feckless poor would spend the money on grog, had inserted a clause into the Act prohibiting Licensed Victuallers from supplying any old age pensioner with liquor.

The maximum New South Wales pension was £26 pa for single persons with an income of £26 or under from other sources. For every additonal £1 over this sum, £1 was deducted from the pension. Thus anyone with an income of £52 pa was ineligible for a state pension. The maximum for married couples was £39.

So fearful were the legislators that the State's money might be squandered, pensions boards were authorised to pay over the money to a clergyman or JP if they suspected the applicant might be spendthrift. Those who were allowed to draw the money for themselves had to go to a bank for payment and it was noted that few of the applicants were able to write their own names, a mark having to suffice. The *Sydney Daily Telegraph* reported of the first pensions day; 'It was curious that none of the applicants asked for the money to be given in any particular form, as is customary at banks. It was taken as it was offered — without question. The only anxiety was to get it. Many retired grasping the coins as with a vice, murmering blessings on all and sundry. In many instances the recipients expressed themselves as being profoundly grateful to the bank clerks, as though they thought the money had come from their pockets. Since the authorities had arranged for every bank to be picketed by the police, in case of unruly behaviour, and since few of the applicants had ever been into a bank before in their lives, it is scarcely surprising that some were a trifle overawed by the experience.

A federal pensions system was instituted with the Commonwealth Invalid and Old Age Pensions Act in 1908.

## OLIVE OIL

was produced by G. W. Francis from local olives at Adelaide in 1851. He sent his oil to the Great Exhibition in London, where it received an Honourable Mention.

## OLIVE TREE

was brought to South Australia by Governor Hindmarsh aboard the *Buffalo* on 28 December 1836 and planted at Adelaide.

## OLYMPICS

The first Olympic gold medallist was E. H. Flack of Victoria, who comprised the entire Australian team at the first modern Olympics which were held at Athens in 1896. On 7 April Flack won the 1500 metres in a time of 4 mins 33 secs and two days later won another gold for the 800 metres in 2 mins 11 secs. He was not, however, the first man to stand on the victory podium while the Australian flag unfurled. This was because the organizers were unable to produce such a thing and ran up the Austrian flag instead. Australia had competed in every Olympics since, one of only four nations (the others are Britain, Switzerland and Greece) to have done so.

*The first Australian woman to win a gold* was Fanny Durack for the 100 metres freestyle swimming event at Stockholm on 13 July 1912, for which she established a world record of 1 min 19.8 secs.

*The first Australian woman to compete in track or field events* was Miss E.F. Robinson, the only female member of the Australian squad at Amsterdam in August 1928, who came third in the semi-final of the women's 100 metres. First to win an individual medal was Shirley Strickland, who took the bronze for both the 100 metres and the 80 metres hurdles at London in August 1948. First winner of a gold medal was Marjorie Jackson, who triumphed in the 100 metres finals at Helsinki on 22 July 1952. Her time of 11.5 secs equalled the world record. She also won the 200 metres event, setting a new Olympic record in 23.7 secs.

*The first Olympics held in Australia,* the 16th Olympiad, opened in Melbourne on 22 November 1956. Australia won 13 gold, 8 silver and 4 bronze medals.

# The first ...

New Zealand the previous year. Britain followed suit in 1931.

## OPERA

performed in Australia was *Giovanni in London*, presented at the Theatre Royal, Sydney, on 4 September 1834.

**The first Italian opera** was *The Barber of Seville*, performed at Sydney in June 1843, with Mrs Gibbs as Rosina.

**The first Opera composed and performed in Australia** was *Don Juan of Austria* with music by Isaac Nathan and libretto by Jacob Montefiore, which was premiered at the Victoria Theatre, Sydney, on 3 May 1847. The principal performers were the Howson brothers and Mrs Guerin. *Heads of the People* dammed it with faint praise: 'The music is scientifically composed throughout, but is too scarce of simple melodies to render it a favourite with the audience of a Sydney theatre.'

**The first regular opera company** in Australia was William Saurin Lyster's, which arrived from California on 1 March 1861 and opened at Melbourne on 25 March. Among their repertoire was *Don Giovanni*, the first Mozart opera to be staged in its entirety in Australia. The company performed 42 different operas during the seven years of its existence.

## OPERA HOUSE

was the English Opera House, Sydney, formerly the Prince of Wales Theatre, which assumed its new function in 1855. Frank Fowler recorded in *Southern Lights and Shades*: 'There I have heard Bellini, Meyerbeer, and even Verdi and Beethoven as carefully rendered as at any theatre in London; the two Italian opera houses are excepted. Madame Anna Bishop was generally first-lady, Miss Sarah Flower contralto; Messrs Laglaise and Conlon — not quite unknown names — tenor and base; and Messrs Lavenu and Loder, men of some English reputation, leaders of the orchestra.'

## OPERETTA

composed and performed in Australia was *The Currency Lass*, presented at the Royal Victoria Theatre, Sydney, on 30 May 1844. The composer and librettist is believed to have been the Irish playwright A. G. Geoghegan, to whom the first Australian play (q.v.) is also attributed.

*Isaac Nathan, composer of the opera* Don Juan of Austria.

## OMBUDSMAN

was Mr Oliver Dixon, appointed by the Western Australian government on 24 April 1971. Others were appointed in SA in 1972, Vic in 1973, NSW in 1974 and Qld in 1977.

## OPALS

were discovered near Angaston, SA, in 1849. The first precious opal was found at Avadale, Queensland in 1872.

## OPEN PRISON

was established in New South Wales in 1914. The first in the world had been founded in

## ORATORIO

composed in Australia was Charles Parker's *The Second Advent*, whose premiere performance was given in Melbourne in 1859.

## ORCHESTRA

was established by J. Livingstone, Choirmaster of St David's Church, Hobart Town, in 1821. Although this wind ensemble was principally for accompanying the church choir, it would seem that it was also employed for more secular occasions, as in 1826 when the *Hobart Town Gazette* reported the performance of 'A new and beautiful Australian air in honour of our sister colony of New South Wales'.

**The first symphony orchestra** was founded by Frederick H. Cowen, a conductor from England, in 1888. It was formed originally to give concerts in connection with the Melbourne Exhibition, but continued in operation for some time afterwards.

**The first overseas symphony orchestra to tour Australia** was the Czech Philharmonic in 1959. The first Australian symphony orchestra to make an extensive overseas tour was the Sydney Symphony Orchestra, which visited Japan, the Philippines, Hong Kong and the UK during September-October 1965.

## ORIENTEERING

was introduced from Sweden by Melbourne athlete Tom Andrews, who organized the first Australian event in the hills around Upper Beaconsfield, south-east of Melbourne, in August 1969. The sport had originated in Sweden in 1918.

## ORGAN

was installed at St David's Church, Hobart Town, in 1825. The organist was John Phillip Deane.

The first pipe organ built in Australia was installed at St Matthew's, Windsor, NSW, in 1840. It is still in regular use.

## ORPHANAGE

was established by Governor King on his own initiative and opened on 8 August 1801. A kindly and humane man, King was shocked at the number of homeless waifs living on the streets of early Sydney. He wrote in March 1802: 'There are 1,007 children in the colony, and finer or more neglected children were not to be met with in any part of the world. Soon after I arrived here the sight of so many girls, between the ages of eight and twelve, verging on the brink of ruin and prostitution which several had fallen into, induced me to set about rescuing the elder girls from the snares laid for them, and which the horrible example of their parents hurried them into. A spacious brick house, built by Lieut. Kent, offered an immediate asylum ... Forty-nine girls from seven to fourteen years old were received into the charge of as eligible people for that purpose as could be found in this colony. They are victualled by the Crown, but every other expense has been defrayed by contributions, fines, duties on shipping, etc., with no other expense to the public except the house. The children are taught needlework, reading, spinning and some few writing'. The shipping dues to which the Governor referred were levied specially for this purpose by an order of 10 October 1800 and were one of the first forms of taxation introduced in Australia. The price paid for the building, which stood on the site now occupied by Anchor House at the corner of Bridge Street and George Street, was £1,539 — a very considerable sum which suggests that it must have been one of the most substantial properties in Sydney.

The orphans were looked after by a matron, cook, house-keeper, porter, servant and three teachers who earned 6 gns a year each. The quality of teaching can be gauged by the fact that one of the teachers was unable to write even her own name. Nor was the quality of the superintendents much better. Governor Bligh appointed to the post a man whose habit it was to preach on Sundays and 'take unwarrantable liberties with the Girls on Mondays'. According to Rev. William Crook, who turned the job down because of the depravity of the school, most of the orphans became prostitutes when they left.

The first of the orphans to avoid this fate by getting married — doubtless the ambition of them all — was one M. Peat, whose wedding to a baker called Laurence Brady took place at St John's Church, Parramatta, on 31 August 1803.

**The first orphanage for boys** was established at Parramatta on 1 January 1819.

## OSTRICH FARM

was established in 1875 by Suetonius Henry Officer at Murray Downs, near Swan Hill, Vic.

# The first . . .

## P PLATES

became compulsory in Victoria on 1 March 1969.

## PAINTING

The first oil painting of an Australian scene was *A Direct North General View of Sydney Cove*, executed in 1794 by the convict artist Thomas Watling. The painting found its way to England, where it was purchased from a dealer's shop in Liverpool on behalf of the Dixson Gallery, Sydney.

**The first Artist to make a living from painting in Australia** was John William Lewin, who arrived at Sydney on 11 January 1800. He established the first art school (q.v.) and executed the first engraving (q.v.) in Australia.

**The first known portraits** of white residents of Australia were the work of convict Richard Read Sr, who arrived in Sydney on 7 October 1813 and established a drawing school at 37 Pitt Street. His earliest known portrait is a watercolour of John Buckland, a settler with property near Campbelltown, painted in May 1814. This is now in the Newcastle Region Art Gallery. During the same year he also painted Elizabeth Isabell Broughton, a child of about 7 who had enjoyed a remarkable escape from shipwreck and the onslaught of Maori warriors in New Zealand. This is the earliest known female portrait and is in the National Library of Australia, Canberra. Other por-

traits by Read include Judge Barron Field, Mrs Samuel Marsden, Governor Macquarie and his wife Elizabeth Macquarie and the 'Colonial poet laureate' Michael Massey Robinson. As early as 1808, J. W. Lewin had offered to execute miniatures at 5 gns each and portraits at 40s. It is not known whether he received any commissions.

**The first Australian-born artist** was the portrait painter William Pitt Wilshire, born in Sydney in 1807.

**The first Australian abstract paintings** were exhibited by Roland Wakelin and Roy de Moistre, both alumni of Dattilo Rubbo's art school in Sydney, in 1919.

## PANTIHOSE

were introduced by Holeproof at £2 a pair in 1967. Australia was slow to discard stockings and suspenders, British girls having started to wear tights as early as 1961. Once the mini-skirt arrived in this country, early in 1966, there was a compelling need to discard suspenders — they showed whenever you bent over. Jean Shrimpton, the English model who first wore the mini in Australia, had an altogether simpler solution — bare legs.

## PAPER

was manufactured by partners Frederick Fisher, George Duncan and John Walker at Bank Mill, on a site near the present Bourke Street, Sydney, which was announced as operational in the *Sydney Gazette* of 18 April 1818. A scrap of this paper was discovered in the Equity Court Papers at the New South Wales Archives in 1965.

## PAPER DRESS PATTERNS

were published by Madame Weigel of Richmond, Vic, in 1880. They came in six sizes and cost 1s 6d each.

## PAPERBACK NOVELS

published as a series were issued by the New South Wales Bookstall Co. of Sydney starting in 1898. Between that year and 1920 they issued some 200 works of fiction, selling 5 million copies at 1s each.

## PARACHUTE DESCENT

was made by Henry L'Estrange on 14 April 1879 when his balloon burst over Melbourne. The 'chute was attached to the balloon and allowed the wreckage to descend at a safe speed.

First to make a parachute jump was J. T. Williams from a balloon 6,000 ft above the recreation grounds at Ashfield, NSW, on 31 October 1882.

## PARKING METERS

were introduced in Collins Street, Hobart, on 1 April 1955. This was 20 years after they had first exasperated motorists in Oklahoma City. Sydney followed Hobart's lead in 1956.

## PARKING OFFICERS

were disabled ex-servicemen employed by the City of Sydney in 1946 to enforce local parking restrictions.

## PARLIAMENT

was the Legislative Council of New South Wales, which was first convened under the leadership of the Lieutenant Governor, William Stewart, on 11 August 1824. All the members were ex-officio.

*The first representative parliament* was the Legislature of New South Wales, with 24 elected members and 12 others, which met on 2 August 1843. It was still subject to the direction of the Governor of the colony.

*The first Parliament opened under responsible Government* was the Legislative Assembly of New South Wales of 22 May 1856. This had 54 elected members, while a separate Legislative Council was comprised of members appointed for life by the Governor. Responsible government came to Victoria and Tasmania later the same year.

*The first Federal Parliament* opened on 9 May 1901 in the Exhibition Building at Melbourne. Among the distinguished members was one who had come to Australia as a convict. William Henry Groom (1833-1901) was a Plymouth baker's apprentice who had been transported at the age of 13 for stealing. He sat in the Queensland Legislative Assembly from 1862 and was elected first Federal member for Darling Downs in 1901.

*The first Parliament at Canberra* sat on 9 May 1927.

See also Elections, Parliamentary.

## PATENTS

were first registered under the laws of Victoria in 1855. The cost of registration was £100, and only 22 patents were filled during the two years the original patent law remained in force.

Patents applying throughout Australia were accepted under the Commonwealth Patents Act from 1 June 1904. By this day 756 applications had already been received.

## PAVED STREET

was George Street, Sydney, which was laid with a macadamized surface of granite in or shortly before 1838. George Street is also the oldest street in Australia, its line following the very first track cleared through the woods immediately after the arrival of the First Fleet at Sydney Cove on 26 January 1788. It remained little more than a cart-track, in common with the other streets of Sydney, until the year 1817, when it was levelled and made good in a manner befitting the principal thoroughfare of the infant city.

## PAVLOVA

in the world was created in 1934 at the Esplanade Hotel, Perth, by Bert Sachse, who added cornflower, vinegar and vanilla to a meringue mixture of egg white and sugar to produce Australia's only notable contribution to international cuisine. The great ballerina Pavlova had visited Australia in 1926 and 1929 and according to Bert Sachse, it was the manager of the Esplanade, Harry Nairn, who coined the name by declaring that the meringue confection was 'as light as Pavlova'.

## PAY-ROLL TAX

was introduced by the Commonwealth Government at the rate of 2½% on 30 June 1941. It was transferred to the States in 1971.

## PEARL CULTURE FARM

was established at Kuri Bay, 420 km north of Broom, WA, in 1956.

## PEARLS

were first collected in quantity as a commercial venture by the *Flying Fram*, which gathered 910 shells off Nichol Bay, WA, in 1861 with a yield of 150 pearls.

## PEDICABS

were introduced in Adelaide in October 1986, closely followed by Melbourne in December. The three-wheeler machines cost a not inconsiderable $4,500 each and the fare was around $4 a km or $20 an hour. The main qualification for being a Pedicab driver was said by the *Melbourne Sun* to be 'affability'.

# The first ...

News Ltd

*Howard Florey developed penicillin in a purified form for clinical use.*

## PEER OF THE REALM

The first native-born Australian to be raised to the peerage was Sir John Forrest, first Premier of Western Australia, who was born the son of a flour-miller at Bunbury, Western Australia, in 1847, and educated at Bishop Hale's School in Perth. Forrest was also the first native of Western Australia to become a member of the colonial government, in 1883, and he was appointed Premier in 1890 when Western Australia was granted self-government. He was created Lord Forrest of Bunbury on 7 February 1918, a month after the creation of the first non-white peer, Lord Sinha of Raipur. Sadly he never took his seat in the House of Lords, dying at sea off Sierre Leone on 3 September 1918 during the voyage to England. His body was brought back to Perth for burial at Karrakatta Cemetary.

*The first Australian peer to take his seat in the House of Lords* was Viscount Bruce of Melbourne (1883-1967) formerly the Rt Hon Stanley Melbourne Bruce, CH, MC, on 26 March 1947.

## PENICILLIN

was produced in commercial quantities by the Commonwealth Serum Laboratories at Melbourne in 1943, two years after the first large scale plant in the world had been set up at the Sir William Dunn School of Pathology at Oxford University. In Britain penicillin was reserved mainly for military use and Australia was the first country in the world to make it commercially available to civilians. Although penicillin had been discovered by Dr Alexander Fleming as early as 1928, it was not until Australian pathologist Prof. Howard Florey of Adelaide developed the antibiotic in a purified form at Oxford in 1940 that it was able to be put to regular clinical use.

## PETROL PUMPS

were installed by a service station in Melbourne in 1920. Formerly petrol had only been sold in cans.

*The first Automatic pump* was an Erie electric pump imported from the USA by AMP of Sydney and installed at a service station in Liverpool road, Enfield, NSW in January 1937.

## PHARMACIST

was emancipated convict John Tawell, who was granted a certificate of competency by a specially convened board of physicians in 1820 and set up a pharmacy in Hunter Street, Sydney. Tawell was one of Australia's original 'wowsers' and distinguished himself in 1836 by emptying 600 gallons of rum into Sydney Cove.

## PHOTOGRAPH

The first photograph taken in Australia, and one of the earliest street scenes in the world, was a study of Bridge Street and part of George Street, Sydney, taken by an unknown French photographer from the fountain in Macquarie Place on 13 May 1841. This was less than two years after the disclosure of the Daguerreotype process by Daguerre in Paris in August 1839. The picture was probably taken back to France, where it is possible it may still exist.

*The first portrait studio* was opened by a Mr G. B. Goodman on 12 December 1842 at the *Royal Hotel*, George Street, Sydney. The portraits, which cost a guinea 'exclusive of frame', were taken on the flat roof of the hotel, each exposure lasting about five seconds. Goodman visited Hobart in August 1843, where in addition to portraits he took what the *Hobart Town Courier* described as 'some very beautifully executed views of our rising metropolis'. He spent several months of 1844 photographing the leading citizens of Launceston and early in 1845 took himself to Bathurst, from whence, despite a population of only 3,000, he had already received a hundred orders in advance of his arrival. He travelled on to Melbourne, where he spent four and a half months in the raw little town of 15,000 souls, then proceeded to Adelaide before returning to Sydney. In each of these places, with the exception of Adelaide, his were the first photographs ever taken.

**The first Australian-born professional photographer** was Thomas Bock (1835-1920), who established the first permanent photographic studio in Tasmania at Hobart in 1847.

**The first native-born amateur photographer** was Sir William Macarthur (1800-82), son of John Macarthur of Merino sheep fame. He took up the hobby about 1857 when he photographed Aborigines around Albany Bay. The following year he was making many studies of the developing city of Sydney, including one of stonemasons at work on the gargoyles for Sydney University and another of a bullock wagon in George Street laden with wool from Camden. Also in 1858 he took pictures of the surveying party in the Valley of the Grose and of camp life in the Blue Mountains, as well as family pictures in the gardens at Camden and at the Macarthurs' town house at Elizabeth Bay. One of his 'snapshots', taken on the verandah at Camden in 1857, shows a man smiling — one of the earliest instances of a smiling figure in a photograph anywhere in the world.

**The first colour photographs** were taken by Mark Blow using a British-made Ives Kromskop camera and displayed at the Crown Studio, Sydney, on 1 August 1899.

The process involved making three transparencies each in a different primary colour, and combining these in a special viewer called a Photochromoscope which gave a single image in natural colour. Single-plate colour photography was not introduced to Australia until the advent of the Lumiere brothers' Autochrome plates in 1907.

**The first aerial photograph** was a panorama of Sydney taken by Melvin Vaniman in 1904 from a balloon tethered 900 ft above the City.

## PIANO

was brought to New South Wales on 9 May 1789 by George Bouchier Worgan, surgeon aboard the *Sirius*. Early in 1791, shortly before his return to England, he presented the instrument to the Macarthurs, who had just moved into a new house. Mrs Macarthur learned to play *God Save the King* and Foot's *Minuet* on it, but with her teacher, Mr Worgan, about to depart, declared that 'I fear without my Master I shall not make any great proficiency'.

The first pianos manufactured in Australia were made by John Benham of Pitt Street, Sydney, who was in business by 1832. The oldest extant example of his work dates from c.1835 and is in the Mint Museum.

The winner of the first Sydney International Piano Competition was Irina Plotnikova on 3 August 1977.

## PIZZA

was introduced to Australia in 1961 by John Battista, an Italian formerly of Toronto, who began baking pizzas in a specially constructed oven he installed in a converted cake-shop in the Sydney suburb of Kensington. The first pizza restaurant was Toto's in Lygon Street, Melbourne, opened by Salvatore Della Bruna on 7 July 1966.

The first Pizza Hut restaurant in Australia was opened at Belfield, NSW, on 19 April 1970.

## PLANNING PERMISSION

for the erection of buildings was first required in the town of Sydney by an order of Governor Macquarie of 11 August 1810. Applications had to be made to the Acting Surveyor and anyone failing to do so would 'have their Houses pulled down, and further incur the Governor's displeasure'. This innovation was part of Macquarie's plan for rebuilding Sydney, with uniform houses in the main residential streets, road widening to a breadth of 50 ft, and a quantity of imposing public buildings. Planning permission was extended to Parramatta and Windsor with effect from 11 May 1811.

## PLATYPUS

to be observed by white men was seen near the Hawkesbury River in 1797. David Collins, who was not in Australia in that year, noted the finding of 'an amphibious animal, of the mole species' and remarked on it having the mandibles of a duck, but did not say who had first seen the creature. It is difficult for the platypus to survive outside its native habitat, so very few have been sent overseas. The

# The first ...

first to be exhibited alive outside Australia was put on show at New York Zoological Park in July 1922, surviving for 49 days. The first to be bred in captivity was born at Healesville, Vic, in 1943.

## PLAY

performed in Australia was Farquhar's comedy *The Recruiting Officer*, performed by a group of convicts at Sydney Cove before the Governor and officers of the garrison on the occasion of the King's birthday, 4 June 1789. It took place in a hut specially fitted up as a temporary theatre. One of those present said that the convict actors 'professed no higher aim than "humbly to excite a smile", and their efforts were not unattended with applause'. Another member of the audience, Capt. Tench of the Royal Marines reported: 'Some of the actors acquitted themselves with great spirit, and received the praises of the audience. A prologue and an epilogue, written by one of the performers, were also spoken on the occasion'.

The first Play set in Australia was *Les Emigrés aux Terres Australes* by 'Citoyen Games', performed in Paris on 24 November 1792. In keeping with the revolutionary times it told an individualistic tale of how an artisan cast away in Australia together with an assembly of bourgeois characters demonstrates his natural superiority — much as the butler in *The Admirable Crichton* was shown, upon a desert isle, to be superior to those he had formerly served. Citoyen Games had a strange idea of Australia; in his play it was infested with fierce tigers. The first play in English about Australia, and the first with some bearing on the Australia of reality was David Burn's *The Bushrangers*, based on the story of escaped convict Matthew Brady, the Tasmanian bushranger, which was staged at Edinburgh, Scotland, in 1829. Burn had witnessed Brady's execution shortly after his arrival in Tasmania three years earlier. The play was not performed in Australia until 1971, when it was put on by a high school in Sydney.

*The first play written and performed in Australia* was Henry Melville's *The Bushrangers; or, Norwood Vale*, presented at the Argyle Rooms in Argyle Street, Hobart Town, on 29 May 1834. Unlike the earlier play of the same title, in this one the bushrangers were the villains, a migrant youth and the daughter of a gentleman settler affording hero and heroine. The play was published in the *Hobart Town Magazine* in 1834.

*The first play by a native born Australian* was yet another *The Bushrangers*, a verse drama by Charles Harpur set around Windsor and Richmond in New South Wales, of which extensive extracts were published in five successive issues of *The Sydney Monitor* under the title of *The Tragedy of Donohre* during February 1835.

Probably the first play by an Australian-born playwright to be performed on stage was *The Heir of the Sept; or; Ireland in the Eleventh Century*, presented at the Queens Theatre, Melbourne, on 15 September 1845. The authorship of the piece was anonymous, the dramatist signing himself 'A Native'.

*The first play by a woman playwright* to be written and performed in Australia was Mrs T. A. Hetherington's *The Stage Struck Digger, or Life on Ballarat*, which ran at the Ballarat Theatre Royal in November 1854. Mrs Hetherington was the wife of the *Theatre Royal's* manager.

*The first play by an Australian playwright to be performed* overseas was Francis Hopkins 'All For Gold, or Fifty Millions of Money', presented in Sydney in 1877 and London in 1881.

## PLOUGH

was introduced by John Macarthur at Elizabeth Farm, Parramatta. Elizabeth Macarthur wrote to her friend Miss Kingdom on 1 September 1795: 'Mr Macarthur has also set a Plough at work, the first which has been used in the country, and it is drawn sometimes by oxen and at others by horses. The ground was before tilled with the hoe. These details I am sensible have not other interest than as far as they serve to show the progressive state of this yet infant settlement.'

## PLOUGHING MATCH

was held at Bong Bong, NSW, in August 1828.

## PNEUMATIC TYRES

were Dunlops fitted to six bicycles by Melbourne cycle dealer E. W. Rudd in 1889, less than a year after the Belfast veterinary surgeon John Boyd Dunlop had produced his first full size tyre. Rudd subsequently became Dunlop's agent in Australia.

*The first motor car fitted with pneumatics* was the Thomson Steam Motor Buggy at

Armadale, Vic, in 1896.

**Production of all-Australian pneumatic cycle and motor tyres** was inaugurated by the Dunlop Pneumatic Tyre Company of Australasia Ltd at its South Melbourne plant in 1899.

## POEM

to appear in print was *The Vision of Melancholy*, a 34-line verse in rhyming couplets, which appeared above the initials 'C.S.' in the *Sydney Gazette* for 4 March 1804. (A few doggerel verses had been published earlier, but it is doubtful whether these were of local composition.)

The first poem on a subject of Australian interest appeared in the same publication on 29 July 1804. This was a four-verse *Epitaph on a Monkey that usually occupied the summit of a high post in the yard of a Gentleman in Sydney.* The author of this poem was anonymous, the monkey's name was Pug.

Poetry continued to appear in the pages of the *Sydney Gazette* on an occasional basis, but all of it anonymous until the publication of an *Ode for His Majesty's Birthday* on 9 June 1810. The poet was Michael Massey Robinson, first clerk in the Government Secretary's Office. Since it would appear, from the style, that Robinson was the author of all the other unsigned poems published in the *Gazette* at this period, he may fairly be regarded as Australia's first poet.

Robinson used to compose odes for each of the King and Queen's birthdays and recite them at the local celebrations of these occasions in Sydney. For this he won himself the unofficial title of Poet Laureate and was granted, not the traditional butt of sack accorded the English Poet Laureate, but two cows from the government herd.

**The first book of poetry published in Australia** was Barron Field's *First Fruits of Australian Verse*, published by George Howe at Sydney in 1819. It contained two poems; 'Botany Bay Flowers' and 'Kangaroo'. David Scott Mitchell, whose collection of Australiana formed the basis of Sydney's justly celebrated Mitchell Library, spent his entire life seeking a copy of the first edition of *First Fruits*. It was in fact the last book he ever bought, on the day of his death, and he died happy clasping it in his hands.

**The first book of verse by an Australian born poet** was *Australasia*, containing a single long poem by William Charles Wentworth (born Norfolk Island 1791), which was published in London in 1823.

**The first book of poetry by an Australian born poet published in Australia** was Charles Thompson's *Wild Notes from the Lyre of a Native Minstrel*, which was issued by Robert Howe at Sydney in 1826. Thompson was the son of a Sydney innkeeper. Born in 1806, he was brought up at Castlereagh, eight miles north of Penrith, where his father had a farm and privately educated by a local clergyman and classical scholar, the Rev. Henry Fulson. He married at the early age of 16 a girl called Jane Moris who was also a native of the colony but a dozen years older than himself. The poet made his career in the government service, part of it as a parliamentary clerk in the NSW Legislature. Although he continued to write verse, Thompson published no further volumes of poetry. He died aged 75 in 1883.

**The first book of verse by a woman poet** to be published in Australia was *Poems and Recollections of the Past*, by Fidelia S.T. Hill 'late of Adelaide', Sydney, 1840.

## POLICE FORCE

was established at Sydney on 7 August 1789, being composed of 12 'trusties', all of them convicts, who were to act as a night watch. The idea was proposed to the Judge-Advocate by a convict called Harris as means of preventing the robberies which took place with such relentless frequency. These depredations were often occasioned by the fact that the convicts, who received their rations weekly, did not know how to apportion the food to last seven days; and having consumed their all in but three or four days, set out to replenish their larders from their more frugal neighbours' stores of provisions.

**The first salaried Police Officers** were appointed by Governor Macquarie with effect from 1 January 1811. The first Superintendent of Police was D'Arcy Wentworth (unsalaried), assisted by Robert Jones, Assistant to the Superintendent, at £60 pa, and John Redmond, Chief Constable, also at £60 pa. The police force consisted of 50 constables, divided between five police districts in Sydney. These men were not paid but received government rations, a Watch-Coat and 'the usual quantity of Slop Clothing annually'. In addition they were periodically granted the privilege of buying rum at advantageous rates — Head Constables being allowed 10 gallons and District Constables 5 gallons at 12s a gallon.

The constables were armed with cutlasses and each man carried a rattle to raise the alarm. Amongst their duties was seeing that

# The first . . .

all public houses were closed by 9 pm and entering 'all Houses which they suspected to be Houses of ill fame'.

**The first uniformed force** was formed under the Sydney Police Act of 1833. As in London, constables wore stove-pipe hats. These were reinforced so that they could be used to stand on to look over walls. Pay was 2s 10d a day for constables, 3s 3d for sergeants. Hours were prodigious — constables spent only one night in three in bed, the other nights, as well as the days, being devoted to patrol duties.

**The first native police force** was established under the command of C.L.J. de Villiers at Narre Warren, near Dandenong, Vic, c. 1838. It lasted only about a year, but was revived in 1842.

**The first detectives** were appointed to the Melbourne Police Force by Chief Constable Sugden in 1848.

**The Commonwealth Police Force** was established on 12 December 1917 following an incident at Warwick, Queensland, when Prime Minister Billy Hughes was hit by an egg at a meeting. The Labor Government of Queensland having refused any action by the Queensland Police, Hughes set up a Federal force.

## POLICE PATROL CAR

was a 20 hp Ford acquired by the WA Police Department in 1911 and based at the Roe Street police HQ in Perth.

The first radio patrol cars were two eight-cylinder 28 hp Lancias of the Victorian Police in Melbourne, equipped with seven-valve receiving sets by Amalgamated Wireless Ltd in May 1923. The idea was instigated by Senior Constable F. W. Downie and the first patrolman to receive a Morse message while on patrol was Constable William Hutchinson, who together with the other radio operators had been given special training at the Marine School of Wireless.

## POLICEWOMEN

were Lilian May Armfield, formerly a nurse at Callan Park Mental Hospital, and Maude Marion Rhodes, an inspector with the NSW Children's Relief Dept, who were selected from 400 applicants and appointed to the NSW Police Department on 1 July 1915. They were attached to No 1 Police Division and given a room to themselves at the Central Police Station, Sydney. Their main duties were to keep young children off the streets, especially at night; prevent truancy; patrol railway stations to protect unaccompanied females; and look after drunken women and their neglected children. Added to these rather mundane responsibilities was an injunction to 'watch the newspapers and to put detectives on the track of those apparently endeavouring to decoy young girls by advertisement or by any other means' and 'to keep an eye on houses of ill-fame and on the wineshops and hotels frequented by women of the town, in order to prevent young girls from being decoyed and drugged with liquor or entrapped'.

Women police were recruited by South Australia in December 1915, by Western Australia in 1917, by Tasmania in 1918, by Victoria in 1924 and by Queensland in 1931.

## POLO

was played at Albert Park, Melbourne on 8 November 1875.

## POPE TO VISIT AUSTRALIA

was Pope Paul VI, who arrived at Sydney on 30 November 1970. The visit was plunged in controversy when the Anglican Archbishop of Sydney, Marcus Loane, refused to attend an ecumenical service with the Pope because of his hatred of Catholicism.

## POSTAGE STAMPS

The first prepaid postal system in the world was pioneered by James Raymond, Colonial Postmaster-General of New South Wales, with the introduction of stamped letter-sheets on 1 November 1838. Sold at 1s 3d a dozen, these sheets bore an embossed stamp comprising the seal of the New South Wales Post Office. Alternatively members of the public could bring their own paper or envelopes to be stamped at a charge of 1s 8d for 25 items. Those who preferred not to pay in advance could opt for payment on delivery, which at this date was 2d within the Sydney area.

**The first adhesive postage stamps** were issued by New South Wales and Victoria on 1 January 1850. The New South Wales stamps, in 1d, 2d and 3d denominations, were designed and engraved by Robert Clayton of Sydney and bore a rather crude image of Sydney, based on part of the design of the Great Seal of New South Wales. Known as

'Sydney Views', they were the first pictorial (as opposed to portrait) stamps in the world.

Tasmania was the next colony to issue adhesive postage stamps, in 1853, followed by Western Australia in 1854, South Australia in 1855 and Queensland in 1860. Until October 1910 these stamps could only be used in the colony/state of issue. They then became interchangeable. The first Commonwealth of Australia stamp was the 'Kangaroo and Map' one penny red issued on 2 in January 1913.

*The first commemorative stamps* were issued by NSW on 26 January 1888 to celebrate the centenary of settlement. The designs differed according to denomination (1d — £1), but each was inscribed with the words 'One hundred Years'. The first commemorative stamps of the Commonwealth of Australia were issued in 1927 on the occasion of the opening of Parliament House, Canberra.

*The first Christmas stamp* was issued in 1957.

*The first decimal stamps* were issued on 7 February 1966 and became valid for postage a week later.

## POSTCARDS

were introduced by the NSW Post office on 1 October 1875. Over 128,000 were sent in the first three months.

*The first picture postcards* were seven halftone views of Adelaide issued by local photographer Ernst Ziegler in May 1898.

## POST CODES

were introduced throughout Australia on 1st July 1967.

## POST OFFICE

was established on the western side of Lower George Street, Sydney, by an order of 25 April 1809. The postmaster was Isaac Nichols, an emancipist who had been transported for stealing a donkey. He was empowered to make a charge of one shilling for every letter from overseas when it was collected by the recipient. The need for this service was occasioned by the fact that letters arriving on ships from England were often sequestered by people to whom they were not addressed before they could be claimed by the rightful recipient. The following June Nichols was authorised to handle domestic mail.

*The first mail service between towns* was established in October 1816 from Hobart to Launceston. A government messenger walked the whole 193 km, setting out from Hobart on a Sunday and leaving for the return

*The first post office was the building on the far left of the picture.*

Australia Post

103

# The first . . .

journey from Launceston the following Sunday.

The first regular postal service between towns on the mainland was established in 1826, mail being carried twice weekly by contractors to and from Sydney and Parramatta, Richmond, Windsor and Liverpool; and by government once-a-week to and from Bathurst. Two years later the mail services were extended to the rest of New South Wales.

A *Sydney-Melbourne mail service* was inaugurated by coach and packhorse by contractor John Hawdon on 2 January 1838.

*The first postman* was appointed in Sydney in March 1828. He both delivered and collected mail.

*The first postmistress* was Mary Ann Rutledge, appointed to supervise the post office at Cassilis, NSW, in 1838.

*The first scheduled mail service to and from the* UK was inaugurated on a monthly basis in 1844, the first vessel to arrive in Australia under this arrangement being the *Mary Sharp* on 11 June.

## PREFERENTIAL VOTING

in the world was introduced by Queensland under its Electoral Act of 5 July 1892. This provided that voters could, if they chose, list second and subsequent favoured candidates on their ballot papers. In elections where only one candidate was to be elected and none had a clear majority, all but the two top candidates were eliminated and the preferences of the other candidates distributed between them.

## PREMIER

was William Clark Haines, who was born in England in 1807, emigrated to Australia in 1848, and formed his first ministry as Premier and Colonial Secretary of Victoria on 28 November 1855.

For the first Labor premier, see Labor Representation.

*The first Prime Minister of Australia* was Sir Edmund Barton, born in Sydney in 1849, who held office from 1 January 1901 to 24 September 1903. He died in 1920.

*The first State Premier to be dismissed from office* was Jack Lang of New South Wales, sacked by Governor Sir Philip Game on 15 May 1932 for refusing to withdraw a confiden-

tial circular to heads of Government Departments instructing them not to pay money into the Commonwealth.

*The first Prime Minister of the Commonwealth to be dismissed from office* was Gough Whitlam, sacked by Governor Sir John Kerr on 11 November 1975 as the culmination of the so called 'Loans Affair'.

## PRESBYTERIAN CHURCH

was the Scots Kirk in Jamison Street, Sydney, of which the foundation stone was laid on 1 July 1824. It was opened in July 1826. The first incumbent was the Rev. John Dunmore Lang, who had arrived in Sydney in May 1823 as the first Presbyterian minister. He served as minister of the Scots Kirk for 52 years, winning a reputation as one of the most outspoken men in Australian public life. Among his distinctions was that of being elected a Member of Parliament while serving a term in gaol, the result of one of the many libel actions brought against him. Lang Street and Lang Park commemorate his name.

## PRICKLY PEAR

One of the worst scourges of Australian horticulture, Prickly Pear was introduced to Australia in 1839 as a decorative pot plant by an inhabitant of Scone, NSW. By 1925 some 50 million acres of arable land in Queensland were infested, of which 30 million acres were completely covered. In that year the Prickly Pear Board released 30,000 of the moth Cactoblastis cactorum, the caterpillars from which would bore into the plant, destroying it. Within 10 years the scourge had been defeated. In 1936 settlers in Boonarga in south-western Queensland erected the Cactoblastis Memorial Hall in gratitude — probably the only monument in the world in honour of an insect.

## PRINTING PRESS

was brought to Australia with the First Fleet in 1788, though there is no record of its use before 1795. In that year a printer called George Hughes began printing Government Orders, of which the earliest known example dates from 16 November of the following year. Titled *Instructions for the Constables of the Country Districts*, it is addressed to James Everitt, constable for the district of Lane Cove. In the meantime Hughes had also started printing playbills, the first recorded specimen being for a performance at the *Sydney Theatre* on 23 July 1796 (see Advertisement). During the following four years he printed some 200 Government Orders, as well as a number of other playbills, but it was left to his successor as Government Printer, George Howe, to publish the first book (q.v.) and the first newspaper (q.v.).

**The first colour printing** executed in Australia consisted of three 5-colour lithographic 'Views of Australia' printed by the artist Augustus Earle at Sydney in 1826.

## PRISON

was a building consisting of four cells which was erected next to the guard-house on the east side of Sydney Cove in July 1794. Imprisonment now became, for the first time in Australia, a judicial punishment. Formerly the penalties for crime had been confined to execution, flogging, the wearing of iron collars and hard labour on the chain gang.

## PRIVY COUNCILLOR

was William Bede Dalley, Acting Premier of NSW, who was so honoured on 28 June 1886 in recognition of his having organized the first Australian expeditionary force, the New South Wales Sudan Contingent of 1885.

## PROCESSED CHEESE

was Kraft, imported from the USA in 1926 by Vegemite pioneer Fred Walker of Melbourne. The introduction of processed cheese, which lasted much longer than natural cheese, increased consumption in Australia from 3 lbs a head to 11 lbs a head per year over the following 50 years.

## PROFESSIONAL JOURNAL

was the *Australian Medical Journal*, Sydney, first published on 1 August 1846 by the Irish lithographer and copperplate engraver William Baker. Baker's medical attainments were somewhat slender, having acted as clerk to the Inspector General of Hospitals until a broken leg forced him to relinquish this employment in 1845.

## PUBLIC BALL

was held in Sydney on 17 October 1810 as part of the Race Week celebrations. Tickets were 7s 6d and the *Sydney Gazette* recorded that it was attended not only by His Excellency the Governor and his Lady, but by 'all the Beauty and Fashion of the Colony'. The report continued: 'Over the door of the Ballroom a Transparency was placed, of the Royal Arms of the United Kingdom; the full band of the 73rd played off 'God Save the King' in exquisite style, and between the country dances filled the room with other melodious and appropriate airs. The business of the meeting could not fail of diffusing a universal glow of satisfaction — the celebration of the first liberal amusement instituted in the Colony, and in the presence of its patron and founder. The Ballroom was occupied till about two o'clock when part of the company retired, and those that chose to remain formed into a supper party.'

**The first fancy dress ball** was held by Alderman Wilshire, Mayor of Sydney, at the Victoria Theatre on 21 August 1844 and was attended by 700 revellers.

## PUBLIC CLOCK

was erected on a 150 ft stone tower at Castle Hill, Sydney, on 31 January 1798.

## PUBLIC HEALTH OFFICER

was John Dobie, Surgeon, R N, appointed Health Officer for the Port of Sydney by Governor Gipps in December 1838.

## PUBLIC HOUSING

was provided in 1900 by the New South Wales Government, which bought a number of dwellings at the Rocks, Sydney to house waterfront workers.

## PUBLIC PARK

was Hyde Park, Sydney, so designated by Governor Macquarie by an Order dated October 1810. In future the open space previously known as 'The Common', 'Exercising Ground', 'Cricket Ground' and 'Race Course' was to be reserved 'for the recreation and amusement of the Inhabitants of the Town, and as a Field of Exercise for the troops'. The Acting Surveyor was instructed to mark out boundaries of the park in order to prevent the encroachment of the Brickfields which lay adjacent to it.

## PUBLISHER

to publish books regularly was George Robertson of Melbourne, who started modestly with a sermon by Dr Macintosh Mackay in 1855 and published some 600 other works during the next 35 years, including Marcus Clark's *His Natural Life* (later retitled *For the Term of His Natural Life*) in 1874. This George Robertson should not be confused with the

# The first...

Sydney-based George Robertson who formed Angus & Robertson in 1886, though in fact the latter was employed by the former when he first came to Australia.

Prior to 1850 most publishing was undertaken by newspaper offices and consisted mainly of almanacs, tracts, pamphlets, broadsides and school books. Excluding almanacs and volumes of parliamentary papers, only 56 full length works (over 100 pages) were published, four in the 1820s, 16 in the 1830s and 36 in the 1840s. These fell into the following categories: agriculture and horticulture — 4; children's books — 1; education — 1; essays and miscellaneous non-fiction — 3; history — 1; law — 4; migration — 2; novels — 6; plays — 1; poetry — 5; politics and economics — 4; reference works — 2; religion — 5; short stories — 1; statistics — 2; text books — 6; travel and topography — 6.

## QUAKER MEETING

was held by James Backhouse and G. W. Walker at Hobart on 12 February 1832. The first Quaker meeting house was opened in Macquarie Street, Sydney on 1 November 1835.

## QUINTUPLETS

were Anabelle, Richard, Faith, Caroline and Geoffrey Braham, born at Brisbane between 5.12 and 6.27 a.m. on 31 December 1967. Geoffrey died 4 days later.

## RABBITS

were introduced with the First Fleet in 1788, and in an official return of livestock made on 9 July it was noted that their number totalled five. The first notice of large numbers of wild rabbits is contained in the *Colonial Times* of 11 May 1827, when it was reported that they were running loose on some estates in Tasmania in their thousands. The 'wild grey' rabbit had been introduced to the island earlier in the decade by Dr William Cowther.

The first rabbits to run wild on the mainland were two dozen animals imported from Britain by a man called Thomas Austin and released at Barwon Park, near Geelong, Vic, on 25 December 1859. Austin's idea was to let them propagate as game. In fact he did the single greatest disservice to agriculture in the history of Australia. The first of the really long rabbit-proof fences was built over a distance of 1,833 km between Port Hedland and Esperance Bay, WA, in 1904, but rabbits still succeeded in penetrating the wheatfields of Western Australia.

*The first artificially-induced myxomatosis epidemic* took hold during February 1951. The virus had been released in warrens at Gunbower in the Murray Valley the previous May and unusually heavy rainfall stimulated the increase in mosquitoes necessary to spread the disease effectively. Rabbits perished by the million wherever there was water, some 90% dying within a month of infection.

## RACEHORSE

was the stallion *Northumberland*, imported to New South Wales aboard HMS *Buffalo* in September 1800.

## RACE MEETING

was held at Parramatta on 30 April 1810. The first race was won by a horse called *Parramatta*, who beat the only other runner, *Belfast*. There was also a trotting race, won by *Miss Kitty*. The *Sydney's Gazette's* correspondent reported that 'on these matches betts to a considerable amount were depending'. The proceedings were enlivened by a number of extra-curricular activities, including cock fighting, wheel-barrow-racing, jumping in a sack, and a novel race between three virgins for a prize of sufficient calico to make a chemise. Given the state of the colony's morals, it was something of an achievement to be able to muster three contestants with the requisite qualification.

The first regular race meeting was instituted at Sydney with a three day event commencing on 14 October 1810 at the 'race course' (now Hyde Park). The inaugural trophy race, The Subscribers' Plate, was won that day by a horse named *Chase*.

**The earliest known race-card** was printed by George Howe for the meeting held under the auspices of the Sydney Race Club on 16 August 1813.

**The first steeplechase** was run over a five mile course between Botany and Coogee, on the outskirts of Sydney, early in 1832. It was won by *Thiefcatcher*, owned by a Mr Williams. Hurdle racing was in vogue by 1838, when there are records of events at Bathurst, NSW, and also in Victoria and Tasmania.

**The first Australian 'classic'** was the St Leger Stakes, inaugurated at the Homebush racecourse near Sydney in 1841, when the winner was Richard Rouse's *Eleanor*. The event was renamed the Australian Derby Stakes in 1865 and has since become known as the A.J.C. Derby.

**The first Melbourne Cup race** was held on 7 November 1861 and won by *Archer* in 3 mins 52 secs, J. Cutts up. Cutts rode *Archer* to victory again in 1862, lopping 5 seconds off his time for the two mile distance. No other horse won two years running until 1968-1969, when *Rain Lover* emulated *Archer's* achievement. *Archer's* owner received a hand-beaten gold watch for his prize for the 1861 victory. Curiously the trophy for the Melbourne Cup was not a cup at all until 1916.

**The first starting gate** in the world was intro-

*Originally called 'driving', the first full meeting was in Melbourne in 1860.*

duced at Ascot Racecourse, Victoria, on 18 August 1893. It was the invention of J. L. Johnstone of Melbourne.

**The first photo-finish camera** was introduced at the STC's Canterbury meeting on 16 March 1946. The first triple dead-heat after the introduction of cameras took place on 3 November 1956, when *Pandie Son*, *Ark Royal* and *Fighting Force* were all first in the Hotham Handicap.

## RADAR

was developed in Australia with the opening of the Radiophysics Laboratory in the grounds of the University of Sydney in March 1940. This followed a visit to Britain the previous year by a senior physicist of the Council for Scientific and Industrial Research to see the progress that had been made on the highly secret science of 'radio location', as it was then called, since (Sir) Robert Watson Watt had first demonstrated the principle in 1935. The first radar equipment produced in Australia was constructed at the Radiophysics Laboratory for the Department of the Army, the 1½ metre wavelength coast-watching units being installed at Australia's most strategically important ports to forewarn of the approach of enemy shipping. Air-warning radar, for the detection of approaching aircraft, was installed at Darwin following the first Japanese raids in February 1942.

# The first...

## RADIO BROADCAST

was transmitted from the offices of Amalgamated Wireless (Australasia) Ltd in Clarence Street, Sydney, to the Royal Society of New South Wales headquarters in Elizabeth Street on 13 August 1919 and consisted of a gramophone record rendering of *God Save the King*. The first live performer to broadcast was Mill L. Walker, who sang *Advance Australia Fair* from the home of Mr L.A. Hooke, Amalgamated Wireless's manager in Melbourne, in a transmission received by an invited audience of notabilities at Queen's Hall on 13 October 1920.

***The first regular broadcasts*** were weekly concerts transmitted by Amalgamated Wireless in Melbourne starting in October 1921.

***The first broadcast by a Prime Minister*** anywhere in the world was a speech by Billy Hughes transmitted from a public hall in Bendigo on 1922.

***The first broadcasting station*** to offer a public service was 2SB Sydney, which started transmission on 23 November 1923. The inaugural programme consisted of Miss Deering, soprano; Sydney Pick, bass; Miss Druitt, contralto; George Saunders, baritone; Mr Thorp, cellist; and the St Andrew Quartet. Purchasers of sets had to pay a 10s subscription and the radio was sealed so that it was impossible to tune it to any other station. All the early stations operated the same system, which had a negative effect on sales and forced the introduction of alternative commercial stations carrying advertising.

***The first play to be broadcast*** was the musical comedy *The Southern Maid* by 2FC Sydney on 5 December 1923. The performance was live from *Her Majesty's Theatre*.

***The first radio commercials*** were broadcast by 2BE Sydney, commencing on 7 November 1924.

***The first racing commentary in the world*** was broadcast by Arnold Treloar from Cheltenham Park, SA, via 5CL Adelaide on 29 November 1924.

***The first play written for radio*** was J H Booth's *The Barbarous Barber*, produced by Stanley Brooks and transmitted by 3LO Melbourne on 21 March 1925.

***The first broadcast from parliament*** in the world was made by 2FC Sydney on 24 March 1925. Regular parliamentary broadcasts from Canberra began on 4 July 1946.

***The first regular newscaster*** was John Robinson for 4QG Brisbane, starting on 27 July 1925.

***The first cricket commentary*** in the world was broadcast by L.G. Watt on 2FC Sydney at the Australia v The Rest match on 4 December 1925.

***The first overseas broadcast*** was made by short-wave to Britain and Europe from VK2ME Sydney on 5 September 1927. Two other short-wave stations also began broadcasting overseas, VK3ME Melbourne in November 1927, and VK6ME Perth in March 1937. These three maintained a regular service until the outbreak of WWII and each used a common 'signature', the call of the kookaburra, so that overseas listeners would instantly know that Australia was calling.

***The first programme for schools*** was the *Education Hour*, which began on the station of the Australian Broadcasting Co in 1929. *The School of the Air* broadcasts for outback children were inaugurated under the direction of Molly Ferguson from the Flying Doctor base at Alice Springs in 1951.

***The Australian Broadcasting Commission*** was established on 1 July 1932 to assume control of the twelve non-commercial radio stations. These stations, originally privately owned and financed from licence fees, had

ABC Library

*George Saunders, who sang in the first programme on the first broadcasting station was also the first ABC announcer.*

*A re-creation of the first state owned railway train.*

State Rail Authority

been bought out by the Federal Government in 1929, programmes being supplied by the Australian Broadcasting Co until the creation of the Commission. The number of licences at that time was 369,945.

**The first radio station to broadcast round the clock** was 2UW from 22 February 1935. It has never been off the air since.

**The first woman announcer** was Margaret Doyle for ABC Sydney on 2 December 1940.

## RADIOPHOTOGRAPHS

The first service was established between Sydney and Melbourne on 9 September 1929 to enable newspaper photographs to be sent from one State capital to another instantaneously. An Australia-Great Britain service was opened between Melbourne and London on 17 October 1934. Among the earliest users of the services was Gaumont British Newsreel, who transmitted a film of Melbourne's Centenary Air Race frame by frame for 68 hours at a cost of some £1,000 a foot or over £7,500 for the brief sequence of 160 frames. Five days after the race, the film was being shown in over 1500 British cinemas.

## RAILWAY

was an 8km line with wooden rails running across the Tasman peninsular to link the heads of Norfolk Bay and Long Bay, which was opened on 1 July 1837. Built in order to offer a surface transport alternative to the often stormy sea passage from Hobart round Cape Raoul, the railway carried passengers in open cars pushed by teams of four convicts. Speeds of up to 40mph were achieved on the downward slopes. It remained in operation until 1877.

**The first steam railway** was established by the Melbourne and Hobson's Bay Railway Company and began operating on a 2½ mile line between Flinders Street, Melbourne and Sandridge Pier (Port Melbourne) on 12 September 1854.

The *Melbourne Morning Herald* reported: 'The sun shone yesterday upon perhaps the most important single event that has yet transpired in Victoria — the opening of the first railway. The station and the engine were decorated with flags and flowers, and all things wore a gay appearance . . . The Company was conveyed to Sandridge in three trains of four carriages each. The engine be-

# The first . . .

haved very well throughout, but was subject to some difficulties from the state of the line, which was imperfectly laid. The curve between the bridge and the Melbourne station is a very awkward one, and the rails are very uneven ... The speed attained yesterday with carriages did not exceed twenty one miles an hour, but the engine travelled much faster when alone.'

This engine had been built by Robertson, Martin & Smith of Melbourne, but it broke down after a few days and the line was closed until the arrival of two locomotives imported from England. Fares were 1s 6d for first class, 1s for second class.

**The first state-owned railway** was opened between the Sydney suburbs of Redfern and Granville on 26 September 1855. The line was extended to Liverpool the following year and to Campbelltown in 1858.

**The first trains from Melbourne to Sydney** ran on 21 August 1883, following the completion of the railway bridge spanning the Murray River at Albury. Passengers had to change trains at Albury because the New South Wales and Victorian railway system used different gauges.

*Artists impression of the first railway station in Sydney.*

State Rail Authority

**The trans-continental line** linking Sydney in the east with Perth in the west was opened for service on 22 October 1917. This inlcuded the famous straight stretch of line across the Nullarbor Plain, at 478 km the longest in the world without a curve. The first trans-continental through passenger train was the *Indian Pacific*, which made its maiden Sydney-Perth haul on 1 March 1970, taking 65

hours for the 3,961 km journey. This followed the final completion of the standard gauge railway track on the east-west route, a task that was begun in 1921.

**The first electric railway** was established with the inauguration of electric locomotives on Melbourne's suburban system, beginning with the section from Newmarket to Flemington Racecourse on 6 October 1918. Most of the suburban system had been electrified by 1926, the year that Sydney began electrification.

**The first Australian-made electric locomotive,** which was built at Newport, Vic, and electrically equipped at Jolimont Workshops, went into service on 20 July 1923.

State Rail Authority

*The driver and fireman of the first train in NSW.*

**The first mainline electrification** was on the Dandenong to Warragul line in Victoria's Gippsland, which was completed on 21 July 1954.

**The first air-conditioned train** was Victorian Railway's *Spirit of Progress*, which began running between Melbourne and Albury on 23 November 1937. New South Wales did not have an air-conditioned train until 1951.

**The first train with fluorescent lighting** was the *Australian Express*, which began running between Perth and Bunbury, WA, in November 1947.

**The first mainline diesel locomotive** was the Commonwealth Railways' *Robert Gordon Menzies*, which made its first run between Port Pirie and Kalgoorlie on 12 Sept 1951.

**The first double-decker passenger carriages** were placed in service on the Sydney suburban system on 6 January 1969.

**The first high speed XPT passenger train** made its inaugural run from Sydney to Dubbo on 8 April 1982

## RAILWAY ACCIDENT

involving loss of life occurred at Haslem's

Creek, now Lidcombe, NSW, on 10 July 1858, when the train from Campbeltown was derailed as it took a curve at excessive speed. Two passengers were killed and 13 injured.

## RAINFALL, ARTIFICIAL

was induced over the Blue Mounains, NSW, by the CSIR Radiophysics Laboratory during cloud-seeding experiments on 5 February 1945.

## RAPE CRISIS CENTRE

was set up in March 1974 to provide aid and counselling to rape victims.

## RAPE IN MARRIAGE AS A CRIMINAL OFFENCE

was proclaimed by the South Australian Parliament on 30 November 1976. It was the first such measure in the English speaking world.

## RECORD PLAYER

was presented before the Royal Society of Victoria in Melbourne by Mr A. Sutherland on 13 June 1878, less than six months after Edison had shown off his latest miracle of science of the USA. This was not a very successful demonstration, since only 'some incoherent sounds were heard, resembling the squeaking of a small animal'. Two months later he tried again, and this time was able to render 'He's a Jolly Good Fellow' in 'a wonderful distinct manner'.

*The first records made in Australia* were produced under the Brunswick label by B. Davis & Co. of Sydney in 1924.

*The first jazz recording* was *Melinburg Joys* featuring Frank Coughlan and the Californians, made in 1925.

*The first 45 rpm singles* released in Australia were Bill Haley & His Comets' *Rock Around the Clock* and Darryl Stewart's *A Man Called Peter*, both issued on the same day in 1955.

*The first rock record* by an Australian band was *You Hit the Wrong Note* by Johnny O'Keefe and the Dee Jays in July 1957.

*The first all-Australian pop music chart* was the Australian Top 40, started by the radio station 2UE Sydney in March 1958.

*The first Australian pop song in the British charts* was Slim Dusty's *Pub With No Beer* in 1958. **First in the US charts** was Frank Ifield's *I Remember You* in September 1962.

*The first Australian recording to reach* **No 1 in the Australian charts** was *Oh Yeah Uh Huh*, by Col Joye and the Joy Boys on the Festival label, which stayed 20 weeks in the charts from 20 October 1959. The band instruments included a typewriter.

*The Seekers who made the first Australian record to sell over one million copies.*

# The first . . .

*The first Australian record with worldwide sales of over one million* was the Seekers' *I'll Never Find Another You* in 1965.

## REFERENDUM

was held on 3 June 1898, when the electors of NSW, Victoria and Tasmania were given the opportunity to vote for or against the Bill for the Constitution of the Commonwealth. South Australians voted the following day. All participating colonies voted in favour, but in NSW the majority was insufficient to carry the measure. Total votes cast were 219,712 of which 111,349 were affirmative. A further referendum was held on the issue the following year, with Queensland added to the participants, and on this occasion the proposals for Federation received a decisive vote in favour in all colonies taking part.

## REFORMATORY

was the *Vernon* training ship, Sydney Harbour, which admitted its first intake of juvenile malefactors on 20 May 1867. This offered the earliest alternative to imprisonment or corporal punishment for young offenders. During the first 10 years of operation, 668 boys were received on board.

**The first reformatory for girls** was established as part of the Girls' Industrial School at Newcastle, NSW, by a proclamation of 22 January 1869. The school had opened some 16 months earlier in a former military barracks. In March 1871 the inmates rioted, according to the police report 'singing obscene songs, others cursing and swearing, others cutting up their beds and bedding and throwing it out of the windows, others . . . breaking the iron bedsteads and (others) also destroyed the chamber utensils, scattering the contents on the floor . . . (others) stripped naked and danced in view of the street'.

## REFRIGERATION PLANT

in the world was built by James Harrison, a former editor of the *Melbourne Age*, at Rodey Point on the Barwon River in Victoria in 1850. The process of refrigeration developed by Harrison depended on the formation of ice by the evaporation of ether. The following year he made his first sale of refrigerating equipment to a Bendigo brewery, Messrs Glasgow and Co. Regular manufacture of

Harrison freezers was undertaken by P. N. Russell of Sydney in 1859. The same year Harrison brought back to Australia a much larger refrigerating apparatus which had been built in England to his specification and installed this at a plant in Franklin Street, Melbourne. Here he produced up to 10 tons of ice a day, but the venture did not prove successful and two years later he was declared bankrupt. In 1873 Harrison developed the first successful technique for freezing meat, an innovation that was to open up a vast new export trade for Australia. At the same time E. D. Nicolle was working on the problem of the refrigeration of meat, which had failed in the past because the carcasses had never been exposed to a low enough temperature. Harrison and Nicolle's work was commercially exploited by the engineer and shipbuilder T. S. Mort, who built extensive meat freezing plants at Darling Harbour and in the Lithgow Valley in the Blue Mountains. On 2 September 1875, Mort took a large party of guests on an inspection of the Darling Harbour works, followed by a train trip to the Lithgow Valley. There the guests sat down to a banquet entirely composed of frozen food, including fish, game, meat, and vegetables. It was the first such meal served anywhere in the world.

## REFRIGERATOR

for domestic use was a kerosene model manufactured by Edward Hallstrom at Sydney in 1923.

**The first electric refrigerator** on sale in Australia was the Kelvinator, imported from the USA in 1926.

The first electric refrigerator of all-Australian manufacture was the Electrice, produced by the Emmco Pty Ltd in 1927

## REINFORCED CONCRETE

was the first used in the construction of the Monier Pipe aqueduct at Annandale, NSW, in 1896. It was first used in a building for the floor of the Central Railway Terminal, Sydney, opened on 4 August 1906.

## RESTAURANT

was Mann's Room, Sydney, opened on 6 June 1803. Dinners would also be provided in patron's own homes 'on the shortest notice'. David Dickinson Mann was an ex-convict who had been transported for forgery in 1798 when he was 22. At the time of the restaurant venture he was also a clerk in the government service. Later that same month Rosetta Stabler opened a rival concern at the Rocks, with 'victuals dressed in the English way'. Boiled mutton and broths were served every day at noon and a roast joint at one o'clock. The price of a cut off the latter was 1s 6d. Mann's sometimes offered more exotic fare, a 'Fine real Green Turtle' being the speciality of the day on 20 July 1803.

## RETURNED SERVICEMEN'S ORGANIZATION

was the 'New South Soudan Contingent Association of 1885', founded by veterans of Australia's first expeditionary force soon after their return home. It was still in existence in 1945, a few survivors of the original 600 troops being still alive. The last member was George Rauchle, who died in 1963 aged 96. Ex-service organizations began to become a powerful community force following the founding of the RSL in 1916.

## RICE

was planted in 1922 on a 2.8 ha plot near Leeton in the Murrumbidgee Irrigation Area of New South Wales. Commercial production began two years later and by 1928 Australia was already self-sufficient in rice.

## RIFLE-SHOOTING

as an organized sport began with the founding of the Sydney Rifle Club in 1842. The first interstate match was held at Melbourne on 3 November 1862, when NSW defeated Victoria by 1495 points to 1431.

## ROAD

was built from the present intersection of Bridge and Phillip Streets, Sydney, to a rock crushing battery at Dawes Point and completed in September 1788. The distance was about a mile.
*The first inter-city highway* was built from Sydney to Parramatta, a distance of 14½ miles, and opened in 1794. Later that year it was extended to the Hawkesbury River and became the main artery of early New South Wales. The Lieutenant Governor recorded: 'An officer who is by no means considered as being particularly active undertook for a trifling wager to walk there from Sydney in nine hours, and with great ease to himself performed a journey in eight hours and two minutes which formerly required an exertion of some days to accomplish'.

On 10 April 1811 the Parramatta road became the *first toll road* in Australia, with tollgates sited where the Central Railway Station in Sydney now stands and at Boundary Street, Parramatta. Charges ranged from 3d for a horse up to 3s for a coach and four.

See Freeway

## ROAD SIGNS, METRIC

were introduced in Victoria on 1 July 1974.

## RODEO

was held at Wodonga, Vic, on 11 May 1891. Events included buckjumping and bullock riding.

## ROMAN CATHOLIC CHURCH

see Cathedral.

## ROMAN CATHOLIC MASS

was conducted for the benefit of the Roman Catholic inhabitants of New South Wales by a proclamation of the Governor on 19 April 1803 which authorised the emancipated convict Fr James Dixon to hold services at Sydney. Among the conditions imposed was a requirement that the police should be in attendance to preserve 'strict decorum'. The inaugural public mass was celebrated at Sydney on Sunday 15 May 1803.
*The first Roman Catholic wedding* was solemnized by Fr Dixon on 7 May 1803, when Henry Simpson, shipwright, was married to Catherine Rourke, of the Rocks, widow.

## ROMAN CATHOLIC PRIEST ORDAINED IN AUSTRALIA

was Fr Charles Summer at St Mary's Cathedral, Sydney, by Dr Polding on 9 May 1836.
The first aboriginal R.C. priest was Fr Patrick Dobson, ordained in May 1975.

## ROTARY CLUB

was founded at Melbourne on 21 April 1921. The movement had begun in the USA in 1905, being so named because originally the members met at each others homes or offices in rotation.

## ROTARY CLOTHES HOIST

in the world was invented by blacksmith Gilbert Toyne of East Malvern, Vic, and

# The first . . .

patented on 7 April 1924. Instead of a prop, a winding mechanism consisting of a crown wheel and pinion lifted the clothes to catch the best breezes. Manufacture began at Carnegie, Vic, the same year with two models, a medium size 16ft in diameter at £5 17s 6d and a large size 20ft in diameter at £6 12s 6d.

## ROTARY HOE

in the world was built in a blacksmith's shop at Gilgandra, NSW, by Cliff Howard and his brother Albert in 1920. Manufacture began two years later when Howard established Australian Auto Cultivators Ltd at Moss Vale, NSW, producing a 15ft wide machine capable of ploughing 3½ acres an hour. Powered by a 60 hp 'Buda' petrol engine, the first commercially-built model was sold for £1,200. The first hand-operated machine, the 6 hp 'Junior', was produced in 1924.

## ROTARY LAWN MOWER

was the Victa, first manufactured by Mervyn Victor Richardson in a shed at Concord, NSW, in November 1952. By 1958 some 3,000 mowers a week were being produced at the Victa factory at Silverwater, with one coming off the production line every 48 seconds.

## ROWING CLUB

was Melbourne University Boat Club, founded by Prof. M. H. Irving on 3 September 1859.

*The first women's club* was the Albert Park Ladies' Rowing Club, Melbourne, formed by Mrs Cassie McRitchie in 1907.

## ROWING RACE

took place on 19 August 1811 between Capt. Bodie's whale boat and 'a capital gig' for a stake of 50 gns. The course was from Sydney Cove, 'round the Sow and Pigs, and back again'.

*The first interstate contest* was held between four-oared gigs representing NSW and Victoria on the Parramatta River near Sydney on 4 February 1863. The three-mile race was won by the home crew in a time of 19 mins 25 secs.

*The first sculling championship* took place at Melbourne on the Yarra River on 11 March 1868, Arthur Nicholls of Victoria defeating H.

Freeman of Sydney by six lengths.

*The first race between eights* took place on the Yarra on 20 December 1870, when Melbourne University defeated Sydney University.

## ROYAL FAMILY, MEMBER OF, TO VISIT AUSTRALIA

was 23-year-old Alfred, Duke of Edinburgh, who arrived at Adelaide on 30 October 1867 aboard HMS *Galatea*. He visited all the Australian colonies except Western Australia during his six-month sojourn. The tour was generally reckoned to have been a considerable success except for the assassination attempt at Clontarf, Sydney on 12 March 1868, when a Fenian called O'Farrell shot him in the back at point blank range. No serious injury was caused the young Duke, but O'Farrell was executed for the crime.

*The first reigning monarch to visit Australia* was Queen Elizabeth II, who arrived at Sydney on 3 February 1954 and visited all the States during her two-month tour.

## RUGBY LEAGUE

was introduced to Australia in 1907 as a breakaway movement from Rugby Union. In England the same had happened in 1895, when the League was formed by northern Rugby Clubs whose predominantly working class players needed to be able to accept payment for playing, barred under Rugby Union rules. In New South Wales players of Rugby Union were allowed a maximum of 3s a day while on tour. The breakaway movement began after Sydney Club forward Alec Burden broke an arm and lost wages for time off work as well as having to pay his own medical expenses. A group of players who used to meet at cricketer Victor Trumper's sports store in Sydney decided to form their own League on the English pattern, with payment of 10s a day plus 7s 6d for out-of-pocket expenses. The first League club was Newtown, founded on 8 January 1908.

## RUGBY UNION

was established on a regular basis with the founding of the first club at the University of Sydney in 1864. As there were no other teams, members played each other or against teams from visiting RN vessels.

*The first occasion that Rugby players wore numbers* anywhere in the world was at a match played between Queensland and New Zealand in Brisbane in 1897.

# S

## SAFETY MATCHES

were manufactured by Bryant and May, Bell & Co. Pty Ltd at the Empire Match Works, Richmond, Vic, on 15 December 1909. They were retailed at 3½d a box. At this time consumption of matches in Australia averaged 15 per day per head of population.

## SAILOR, AUSTRALIAN-BORN

was Robert Johnston (1792-1882), who was born at Sydney the son of Major George Johnston (the first soldier to land at Port Jackson in January 1788), and joined the Royal Navy as a midshipman aboard HMS *Malabar* in February 1807 when he was 14. He served in the War of 1812 against the USA and returned to NSW on half-pay in 1816. The remainder of his long life he spent in his native land, dying at Sydney in 1882 at the age of 90. Philip Parker King (1791-1856), was born at Norfolk Island the son of Governor King, joined the Royal Navy in 1807 shortly after Johnston and became the first Australian to attain flag rank when he was promoted Rear-Admiral in 1855. His son Philip Gidley King (1817-1904), born at Parramatta, was the first second-generation Australian to join the Navy when he became a midshipman aboard the *Beagle* in 1831.

## ST JOHN AMBULANCE ASSOCIATION

The first Australian centre was founded in Melbourne in June-July 1883. The first branch to be reconstituted as a Division of the Brig-ade was the Glebe branch (Sydney) registered on 20 March 1903.

## SALES TAX

was introduced by the Commonwealth Government in 1930 to offset decline in revenue caused by the Depression.

## SALT

was produced at Point Maskeleyne (Dawes' Battery), Sydney, in May 1790. Capt. David Collins, Royal Marines, recorded: 'The colony had hitherto been supplied with salt from the public stores, a quantity always being shaken off from the salt provisions, and reserved for use by the store-keepers; but the daily consumption of salt provisions was now so inconsiderable, and they had been so long in store, that little or none of that article was to be procured. Two large iron boilers were therefore erected at the east point of the cove; some people were employed to boil the salt water, and the salt which was produced by this very simple process was issued to the convicts...'

*The first commercial saltworks* was established by John Blaxland in 1807 on a 40-acre enclosed site at the junction of the Duck and Parramatta rivers on his estate at Newington, NSW. A superintendent and a group of skilled workmen were brought out from the Leamington Salt Works in England and very soon Blaxland's salt pans had made New South Wales self-sufficient in salt. They continued to function for some 80 years.

## SALVATION ARMY

meeting was held in the open air by Edward Saunders and John Gore at the Botanic Gardens in Adelaide on 5 September 1880. The two men had both worked under the Army's founder, General Booth, in England and had met by chance in Adelaide the pre-

*St John Ambulance Brigade, Sydney Branch, 1903.*

# The first . . .

vious April. The earliest Corps was founded with the arrival in February 1881 of the first Salvation Army officers, Captain Sutherland and his wife, who had come out to Adelaide at the suggestion of Saunders and Gore.

The 'Salvos' had been founded in London's East End 15 years earlier, but their work was originally confined to evangelising. It was in Australia that the work for which the Sally Army is most celebrated, in the field of social welfare, had its beginnings in 1884 when Major James Barker of Melbourne was appointed its first full-time social worker anywhere in the world.

## SATELLITE, SPACE

was WRE SAT 1, launched from Woomera, SA, aboard a US Redstone rocket on 19 November 1967. It was used to record ultraviolet and x-ray radiation from the sun and to measure high altitude molecular oxygen densities.

## SATELLITE TRACKING STATION

was set up by the Weapons Research Establishment of the Department of Supply at Woomera, SA, in 1957 as Australia's contribution to International Geophysical Year.

## SAVINGS BANK

was Campbell's Bank, founded by pioneer merchant Robert Campbell at Sydney on 17 June 1819. Depositors, the majority of whom were convicts, received 7½% pa interest. The bank merged with the Savings Bank of New South Wales when the latter was established in 1832.

*The first Post Office Savings Bank* was founded at Perth, WA, on 1 July 1863, less than two years after the world's first Post Office Savings Bank had been established in Britain.

*The Savings Department of the Commonwealth Bank* was established in Victoria on 15 July 1912. Its activities were extended to the other States over the following six months.

## SCHOOL

was established by Isabella Rosson, a convict who had been transported for stealing clothes, who began teaching a class of convicts' children at Sydney in 1789. On 5 Sep-

tember that year she married William Richardson of the Royal Marines and the pair of them worked as teachers from the beginning of 1790. The Rev. Richard Johnson recorded in 1792, of the Richardsons and also a schoolmistress of the name of Mary Johnson at Parramatta, that 'they teach the children belonging to the Convicts gratis — the military, officers etc making them some little acknowledgement for their trouble . . .' Schoolbooks had been sent from England 'through the favour of the Society in Bartletts Buildings'. From 1793 onwards the classes in Sydney were conducted in the church and, after it had been burned down in 1798, in a public store-house.

*The first purpose-built school* was erected by order of Governor King at the Green Hills, Hawkesbury (near Windsor), and leased by the Crown to the settlers for a period of 14 years from 1 October 1804. An annual levy of 2d per acre were made on the Hawkesbury settlers for the rent and maintenance of the property, which included a chapel as well as the schoolhouse. The latter was a brick building, 100 ft long, 24 ft wide and 24 ft high, one end of the upper story being made into an apartment for the schoolmaster.

*The first boarding school* was opened by William Pascoe Crook, master of the Public School at Parramatta, who announced on 19 August 1804 that he had lately taken a house in which to accommodate boarders. The curriculum, he said, would be 'adapted to the situation for which the Pupil may be designed', and included written and spoken English, book-keeping, geometry, trigonometry, mensuration, navigation, surveying and gauging as optional subjects, together with history and geography and astronomy as core subjects. Unusually for a schoolmaster of those days, Mr Crook promised to make 'every part of Education as pleasing as possible'. The fees were £27 per annum, or £30 worth of wheat or pork.

William Crook had been a tinworker in his native Devon, later becoming a missionary. He opened the first boarding school for girls at the corner of Hunter and Bligh Street, Sydney, in 1808. In 1810 he and three others established the first congregational church (q.v.) in Australia.

*State education* in Australia had its beginning with the appointment of John Eyre as Schoolmaster in charge of the Parramatta Public School by an Order of Governor Macquarie dated 22 March 1810. Formerly the school had depended on voluntary support, but Eyre was paid from government funds. On 14 April John Davies was similarly appointed schoolmaster of the newly-established Public School at Sydney.

The first legislative provision for education was under the New South Wales Church Act of 1836, under which Government undertook to subsidise church schools by £1 for every £1 raised by the community. The first Regulations for Schools allowed schools established after 1836 the sum of 1d per day per child, or 1¼d in districts of under 2,000 population. There was a limit of £35 per school in any quarter.

Provisions for state education in the supply estimates was first made in 1839, when £3,000 was voted by the New South Wales Legislature for the establishment of a new public school in Sydney and two others outside the capital. In addition £1,000 was allocated for the support of Roman Catholic schools. In 1844 it was reported that there were 7,642 children under instruction in public schools, 4,865 in private schools, and some 13,000 not attending any school.

The first widespread network of state schools was established by the New South Wales National Board, established in 1848. Two-thirds of the cost of each national school, plus the teacher's salary of £40 - £80, was paid by the National Board and one-third by the local community.

**The first state secondary schools** were six high schools established by the New South Wales Department of Public Instruction in 1883 — two at Sydney, two at Bathurst and two at Goulburn.

**The first school for Aborigines** was the Native Institution, Parramatta, founded 18 January 1815 with 12 pupils of both sexes under the tutelage of missionary William Shelley, who had a high fence built round the grounds to prevent the children absconding. A humane man, he ordered the workmen to leave out some of the palings so that the children's parents could look in and see them. The children used the narrow exits to make good their escape.

When 20 pupils of the school competed in the Anniversary School Examination at Parramatta, a 14-year-old Aboriginal girl won the main award in competition with 100 white children. Despite some rare academic successes like this one, their education did little to condition the black children to European society and most of them 'went bush' on graduating.

The school moved in 1823 to Blacktown,

which owes its name to the camp, known to the locals as 'Blacks' Town', set up nearby for the pupils' parents.

**The first Roman Catholic school** was opened by Thomas Byrne in 1822 in a portion of the New Court House, Castlereagh St, Sydney. The first Roman Catholic secondary school was established by Bishop Polding at his residence in Sydney in 1835.

**The first infant school** was founded by the Rev. Richard Hill at Sydney on 16 December 1824.

**The first grammar school,** also the first secondary school to be conducted by trustees rather than by a private proprietor, was the Free Grammar School, Sydney, opened under the headmastership of ex-convict Dr Laurence Halloran in Phillip Street on 19 November 1825. Fees were 4 gns for 'free' boys; others paid whatever fee was determined by the headmaster. The enterprise lasted less than a year, being killed off by drought, depression and the cupidity of the trustees. The grammar school movement was successfully revived in 1832 with the founding of the Australian College and the King's School, Parramatta. The latter is now the oldest secondary school in Australia.

**The first Convent school** was opened at Perth by the Sisters of Mercy on 26 January 1846.

**The first school for the blind** was the Asylum-School for the Blind, established in Melbourne in 1860.

**The first school for the deaf** was opened in 1860 with seven pupils at premises in Castlereagh Street, Sydney.

**The first co-educational secondary school** was the Friends School, opened at Hobart on 31 January 1887. It was one of the first schools in Australia to include science in the curriculum, and almost certainly the first to offer this subject to girls.

**The first kindergarten** was established as a department of Redlands, Sydney, in 1888.

**The first 'progressive school'** was Frensham, founded under Winnifred West at Mittagong, NSW, in 1913.

## SCHOOL EXAMINATIONS (EXTERNAL)

were conducted under the aegis of Sydney University in November 1869 and were open to pupils of any public or private school and also to those educated by private tuition. They were based on the Oxford Local and Cambridge Local, which had been instituted in England for the pupils of middle-class schools a few years earlier.

# *The first* . . .

## SCHOOL MAGAZINE

was *The Collegian*, a handwritten weekly paper issued at the Australian College, Sydney, from 1 September 1834. There were twelve numbers, following which the editor, the Rev. Henry Carmichael, set up his own school and continued the magazine as *The Ex-Collegian*.

## SCHOOLTEACHER, AUSTRALIAN BORN

was Charity Evans, born at Sydney on 19 May 1801. She was a teacher at the Female Orphan School, of which she had been an inmate, from about 1813 until her marriage to another schoolteacher in 1823.

*The first Australian-born schoolmaster* was William Edney, born at Parramatta on 17 March 1803, who began teaching at Isaac Wood's Sydney Academy in January 1820. He had trained in the Madras system of teaching at Colombo.

## SCIENTIFIC JOURNAL

was the *Tasmanian Journal of Natural Science*, edited by Ronald C. Gunn and published in Hobart from 1842 until 1849.

## SCIENTOLOGY

was introduced into Australia in 1956 from the USA, where the cult had been established by Ron Hubbard five years earlier.

## SCOUT TROOPS

were formed in Australia as elsewhere soon after the publication of *Scouting for Boys* in England by Maj.-Gen. Robert Baden-Powell in February 1908. The first patrol to be registered was the 1st Mosman Kangaroos. By the end of the year there were already 155 registered patrols in New South Wales.

## SCULPTURE

was executed by the convict artist Daniel Herbert, who carved two heads on either side of the entrance to St Luke's Presbyterian Church at Bothwell, Tas in 1831.

*The first freestanding sculpture* was a bust carved by Benjamin Law of Aboriginal cheif Woureddy in 1836. The first full-length sculpted figure was executed in 1844 by Charles Abrahams, who used Sydney wheelwright Robert Hancock as a model.

*The first large-scale bronze to be cast in Australia* was Charles Summers' *Burke and Wills Memorial*, unveiled in Melbourne on 21 April 1865.

See also Statue.

## SEAPLANE

to be flown in Australia was a Maurice Farman Hydro-aeroplane piloted by Maurice Guillaux at Double Bay, Sydney, on 8 May 1914.

## SEAT BELTS

for motorists were first made compulsory in Victoria on 22 December 1970. The rest of Australia followed suit in 1972.

## SEISMOGRAPH

for the detection of earthquakes was a Milne seismograph installed at Adelaide Observatory in 1908.

## SERVICE PENSIONS

were introduced on 1 January 1936 for ex-servicemen reaching the age of 60, or becoming permanently unemployable, or suffering from pulmonary tuberculosis. Those incapacitated by war service were already eligible for war pensions.

## SEVENTH-DAY ADVENTISTS

arrived in Melbourne from the USA in June 1885 and held their first service in a tent on the corner of Brunswick and Streets, North Fitzroy on 10 January 1886. There were originally 28 members. The first Adventist church was erected in Alfred Crescent, North Fitzroy and opened on 13 September 1896.

## SEX CHANGE CLINIC

was established at Sydney's Prince Henry Hospital during 1971.

## SEX PROBLEM CLINIC

was opened in Perth in December 1981.

## SEX SHOP

was opened in Sydney's Darlinghurst Road during October 1971.

## SHARK ATTACK, FATAL

in Australian waters resulting in the death of a non-aborigine took place at Faure Island, Hamelin Harbour, WA in 1803. The victim was a M. Lefevre, a member of the French expedition led by Nicholas Baudin to explore the South Seas. There were only 12 shark fatalities in the 19th century, but no less than 66 in the first 50 years of the present century — an increase occasioned not only by greater population, but also the propensity for bathing. The worst year for fatal shark attacks was 1929 with eight. Meshing nets began to be used at night time off Sydney beaches in 1937 and this considerably reduced the number of sharks in the area, those getting entangled in the nets being destroyed the next morning.

## SHEARING MACHINE

to be successfully manufactured anywhere in the world was developed by Frederick York Wolseley over a twelve-year period starting in 1873. The breakthrough came when Wolseley purchased the patent of another English-born inventor, John Howard, and combined the best features of both designs. In 1885 the two men gave the first public demonstration of mechanical shearing in Goldsborough and Co's wool store in Melbourne, the Wolseley-Howard machine being pitted against a hand shearer. When the hand shearer finished before the machine, it looked as if once again power shearing was nothing but a dream — until the mechanical shears were run over the three shorn sheep and yielded another 2½ lbs of wool. Manufacture began soon afterwards, Wolseley engaging the firm of R. P. Park to construct the machines and in 1887 he established the Wolseley Sheep Shearing Co at 19 Phillip Street, Sydney. Among those employed by the firm was a young Englishman called Herbert Austin, who later designed and built the first Wolseley car and went on to produce Britain's first mass-produced car, the Austin 7 of 1922. But for the invention of mechanical sheep-shearing in Australia, motoring for the millions in Britain would doubtless have been much longer delayed.

*The first complete shearing by machine* anywhere in the world took place at Dunlop Station, Louth, NSW, in 1888.

## SHEEPDOG TRIALS

in the world were held at Forbes, NSW, in 1871. The winner, a bitch called Kelpie, was one of the founders of Australia's kelpie breed. The first such event outside Australia was at Bala, Wales, in 1873.

## SHIP

wholly built in Australia was the 26-ton armed Colonial Schooner *Cumberland*, built at Sydney in 1801 and put to use early the following year carrying grain from the Hawkesbury and later in 1802 for exploration in Bass Strait.

*The first steamship in Australian waters* was the *Sophia Jane*, brought out from England aboard another vessel, to make her maiden trip at Port Jackson on 17 June 1831. The first built in Australia was a river steamer called the *Surprise*, laid down by Messrs Smith Bros at Neutral Bay, which made her maiden voyage on 23 July 1831. The first sea-going steamer, the *Clonmel*, left Sydney on her maiden voyage to Port Phillip with over 50 passengers aboard on 1 December 1840.

*The first screw-driven steamship in Australian waters* was the *City of Melbourne*, built by Melbourne pioneer George Ward Cole and launched on the Yarra in 1851.

*The first steamship to make the voyage from Britain to Australia* was the P & O liner *Chusan*, which arrived at Port Jackson on 3 August 1852.

*The first iron steamship built in Australia* was the *Ballarat*, assembled by the Australasian Steam Navigation Co. from plates manufactured in Britain and launched at Pyrmont, Sydney, in February 1853.

*The first warship built in Australia* was the armed sloop *Eliza*, which was launched at Port Arthur, Tas, and began patrolling the Derwent River on 17 July 1843 to prevent convicts escaping and to suppress smuggling. The first built for Australian defence was HM Colonial Ketch *Spitfire*, a 65 ton vessel with a single 32-pounder long gun which was launched at Cuthbert's Yard, Port Jackson, on 4 April 1855.

*The first cruiser built in Australia* was HMAS *Brisbane*, launched at Cockatoo Island, Sydney, on 30 September 1916.

*The first minesweeper or corvette built in Australia* was HMAS *Bathurst*, launched at Cockatoo Island, Sydney, on 1 August 1940.

*The world's first purpose-built fully cellular container ship* was the *Kooringa*, which was put into service by Associated Steamships in 1964.

## SHIP'S RADIO

was installed aboard the Queensland gunboat HMQS *Gayundah*, which transmitted its

# The first . . .

inaugural message in Morse on 9 April 1903 to a receiving station at Brisbane: 'Gun drill continued this afternoon and was fairly successful — blowing squally and raining — prize firing tomorrow. Marconi insulators were interfered with by rain but easily rectified and communication since has been good. Good Night.' The aerial was attached to a long bamboo pole lashed to the mast.

*The first merchant vessels equipped with radio* were the *Riverina, Ultimaroa,* and *Zeelandia* in 1905.

## SHOP

was opened in a hut at Sydney Cove shortly after the arrival of the convict transport *Pitt* from England on 14 February 1792, the merchandise consisting of a miscellany of articles brought out on the vessel. Capt. David Collins of the Royal Marines reported that not withstanding 'the high price at which every thing was sold, the avidity with which all descriptions of people grasped at what was to be purchased was extraordinary...' Further shops were opened in both Sydney and Parramatta with the arrival of the *Royal Admiral* in October of the same year.

*The first shop with plate glass windows* was William Moffit's, stationers and bookbinders, Pitt Street, Sydney in 1833. It was reported that people flocked to Pitt Street to see the new window.

*The first department store* is difficult to define, since a number of major Sydney and Melbourne drapers and milliners evolved into big emporiums selling general merchandise during the last quarter of the 19th century. Perhaps the best claim is that of Farmer & Co., Silk Mercers, Linen Drapers and Haberdashers, whose premises at Victoria House in Pitt Street, Sydney, were rebuilt to accommodate separate departments in 1874. Certainly Australia was in the forefront of this development, since the modern department store was also beginning to emerge in London, Paris and New York during the 1870s.

## SHORTHAND

was introduced to Australia by Jacob Pitman, who arrived in Adelaide early in 1838 bearing one hundred copies of his brother Isaac Pitman's recently published work *.italicStenographic Short-hand.* Thus began the worldwide dissemination of the most internationally recognised shorthand system.

## SHOT IN WORLD WAR I

fired by the forces of the British Empire was an artillery shell directed from Fort Nepean at the German vessel *Pfalz* as she sought to escape from Port Phillip, Vic, on the day war was declared by Britain and Australia, 4 August 1914.

## SHOT IN WORLD WAR II

fired by the forces of the British Commonwealth of Nations was an artillery shell directed from Fort Nepean at an unidentified vessel approaching Port Phillip Heads on the day war was declared by Britain and Australia, 3 September 1939.

## SICK LEAVE, PAID

was introduced by New South Wales under an amendment to the Industrial Arbitration Act made on 1 July 1951. One week's sick leave was allowed for each year of service.

## SILVER MINE

was established at Moruya, NSW, in 1864.

## SILVERWARE

The earliest known items of Australian silverware are a pair of teaspoons made by Walter Harley and dated with the Glasgow mark for 1820. A kangaroo substitutes for the Glasgow town mark and clearly identifies the Australian provenance of the spoons. They belonged to Thomas Darcy, Lieutenant Governor of Van Diemen's Land from 1813 until 1820, and bear his crest and initials. Harley was a silversmith from Wexford, Ireland, who had arrived in Sydney as a convict in 1815. He worked for a Mr Austin, jeweller, until 1818, then for Jacob Josephson, jeweller of Pitt Street, before setting up on his own in Castlereagh Street as a manufacturing silversmith in 1820.

## SKATEBOARDS

were introduced to Australia from California by Sydney surfer Midget Farrelly in 1964. The first skateboard track was opened at Albany, WA, in 1976.

## SKIING

originated at the Kiandra goldfields of NSW, the earliest reference appearing in the

*Monaco Mercury* of 29 July 1861: 'Scores of young people are frequently engaged climbing the lofty summits with snow shoes and then sliding down with a volancy that would do credit to some of our railway trains.' It should be noted that during the 19th century skis were generally called snow shoes. In August 1861 the *Sydney Morning Herald* carried a report copied from the *Braidwood Observer* which described them as 'two palings turned up at the front and about four feet long, with straps to put the feet in, and the traveller carries a long stick to balance himself...'

**The first ski races** on record were held at Mt Hotham, Vic, in 1863. Competitors, who used skis made of mountain ash, included Chinese goldminers. This was three years earlier than the first ski races in Europe, held at Iverslokken, Norway in 1866.

**The first ski club** was the Kiandra Snow Shoe Club, believed to have been established in or about 1878.

## SKYSCRAPER

was Melbourne's 20-storey high glass-walled ICI building, designed by Bates, Smart and McCutchem and built in 1958. Sydney responded with the 29-storey, 380ft high AMP building in 1961.

*The ICI building in Melbourne was the first skyscraper.*

## SLICED BREAD

was introduced in 1939 by Harry Gough at his Sunshine Bakeries, Newtown, Sydney. By 1960 about one-third of all the bread sold in Australia was sliced.

## SNOOKER

is claimed to have been introduced in the billiards room at the *Hotel Australia*, Sydney, by Frank Smith in 1887. Smith also claimed to have invented the game, which is palpably untrue, as it originated at Jubbulpore, India, some twelve years earlier.

## SNOWFALL

ever recorded in Australia fell between the hours of 8 and 9 in the morning for about half an hour on 28 June 1836. The *Colonist* reported: 'The fall was by no means considerable in Sydney, although we are told it was several inches deep in Parramatta. It lay for an hour or two on the tops of houses, and in some other situations, and the Sydney boys were seen for the first time in their lives making snow-balls. The day was very cold, throughout.

## SOCIETY

established in Australia was the Anacreontic or Singing Society, founded at Sydney in 1793. Ensign McKellar described its activities in a letter to a fellow officer on Norfolk Island: 'All the unmarried people (with Messrs Hunt Kent and Bell Agts and Surgeons in the Navy) and Capt Foreaux, Clephan and myself are members, Nosy is not, because he would not be admitted. It is carried on thus, every Saturday night they meet alternately at each others houses, and the amusement is singing and drinking grog — every man sings his song, whether he can or no — It is not much thought of by the sober thinking set...'

In September of the same year was founded the Settler's and Land Owners' Society. There were 90 original members, the subscription being 3 bushels of wheat each.

**The first learned society** was the Royal Society of New South Wales, which was founded on 27 June 1821 as the Philosophical Society of Australasia.

**The first agricultural society** was founded in Tasmania in January 1822. It had as its objects not only the protection of flocks and herds and the general encouragement of production from the soil, but also the less earthy intent of inculcating 'improved moral habits among the population'. The first agricultural

# The first ...

society on the mainland was founded the same year, at Parramatta on 5 July 1822.

**The first literary society** was established at Perth, WA, in January 1830. Membership was 2 gns per annum and, unusually for the day, open to both sexes.

**The first society in Australia to be designated 'Royal'**, and the first outside Britain to be accorded this honour, was the Royal Society of Van Diemen's Land for Horticulture, Botany and the Advancement of Science, granted the prefix in 1844.

**The first art society** was the Society for the Promotion of the Fine Arts, established in Sydney under the Presidency of Sir Charles Nicholson Bart in 1847.

**The first gastronomic society** was the Wine and Food Society of Victoria, founded at Melbourne on 5 August 1936. It was the sixth such society in the world.

## SOFTBALL

was introduced in Victoria in 1942 by Sgt W. B. Duvernet of the US Special Services as an off-duty pastime for soldiers and nurses.

## SOLDIER, AUSTRALIAN-BORN

was Thomas Stubbs (1802-78), who was born in New South Wales and went to England in 1812 to join the 24th Regiment as a boy soldier when he was only 10. He served in India for 11 years and returned to Sydney on leaving the army in 1825. He became an innkeeper, an auctioneer, a promoter of concerts and a song-writer, as well as being appointed as honorary secretary of the Philharmonic Society in 1837. Herman Melville, who visited Sydney in 1842, found Stubbs such an engaging personality that characters in two of his novels were modelled on him.

## SOLDIER TO BE KILLED ON ACTIVE SERVICE

was Lieutenant J. S. Perceval of Melbourne, one of 2,500 Australian volunteers to serve in the New Zealand militia during the Maori War of 1863-64, who fell at the battle of Titi Hill, Mauku on 23 October 1863. He had arrived in New Zealand only three weeks earlier and was drafted into the 1st Waikato Regiment. James Cowan recorded in his *New Zealand Wars*: 'In the centre, facing the Maori's front, the gallant Perceval recklessly exposed himself, and it was with difficulty that the Mellsop brothers, three young settlers, prevented him from charging the enemy. Twice they saved his life by pulling him under cover. At last, after shooting several of his opponents, he was shot himself, and fell dead in front of his men.'

## SONG

known to have been composed in Australia was in celebration of Sydney's first race week and was first sung by Francis Williams, a merchant and race steward, at a public dinner held at Mr E. Willis' house in George Street on 19 October 1810. The untitled song was sung to the tune of *To Anachreon in Heav'n* and began;

> 'Oft the Bards of old Times, and the minstrel's gay strains
>
> Have the sports of the Chase, all transcendant reveal'd;
>
> Sung of Nimrod's exploits on the wide spreading plains
>
> And from Dian's bright charms trac'd the charms of the field'.

The author is not recorded.

The first songwriter known by name was G F Moore whose *Western Australia for Me*, was sung by him in its maiden rendition to the tune of *Ballinamona Oro* at the Governor's Ball in Perth on 3 September 1831.

## SONG BOOK

was *The Australian Song Book*, published by R.P. Cregin of Hunter Street, Sydney, at 1s 6d in May 1846.

## SPEAKING CLOCK

telephone service was introduced in Sydney on 13 November 1954. The voice was that of Gordon Gow.

## SPEED LIMIT

for motorists was introduced under South Australia's Motor Traffic Act of 1904. On country roads the limit was 15 mph, but in most of Adelaide only 12 mph and in the two principal shopping streets it was restricted to 4 mph between 7 and 10 p.m. on Saturday nights.

## SPORTING TROPHY

to be competed for annually was the Hyde

Park Race Trophy, a silver cup of Irish origin presented to Mr Emmett, whose horse *Roy Roy* won the first open horse race in Australia. The cup is inscribed:

'Pledge from the cup this first Australian prize,

May each revolving year the races bring,

That training horses from these sport may rise,

Health to the patron and long live the King.

Sydney, May 31st, 1819, given by the inhabitants to the proprietor of the winning horse.'

## SPORTSMAN TO WIN A WORLD CHAMPIONSHIP

was Edward Trickett of Parramatta, who became world sculling champion when he defeated the English oarsman Sadler over a course from Putney to Mortlake on 27 June 1876.

## SQUASH COURT

was opened at the Melbourne Club in July 1913.

## STAGE COACH

service was reported in the *Sydney Gazette* for 10 March 1821: 'Thursday last was the day of the half yearly Fair at Parramatta. The stage coach started for the first time with two Rev.

gentlemen and two bank directors as inside passengers and the Naval Officer (Captain John Piper) and three officers of the 48th Regiment as outside passengers and the bugles in the basket sounding the whole way.'

According to Peter Cunningham in *Two Years in New South Wales* (1827), coaches to Parramatta left Sydney at 8 in the morning and 4 in the afternoon and the fare inside was 6s. The stage, drawn by four horses, carried six passengers within and six without.

**The first long distance coach service** — including an overnight stop — was from Sydney to Bathurst, a distance of 132 miles, and was inaugurated by Thomas Rose in 1824. The coach left Sydney at 6 a.m., stopped at Parramatta for breakfast at 8 a.m., at Penrith for lunch at 11.30 a.m., and stopped at Wentworth Falls for the night at 7 p.m.; leaving again at 6am, it arrived at Bathurst at 7 p.m.

**Cobb & Co's coaching service** was inaugurated by the American Freeman Cobb on 30 January 1853 with a Melbourne-Forest Creek (now Castlemaine, Vic) run. They had the distinction of operating the largest ever stage-coach, a monster called the *Leviathan* which could accommodate over 90 passengers, and was drawn by eight horses. It ran between Ballarat and Geelong in the 1860s.

Stage coaches continued to run in Australia longer than any other country in the world. As late as 1921 there was a 3d coach guide to horse-drawn services connecting

*Artist's impression of the Cobb & Co coach* Leviathan.

La Trobe Collection

# The first ...

bush towns in backblocks Victoria. The last stage coach was still running on the Casterton-Mount Gambier route in 1925. Its proprietor, Tom Cawher, had started as a coach-driver 50 years earlier.

## STAMP COLLECTING JOURNALS

were *The Australian Stamp Collectors' Journal*, Adelaide, and *The New South Wales Stamp Collectors' Magazine*, Sydney, both founded in 1879.

## STAMP COLLECTING SOCIETY

was the Philatelic Society of Sydney, established 10 September 1885.

## STATIONER

(recorded) was Thomas Broughton of Sydney, who advertised his services in the *Sydney Gazette* for 8 May 1803. He was also a bookbinder.

## STATISTICAL YEARBOOK

appeared in 1829 under the title of *The Colony of New South Wales for the Year* 1828. The 200 pages of contents included 'Taxes, Duties etc., Fees Revenue and Expenditure; Local Revenues; Observations on the Abstracts of the Revenue and Expenditure for 1828; Military Returns; Public Works; Civil Establish-ment; Pensions, Lists of Officers; Population; Ecclesiastical Return; Education; Exchanges, Monies, Weights; Imports and Exports, Agriculture; Manufactures, Mines and Fisheries; Grants of Land; Gaols and Prisons.' Published by order of the Colonial Secretary, this was the first government publication of such magnitude, earlier government printing having been confined to proclamations, Acts in Council and Government Orders.

## STATUE

was a representation in bronze by E. H. Baily of Sir Richard Bourke, Governor of New South Wales 1831-37, which was unveiled in the Domain at Sydney on 11 April 1842. Sir Richard enjoyed the notable distinction of being so immortalised while he was still alive. The unveiling was attended by what was then the largest crowd ever to assemble in Australia, estimated at between 7,000 and 10,000. There were also some 120 carriages 'filled with ladies'. The pedestal of the statue, which still stands, is claimed to have the longest inscription of any statue in the world, running to 303 fulsome words.

*The first statue to a private citizen* commemorated Thomas Sutcliffe Mort (1816-1878), a shipbuilder and engineer who also conducted some of the earliest wool auctions in Australia, pioneered the refrigeration of meat, and was the first to offer company shares to his employees. His monument, paid for by his grateful staff, stands in Macquarie Place, Sydney, and was unveiled on 9 June 1883.

*The world's first pre-paid letter with embossed stamps*

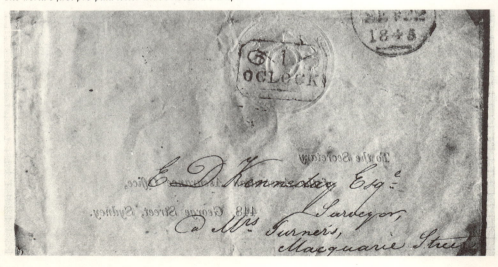

Australia Post

## STEAM ENGINE

was brought to Sydney by miller John Dickson in 1813. The engine was of considerable size, being valued at £5,200. It was installed at Dickson's mill at Cockle Bay and on 29 May 1815 began driving a pair of stones which ground 10 bushels of wheat an hour. This was 20 times the volume of wheat that could be ground per hour in a hand mill and five or six times the capacity of a horse-driven mill.

## STEEL

was produced in 1854 by ironfounder Peter Nicol Russell at his Pyrmont Iron Works at Sydney, where small quantities were made into cutlery.

The first large-scale production of steel was undertaken by William Sandford, who built a four-ton Siemens-Martin open hearth steel furnace at Eskbank works, Lithgow, NSW, and began tapping steel on 24 April 1900.

## STEEL-FRAMED BUILDING

was Nelson House, Clarence Street, Sydney, a nine-storey art nouveau edifice designed by L. S. Robertson and built in 1910 at a cost of £12,758. The world's first steel-framed building, sometimes described as the first skyscraper, was the Home Insurance Co office built in Chicago by William Le Baron Jenney in 1885.

## STOCKBROKER

was William Barton, who began trading in stocks and shares at Sydney in 1852.

## STOCK EXCHANGE

was established in the Hall of Commerce, Melbourne, in October 1859 with John Binns Were as Chairman. Others include Sydney (1872), Bendigo (1873), Launceston (1881), Hobart (1882), Brisbane (1885), Ballarat (1885), Perth (1889), Rockhampton (1926) and Newcastle (1937). Sydney claims to be the oldest, as the Melbourne Stock Exchange was refounded in 1885 after a dispute about advertising.
*The first stock exchanges to operate screen trading* were Melbourne and Sydney, which jointly introduced a $68 million automated trading system in July 1987. Trading floor activity is expected to be eliminated within five years.

## STREET LAMPS

were oil lamps erected in Macquarie Place, Sydney, and first lit on 7 April 1828.

See also Gas Lighting; Electric Lighting.

## STRIPPER

or harvesting machine was successfully demonstrated by John Ridley on his 70-acre wheat farm near Adelaide in November 1843. This incorporated a system of 'comb and beaters' which enabled threshing of the grain from the ears of the standing crop, an idea originated the previous year by John Wrathall Bull. The Stripper reduced harvesting cost from £2 an acre to about 5s 6d an acre and transformed the Australian wheat industry from an uneconomic and labour intensive enterprise to one that opened up vast new lands to profitable cultivation.

See also Combine Harvester.

## STUD

was established by an order of the Commissary's Office at Sydney dated 2 June 1804. This stated that the Arabian stallion *Shark*, which had been brought to New South Wales aboard the *Mersey*, had been purchased by the Governor and 'transferred to Government for the purpose of improving the Breed of Horses in this Colony'. Shark was available to service mares at a fee of 10 bushels of wheat 'for the public use' and 30s to 'the Persons having the care of the Horse'.
*The first stud farm for the breeding of racehorses* was Bungarribee, established by Charles Smith near Sydney in 1830.

## STUMP-JUMP PLOUGH

in the world was the 'Vixen', designed by Robert Bowyer Smith of Kalkabury, SA, and first demonstrated on 'Section 58 Hundred of Tiparra' in August 1876. A three-furrow plough, it was designed to jump over stumps of the kind that characterised Smith's own scrub land holding at Yorke Peninsula and made it difficult to work with a conventional plough. The effect of the invention was the cultivation of lands formerly considered incapable of being worked profitably and the springing up of towns to serve these formerly barren areas.

# The first . . .

## SUBMACHINE GUN

designed and built in Australia was the Owen Gun, invented by motor mechanic Evelyn Owen of Wollongong, NSW, in 1938, the same year as the Bren Gun was introduced in Czechoslovakia. Having failed to interest the military authorities, Owen volunteered for the AIF on the outbreak of war. The last thing he did before leaving home to join his unit was to place his prototype gun, wrapped in a sugar bag, on the steps of his next-door neighbour, Mr V. A. Wardell, the manager of Lysaght's steel works at Port Kembla. Wardell was surprised to find this weapon of war dumped on his doorstep, but impressed with its simplicity and neat appearance. At that time there were only two submachine guns in the whole of Australia — a Schmeisser confiscated from a German by a customs officer and a World War I German machine pistol in a museum.

After Wardell had demonstrated the Owen Gun to the Director General of Munitions, a number of experimental models were commissioned from Lysaght's and tested against the American Thompson Submachine-Gun and the British Sten Gun. It was found that the Owen performed better in battle conditions, particularly when the parts were congested with mud, and in 1942 the first production models were issued to Australian troops in New Guinea as replacements for the heavier Thompson. In time it also replaced the Sten. The Owen could fire ten shots a second and had a 33-round vertical fed magazine. Nearly 50,000 were produced, earning Evelyn Owen some £12,000 in royalties.

## SUBMARINES

were HMAS AE1 and AE2, both of them E class vessels built in Britain, which arrived in Darwin Harbour on 6 May 1914 after the longest voyage ever undertaken by submarines.

AE1 disappeared off the coast of New Britain on 14 September 1914 together with her 35 man crew. This was the first occasion an Australian vessel was lost in warfare.

## SUGAR

was produced from 243 hectares of cane planted on the banks of the Wilson River, near Port Macquarie, NSW, by Thomas Scott in 1822. Some 7 tons of sugar were obtained from the crop, though the cane was

*Evelyn Owen (right) holds his invention the Owen gun.*

Australian War Memorial

insufficiently matured due to the unsatisfactory climate.

**The first sugar refinery** was established by the Australian Sugar Co. at Canterbury, NSW, in 1841.

**Cultivation of sugar on a commercial scale** in Australia began when Captain the Hon. Louis Hope built the first raw sugar mill at his Ormiston plantation near Brisbane in 1864. He had planted 8 hectares of cane the previous year. *Beet sugar* was first refined at Maffra, Vic, in 1897.

## SUICIDE

was James Downey, a time-expired convict of the First Fleet, who hanged himself in his hut on 31 October 1791. A labourer in the bricklayers' gang and 'in general considered as a harmless fellow', he committed suicide for fear of being arraigned on a charge of theft.

## SUNDAY SCHOOL

was founded by Thomas Hassall at his father's house in Parramatta in May 1813.

## SUPERPHOSPHATE

was produced by Cumming Smith & Co from bone char, a by-product of sugar refining, at Yarraville, Vic, in 1878. The fertiliser was shipped to Madagascar aboard the vessels which brought the raw sugar to Australia.

## SURFBOARD

in Australia was made by Alick Wickham, the Solomon Islander who introduced the crawl to Australia. He first rode it at Curl Curl Beach, north of Sydney, in 1908. Frank and Charlie Bell rode a homemade board at Freshwater Beach, Sydney the same year. The sport made little progress until the arrival in 1915 of Hawaiian champion swimmer and surfer Duke Kahanamoku, who had a board made from sugar-pine at Hudson's timberyard in Sydney. Finishing it himself with a sand polisher, Kahanamoku then took it to Freshwater and gave a three-hour display of virtuoso boardriding that immediately established a new Australian sport. When he left Sydney, he gave the board to Claude West, the best of the local riders. It is preserved today at the clubhouse of the Freshwater Surf Club.

**The first woman surfboard rider** was 15-year-old Isabel Letham at Freshwater Beach in 1915. Isabel was introduced to surfing by Duke Kahanamoku, who had carried her on his shoulders as he rode his Hawaiian-style long board in the demonstration quoted above.

**The first Malibu board** — a mere 8 ft 6ins against the 20 ft length of most Australian boards — was demonstrated at North Bondi by Hollywood actor Peter Lawford in 1954. Within three or four years the short, highly manoueverable balsa boards with a fin had completely replaced the giant hollow plywood boards.

**The first Australian to become world champion** was Midget Farrelly at Manly, NSW, in May 1964.

## SURF BOAT RACE

took place in January 1908 at the Southern end of Manly Beach between two ship's boats borrowed by members of the Manly Surf Life Saving Club.

## SURGEONS

were Surgeon-General John White, Dennis Considen, William Balmain and Thomas Arndell, who arrived at Port Jackson with the First Fleet on 26 January 1788 and together with John Irving, who acted as an assistant, comprised the original medical staff of the New South Wales government establishment.

**The first Australian-born surgeon** was William Sherwin of Sydney, who studied under Dr William Bland and qualified as a Member of the Royal College of Surgeons in 1823.

**The first woman surgeon** was Laura Margaret Fowler, who became House Surgeon at Adelaide Children's Hospital on 6 February 1892. She subsequently worked in India.

## SWIMMING POOL

was established on the bay beyond the Government Domain, Sydney, in 1830. There were separate pools for men and women, the latter fully enclosed so that 'the ladies are safely secured from all intrusion and they can duck and gambol unseen and unmolested.'

## SWIMMING RACE

was held at Robinson's Baths at the edge of the Domain, Sydney, on 14 February 1846 and won by W. Redman in a time of 8 min 43 sec over 440 yards.

**The first international championship race** in the world took place at St Kilda, Melbourne, on 9 February 1858, when Jo Bennett of Australia defeated Charles Stedman of England.

# The first...

## TANKS
were four Vickers Medium Mark II's, purchased from Britain for £72,000, which went into service with the newly-formed Australian Tank Corps at Randwick, NSW, in September 1929.
*The first tank designed and manufactured in Australia* was the 27 ton AC 1 or *Sentinel*. Production of the series began in August 1942 in South Melbourne. It carried a crew of five and was powered by three Cadillac petrol motors in clover-leaf mounting. It was armed with a 2-pounder gun.

## TANNERY
was established by James Wilshire in 1803 at Brickfield Hill, Sydney, where it remained in business until 1861. Wilshire's leather was such high quality that it was reported the soldiers were selling the army issue shoes sent out from England at 2s 6d to 3s 6d a pair and buying his leather instead.

## TAXES
were introduced in January 1800 at the rate of 1s per gallon on spirits, 6d on wine and 3d on porter or strong beer. The revenue went to the Gaol Fund, several of the settlers having refused to contribute to the cost of rebuilding the gaol at Parramatta after it had been burned down.

## TAXIS
began plying for hire in Sydney in 1904. Three were licensed that year. After a while they were withdrawn and it was only in 1909 that both Sydney and Melbourne got their first permanent taxi fleets. In March of that year a correspondent in *The Australian Motorist* wrote of Melbourne's taxis: 'I notice that many working girls, and boys also, are gaining their first taste of the delights of motoring by their means. They save up and club together, and hire a taxi for as long as their money will suffice, and do the grand tour on their weekly half-holiday or, at times, in the evenings.'

## TEACHER TRAINING COLLEGE
was the Normal Institution, Sydney, founded by Henry Carmichael in December 1834 to train teachers for the proposed new system of National Schools.

## TECHNICAL SCHOOL
was the Van Diemen's Land Mechanics' Institute, opened at Hobart in 1829.

## TELEPHONE
in regular use connected the head office of hardware importers McLean Bros and Rigg in Elizabeth Street, Melbourne, with their Spencer Street store and was installed on 2 January 1878.
*The first telephone call over an extended distance* was made on 9 January 1878 by customs inspector W. J. Thomas, who spoke over a wire from Geelong to Queenscliff.
*The first telephone number* was issued to the Melbourne engineering company Robinson Bros, who had telephones installed at their Flinders Street head office and their foundry in South Melbourne in July 1879. Their telephone number was Melbourne 1, which they retained until the 1920s, when it was transferred to St Patrick's Cathedral.
*The first telephone exchange* was established in Collins Street with a 100-line switchboard by the Melbourne Telephone Exchange Co on 10 May 1880. In August the company issued Australia's *first telephone directory*, listing all 44 subscribers. Other exchanges followed at Brisbane in October of the same year, at Sydney in March 1882, at Adelaide, Hobart and Launceston in 1883 and Perth in 1887. Brisbane's was the first exchange operated by the Post Office.
*The first trunk line* was opened between Adelaide and Port Adelaide, a distance of 16 km, in 1886. The first interstate trunk line

connected Nelson, Vic and Mt Gambier, SA, in 1902. Sydney and Melbourne were connected 10 July 1907, Melbourne and Adelaide in 1914, Sydney and Brisbane in 1923 and Adelaide and Perth in 1930.

**The first automatic telephone exchange** for public use began operating at Geelong, Vic, on 6 July 1912. The first State to have a wholly automatic network was Tasmania in June 1977, when the last manual exchange, Swansea, was replaced.

**The first PABX** was installed at the Hotel Australia in Sydney in 1914.

**The first telephone service between Britain and Australia** was inaugurated on 30 April 1930 with a call from British Prime Minister Ramsay MacDonald in London to Australian Prime Minister Hugh Scullin in Canberra.

**The first STD services** were introduced between St Mary's and Sydney and between Dandenong and Melbourne in 1956. International STD enabled Sydney subscribers to dial direct to 13 countries for the first time on 1 April 1976.

**Reverse charge calls** and *payment by credit* were both introduced throughout Australia on 1 January 1961.

## TELEPHONE BOX, PUBLIC

was installed at Sydney General Post Office on 8 March 1893.

## TELEPHONE COUNSELLING SERVICE

was Lifeline, inaugurated by Alan Walker of the Central Methodist Mission in Sydney in 1963.

## TELEPRINTER

for recording telegraph messages direct on to a tape in printed form was invented by Donald Murray in Sydney in 1898 and first employed commercially in Britain in 1902.

## TELETEXT

service to domestic TV sets began on 4 February 1980.

## TELEVISION

transmission was made by ex-aircraft engineer Gilbert Miles on 10 January 1929 at Television and Radio Laboratories via Station 3UZ in Melbourne. His equipment consisted of a Nipkow disc scanner and a Baird-type 28-line receiver, giving a picture which magnified to about the size of a postcard. John Logie Baird had first demonstrated his low definition television system in London three years earlier. At the time that Gilbert Miles was making his pioneer transmissions, which continued for several weeks, Baird had just started the first scheduled programme service, with an hour of music and songs by the 'Baird Concert Party' every Tuesday night. Miles' transmissions were rather more rudimentary. *Radiovision*, Australia's earliest TV journal, reported that 'subjects at present being broadcast comprise geometric designs and "move" subjects in black and white, and as such are particularly suitable for tuning and adjustment'. The moving images consisted of simple silhouettes of such items as a windmill with its sails rotating and a boy playing on a swing. Also transmitted were 'definitely graduated half-tone test slips' and animated films of model animals.

Shortly after the broadcasts began, Gilbert Miles was married and a congratulatory message was transmitted to a receiver on the wedding breakfast table by the staff of Television and Radio Laboratories. Subsequently he made telecasts from the laboratories in South Melbourne to his home in Glen Iris, where the pictures were picked up by his wife on Australia's first domestic TV set.

**The first electronic television transmissions** were made experimentally by Val McDowall on 6 May 1934 from the old Brisbane Observatory. McDowall was the first to transmit a film when he showed a Janet Gaynor movie.

**The first television station** was TCN-9 Sydney, which began regular transmission on 16 September 1956. This was almost exactly 20 years after the world's first public high-definition TV service had been inaugurated by the BBC. The first face to be seen on screen was that of Australia's first TV announcer, Bruce Gyngell, in a dinner jacket with his tie skew-whiff, who presented the opening night's programmes from St David's Church Hall, Surry Hills. This makeshift accommodation served as a studio for a couple of months until the purpose-built studios at Willoughby were ready. The floorboards at St. David's being uneven, every time a camera tracked the picture jumped. Most of the early programmes consisted of canned American material, but there were brave attempts at home-grown entertainment with *The Johnny O' Connor Show*, *Accent on Strings* and *Campfire Favorites*, and the first TV game shows *What's My Line* and *Name That Tune*. Apart from an 'intro' called *This is Television*,

# The first ...

The *Johnny O'Connor Show* was the first programmed broadcast on TCN-9's opening night.

**The first television news** was transmitted by TCN-9 Sydney and presented by television's first newsreader Chuck Faulkner in what was called an 'Irish-Australian-American accent' at 7 p.m. on 16 September 1956.

**The first sports transmission** was the Pelaco Golf Tournament by TCN-9 Sydney in November 1956. Traffic was brought to a halt during the four-day telecast as huge crowds gathered to watch sets in shop windows and the police asked for transmission to be halted. It went on.

**The first current affairs programme** was Seven on Seven, presented by Howard Craven on ATN-7 Sydney starting in late 1956.

**The first television play** was J. M. Barrie's *The Twelve Pound Look*, produced by Paul O'Loughlin with a cast of four at a cost of £335 4s 7d and transmitted on Channel 2, Sydney, on 5 November 1956. The rights to the play slightly exceeded the sum in the title — they cost twelve guineas.

**The first Prime Minister to appear on television live** was Robert Menzies on the opening night of ABN-2 Sydney, 5 November 1956.

**The first Australian play presented on television** was Leslie Rees's newspaper drama *The Sub-Editors' Room*, produced by the author and aired by ABC Sydney on 18 December 1956.

**The first Shakespeare plays on television** were *Hamlet*, starring William Job as the Prince of Denmark, which was aired by ABC Sydney on 17 June 1959; and *Anthony and Cleopatra*, starring Keith Eden and Bettine Kauffman, aired by ABC Melbourne the same night.

**The first Sydney-Melbourne transmission** took place on 10 January 1959, when the Third Test was telecast by GTV-9 Melbourne from the Sydney Cricket Ground. One commentator was moved to observe that 'it was typical of the Australian way of life that sport provided the incentive for long distance telecasting'. The first transmission in the reverse direction was of the Melbourne Cup by TCN-9 later the same year.

**The first dramatic series** made in Australia were the soap opera *Autumn Affair*, starring radio star Muriel Steinbeck as an authoress in love with a fashion photographer, which began transmission on ATN-7 Sydney and GTV-9 Melbourne during 1959; and the hospital drama *Emergency*, starring Brian James, which ran concurrently on the same channels.

**The first Australian series to appear in the National Top Ten ratings** was the Graham Kennedy Channel Nine Show, which was 8th in 1960. Previously all top-rated shows had been American imports. By 1965 an Australian programme, *The Mavis Bramston Show*, was scoring the highest ratings of any TV series (only Saturday night movies scored higher), and it was the same year that British programmes started entering the Top Ten for the first time, with *The Saint* at No 3 and *Coronation Street* at No 8. Australian and British series continued to find favour to the detriment of American product and in 1972 there was not a single US series in the Top Ten.

**The first and only Australian series to top the ratings overseas** was *Boney*, with New Zealander James Laurenson as a half-caste Aboriginal bush detective, which hit the No 1 spot in Scotland in 1973.

**The first international television transmission** was a two-way exchange of programmes between Australia and Britain via the Intelstat 2 space satellite on 24 November 1966.

**The first television transmission of a parliamentary debate** took place from Canberra on 6 August 1974, when ABC broadcast a joint sitting of both Houses. The Federal Budget speech was televised live for the first time on 21 August 1984.

**The first colour television programmes** were transmitted on 1 March 1975.

**The first woman newsreader** was Jan Leeming for Channel 10, Sydney on 5 May 1965. ABC's first regular woman newsreader was Margaret Throsby on air from 12 March 1978.

**The first ethnic programme services** were inaugurated on Channel 0/28 Sydney and Channel 0 Melbourne under the auspices of the Special Broadcasting Service on 24 October 1980.

## TELEVISION COMMERCIAL

was transmitted by TCN-9 Sydney on opening night, 16 September 1956, and advertised Vincent's powders and tablets. Probably the lowest budget commercial of all time, it consisted of three stills which changed over ten seconds. The first live action commercial, which was for Rothman's cigarettes, was transmitted by TCN-9 in a 20-second spot at 7.29 p.m. the same night. It was made by Jackson Wain Advertising.

**The first awards for TV commercials** were presented by the Federation of Australian Television Stations in 1976, when 'Commercial of the Year' was won by a Band-Aid commercial titled *Johnny Comes Marching Home*.

## TELEVISION JOURNAL

was *Radiovision*, published by Television and Radio Laboratories Ltd of Queen Street, Melbourne from September 1928 to October 1929. Priced 6d, each of the 14 issues contained only 4 pages, possibly because of a paucity of news about television progress. It was the second regular TV publication in the world, the first, *Television*, having been founded in London in March 1928.

## TEMPERANCE SOCIETY

was the New South Wales Temperance Society, which held its first public meeting at Mr Hunt's show-room in Jamison Street, Sydney on 6 May 1834.

## TENNIS BALLS

manufactured in Australia were produced by the Dunlop Pneumatic Tyre Co. of Australasia Ltd, Port Melbourne, in 1908.

## TENPIN BOWLING ALLEY

was opened at Glenelg, SA, in May 1960. The first fully automatic bowling alley was opened at Hurstville, Sydney, in October of the same year.

## TERRORIST ASSASSINATION

occurred at Vaucluse, Sydney on 17 December 1981, when two gunmen shot dead the Turkish Consul-General, Sarik Ariyak, and his bodyguard Engin Sever.

## TEST TUBE BABY

was Candice Reed, born at Melbourne's Queen Victoria Medical Centre on 22 June 1980. She was the world's fourth.

## TEXTILES

were samples of locally woven cloth sent by Governor Hunter to Lord Sydney with a covering letter dated 1 June 1799. These consisted of a 'Webb of Linen . . . made from the Wild Native flax', 'a Webb of Woolen . . . from the Coats of the Sheep bred in the Colony' and 'a piece of Coarse Sacking very carelessly made in an attempt at making Cloth from the Bark of a Tree which grows on the Banks of the River Hawkesbury'.

Regular manufacture of textiles began with the production of linen and woollen cloth in a small factory established in Sydney on the orders of Governor King in October 1800. Forty two women convicts were employed for spinning and 22 male convicts as weavers at 1d a yard. The two superintendents were given the promise of emancipation after a year if their conduct merited it, but one of them, an Irishman, was later reported to be 'a worthless character'. In August 1801 King wrote that 306 yards of blanketing and 472 yards of linen had been produced in the previous five months. Wild flax was used for the linen, while the wool came from the government flock and from local farmers, the latter being paid in kind with the finished blankets. The supply of wool from free settlers soon dried up, presumably when they had received all the blankets they needed, because a year after the factory had started manufacture the Governor was complaining that no one was prepared to accept the government's price of 2d per pound. Prior to the establishment of this mill, the only manufacturing enterprises had been brickmaking and tanning, both under government control.

## THEATRE

was opened at Sydney under the management of John Sparrow on 16 January 1796 with a performance of Dr Young's tragedy *The Revenge* and *The Hotel* as an afterpiece. The best seats cost a shilling or the equivalent in spirits, flour, meat or anything useful. The Sydney Theatre was extremely popular with the convicts, who would go to almost any length to secure the wherewithal for admission. One ingenious fellow killed a fine greyhound belonging to an officer, skinned it and sold the joints as Kangaroo flesh at 9d a pound. The convicts only attended the theatre, it was said, to see whose houses they might plunder while the family was absent at the play. It proved such a stimulus to crime that in 1798 the Governor of New South Wales ordered the building to be levelled to the ground.

The continuous development of drama in Australia dates from the opening of the **first professional theatre**, the Theatre Royal, es-

# The first . . .

tablished in Sydney by Barnett Levey, which opened with a performance of *The Miller and His Men* together with a farce *The Irishman in London*, on 5 October 1833. It was here that Australia's first international star of the stage, Eliza Winstanley, made her debut at the age of 16 in *Clari or the Maid of Milan* on 31 October 1834. She was to establish a reputation as a Shakespearian actress in Britain and the United States, performed before Queen Victoria at Windsor, and became a popular novelist and editor of a weekly magazine, before finally retiring to Australia in 1880.

*The first theatre in the world with a sliding roof* — for opening in the summer — was the Princess Theatre, Melbourne, designed by William Pitt in 1887.

## THEOLOGICAL COLLEGE

was St James' College, Lydhurst, which was established in December 1846 in 'a neat stone mansion', formerly a private residence, off the Glebe Road, Sydney. The Principal was the Rev. R. Allwood. The venture proved to be premature. Four graduates were ordained by the Bishop of Sydney but in April 1849 the College found itself without a single student and it was subsequently closed.

See also Seminary.

## TIN

was discovered at Beechworth, Victoria, on 11 March 1843.

*The first tin mine* was established in 1872 near Inverell, NSW, following the discovery of a seam of tin by Joseph Willis the previous year. Soon afterwards other discoveries were made in New South Wales, and with the opening of the Mount Bischoff mine in Tasmania and another at Stanhope, Queensland, by the mid-1870s Australia had become the world's major producer of tin.

## TOPLESS SUNBATHER

to appear on an Australian beach was 20-year-old Finnish model Tuija Pakerinen at Mona Vale, near Sydney, in July 1964.

## TOTALISATOR

was installed at the Sportsmen's Club in Bourke Street, Melbourne, in 1882. This was a manually operated device based on the French Pari-Mutuel system. The automatic tote was devised by (Sir) George Julius of the consulting engineers Julius, Poole & Gibson of Sydney and first set up at Ellerslie Racecourse, Auckland, NZ, in March 1913. Julius was the son of the Bishop of New Zealand. His invention was subsequently developed by Automatic Totalisators Ltd, which installed the first automatic tote in Australia at Gloucester Park race-track, Perth in 1916. The firm later exported the machines to many countries overseas.

*The first off-course* TABs were opened in Victoria in May 1960. WA legalised off-course tote betting the same year, Queensland in 1962, ACT and NSW in 1964, SA in 1967 and Tas in 1975.

## TOWN HALL

was the original Melbourne Town Hall, opened in Swanston Street on 27 March 1854. The oldest Town Hall is Geelong's, which dates from 1855.

## TOWN MAP

was a *Plan de la Ville de Sydney*, engraved by Cloquet after C. A. Lesueur and published in Paris on 31 October 1802. Below the map was a key to 38 places of note in the town.

*The first town map published in Australia* was A *Plan of the Town of Sydney*, drawn by the ex-convict and pioneer surveyor James Meehan in 1807.

## TOWN PLANNER

was Charles C. Reade of Adelaide, appointed by the South Australian government in 1916.

## TRACTOR

manufactured in Australia was the McDonald *Imperial*, produced in Melbourne in 1909.

## TRADE AGREEMENT, INTERNATIONAL

was made with South Africa in 1906.

## TRADE COMMISSIONER

to represent overseas on a permanent basis was Henry Yule Bradden, appointed to the USA in September 1918.

## TRADE UNION

on record was the Cabinet Makers' Society,

founded in Sydney in 1833 to maintain piece work prices in the furniture trade. By 1840 there were ten trade unions in the Australian colonies.

**The first trade union known to have called a strike** was the Australian Society of Compositors, which held a meeting in Sydney on 8 January 1840 at which a resolution was passed seeking to limit the number of apprentices employed in relation to the number of journeymen. The resolution being refused by the employers, a strike was called which curtailed, though it failed to halt, production of the *Sydney Gazette* and the *Sydney Herald*. As a strike breaking measure the employers sent to England for more tractable compositors, though it is doubtful whether they were needed, since the papers soon resumed normal production. The trade unionists were sentenced to two months imprisonment with hard labour for absenting themselves from work without leave. Other strikes were called the same year by the tailors of Sydney and the carpenters and joiners of Melbourne, the former for an advance on their 8s a day wage and the latter for an advance on 12s a day.

**The first attempt to establish a closed shop** was made in December 1840, when three members of the Sydney Shipwright's Society were prosecuted for refusing to work with a non-member.

**The first union of women workers** was the Tailoresses' Union founded at Melbourne on 15 December 1882. The union was a direct outcome of the successful settlement of a strike called by the tailoresses five days earlier, the first such action by female employees in Australia. This achieved not only improved wages and better working conditions, but also aroused public opinion about the use of sweated labour in the industry, leading to the appointment of the Sweating Commission.

**The first white collar union** was the South Australian Association of Clerks, founded in Adelaide in 1905.

**The first general strike** was a 24-hour nationwide stoppage called by ACTU on 12 July 1976 over the Labor Government's modification of Medibank.

It is worthy of note that by 1914, Australia had the highest incidence of trade union membership in the world, with 106 trade unionists per 1000 inhabitants.

## TRADE UNION CONGRESS

was organized by the Sydney Trades' and Labour Council in October 1879 and was attended by 39 delegates representing 11,087 members.

## TRADE UNION JOURNAL

was the *Victorian Typographical Journal*, established by the compositors' union in Melbourne in February 1858.

## TRAFFIC LIGHTS

were installed on the corner of Collins and Swanston Streets in Melbourne in 1928.

## TRAMPOLINES

were homemade models erected at Newtown, NSW, and Oakleigh, Vic, about 1955. The first professionally made model was presented to Melbourne YMCA in 1956 by George Nissen, the American inventor of the modern trampoline.

## TRAMS

were horsedrawn vehicles which ran along Pitt Street, Sydney, from the station at Devonshire Street to Circular Quay, commencing on 23 December 1861. The Government-operated service closed down five years later due to opposition from local shopkeepers.

**The first self-propelled trams** were steam vehicles which replaced horsedrawn trams on the Elizabeth Street tramway in Sydney on 28 September 1879.

**The first electric trams** in regular operation began running between Ridge Street, North Sydney and Spit Junction in September 1893.

## TRANS-AUSTRALIAN CROSSING

was completed by Edward John Eyre with his arrival at Albany, WA, on 7 July 1841.

## TREE-FELLING CONTEST

took place at Ulverstone, Tasmania in 1874 between Joe Smith and Jack Biggs. Using trees four feet in diameter, the two axmen competed for a stake of 5000 palings. The winner was Smith, whose tree hit the ground just as his opponent's was beginning to topple.

## TRIAL BY JURY

was held at the Sydney Sessions on 2 November 1824. Emancipists were held to be ineligible to act as jurors, but this form of discrimi-

# The first...

nation ceased in 1828. The concession was not universally popular. One jury, on entering the court, found slips of paper on the desks before them each inscribed with some forcefully expressed remarks. One read: 'Of all the humbugs in this humbugging world, the most detestable is to sit for hours in a blackguard Botany Bay jury-box, on the same seats that have been polluted by the canaille (Angilce, 'mancipists) listening to the prosing blunders of a superannuated old wig.' The majority of juries continued to be military rather than civil until 1839.

## TRIPLETS
were born to Amelia Rixon of Sydney on 5 January 1806.

## TROLLEY BUSES
began running between Liverpool Street and Potts Point in Sydney on 22 January 1934. The last were withdrawn from service in Brisbane in 1969, ten years after Sydney had abandoned them.

## TROTTING RACE
was held at Parramatta on 30 April 1810 (see Race-meeting). The first full meeting was held at Melbourne on 21 January 1860.
*The first night trotting meeting* was held at the Adelaide Showground on 6 November 1920. Trotting had only a minor following in Australia prior to the introduction of night meetings.
*The first race for women* was the Australian Reinswomen's Championship held at Globe Derby Park, Adelaide, in May 1973, and won by full-time Sydney trainer Mrs Fran Donohoe driving Red Sky.

## TROUSERS WITH PERMANENT CREASES
in the world were produced in 1957 by CSIRO's Division of Textile Industry. The process, patented as Si-ro-set, involved treating wool with a resin which caused a temporary change in the chemical structure of the fibres. The fabric woven from this wool was then steam-pressed and the chemical eliminated. Garments so treated would retain their creases even when soaked and dried again.

## TROUT
were hatched on 5 May 1864 from a consignment of brown trout eggs imported from England on behalf of the Salmon Commission of Tasmania. The importation was shared by the Victorian Government and all brown trout in Australia, and possibly New Zealand also, are descended from fish hatched from these eggs.

## TYPE FOUNDRY
was established at Sydney in 1842. On 7 January 1843 the *Sydney Morning Herald* reported: '*The Government Gazette* is now printed with a font of large primer type cut in the Colony by a Mr Thompson, who arrived here about two years ago. The successful establishment of this foundry will be highly advantageous to the printers, not only of Sydney, but of Port Phillip and the neighbouring colonies, as the old worn-out type can be recast instead of being sent to England at heavy cost.'

*The first electric train in Sydney.*

## UNDERGROUND RAILWAY

was inaugurated in Sydney on 20 December 1926 with the opening of the section between Central and St James.

## UNEMPLOYMENT BENEFIT

was introduced in Queensland in 1923. Contributions from employer, employee and the state provided up to 5 weeks of benefit in a year for unemployed workers. A national system of unemployment benefit was inaugurated in 1944.

## UNEMPLOYMENT FIGURES

were issued by a select Committee of the Legislative Council of NSW in the latter part of 1843 and showed that there were 1,300 labourers and mechanics out of work in Sydney, these men having some 3,000 dependents. A sum of £1,000 was voted by the Council for sending as many as possible into the country districts to seek work. Caroline Chisholm, who was to become celebrated for her philanthropic work in New South Wales, undertook her first efforts on behalf of the poor by settling thirty families of the unemployed at Illawarra.

## UNITARIAN CHURCH

was Macquarie Street Chapel, Sydney, opened 30 October 1853.

## UNITING CHURCH

was founded on 22 June 1977 with the

## TYPEWRITER

was a Remington machine imported from the USA by the NSW Telegraph Department and in use by the middle of 1875. Commercial production in America had begun only a year earlier. It would seem that the Telegraph Department's interest in the apparatus was whether it could be adapted for printing telegrams, because there is no record of typewriters being used for general office work in Australia before 1883. In that year a number were imported by Sydney Stott who opened a commercial school in Sydney to train operators of these 'new-fangled machines', as well as to teach shorthand and book-keeping. At first most operators were men, but it soon became apparent that women were more adept — they were also cheaper. The firm of Enoch Taylor & Co. of Sydney claimed to have been the first to introduce typewriters for office use.

# The first . . .

merging of the Methodist, Congregationalist and most Presbyterian Churches.

## UNIVERSITY

was Sydney University, inaugurated 11 October 1852 in temporary premises formerly occupied by the defunct Sydney College, under the direction of A. J. Hamilton MA, Provost, and Dr (later Sir) Charles Nicholson, Vice Provost and first Chancellor (1854). There were 24 students and three professors at the outset. Among the former was David Scott Mitchell, whose collection of Australiana, started when he was a student, formed the nucleus of the world famous Mitchell Library. The first graduates were A. Renwick, G. Salting, and W. Salting, who received BA degrees in 1857.

*The first female student at an Australian university* was Miss Caroline Boyd of Sandhurst, Vic, the daughter of a doctor, who was accepted as an undergraduate at Melbourne University on 23 March 1880.

*The first female student to graduate from an Australian university* was Miss Bella Guerin, daughter of the governor of Ballarat gaol, who obtained her BA at Melbourne University on 1 December 1883. She had been a teacher before enrolling in the Arts faculty. The first to graduate as a Bachelor of Science was Fanny Hurst from Sydney University in 1888.

*The first free university* anywhere in the British Empire was the University of Western Australia, opened on 13 February 1913. All university fees in Australia were abolished from 1 January 1974.

*The first university to award a Ph.D.* (Doctorate of Philosophy) for post graduate research was Melbourne University in 1946.

## URANIUM MINE

was opened at Radium Hill, SA, in 1909. The carnotite-ilmenite ore mined there was treated for the production of uranium oxide.

## US PRESIDENT TO HAVE VISITED AUSTRALIA

was Herbert Hoover, 31st President 1928-32, who was employed as a mining engineer on the eastern goldfields of Western Australia c.1900.

*The first President of the USA to visit Australia while in office* was Lyndon Johnson,

FORD MODEL 304

(112 INC[

This new utility model has smart with fine interior fittings. Rear

*The 'ute' was designed by Lewis Bandt of Ford Australia in 1933.*

who arrived at Canberra on 20 October 1966. Despite the threats of anti-American demonstrations, he endeared himself to the crowds by calling out through the 'bullhorn' on his car 'Hurrah for Australia!' several times. For Johnson this was a return trip to Australia; he had visited Melbourne as a US Navy officer in 1942.

## UTILITY

in the world was designed by Lewis Bandt, chief body engineer of Ford Australia in Geelong, in response to a letter received from a farmer in 1933. Unable to afford both a car and a truck, the farmer described what he had in mind: 'The front is the coupe, to suit my needs for taking the family to church on Sunday. The back is to be the roadster-utility box so that I can take my pigs to town on Mondays'. The first production models came off the line in 1934.

Bandt worked for Ford for 44 years. Sadly he was killed in 1987 while driving the prototype 1933 ute, which bore the licence plate number UT-001. The wrecked vehicle had 83,900 miles on the clock.

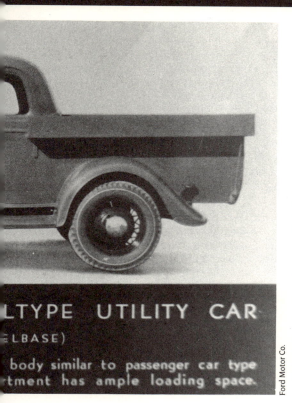

LTYPE UTILITY CAR
ELBASE)

body similar to passenger car type
tment has ample loading space.

Ford Motor Co.

## VACCINATION

was performed in Sydney on 6 May 1804, when three children from the Orphan Asylum were vaccinated by the Principal Surgeon and a number of soldiers' children by the Surgeon of the New South Wales Corps. The vaccines, for the prevention of smallpox, had been sent to New South Wales by the Royal Jennerian Society. Dr Jenner had pioneered vaccination some eight years earlier, but the practice only became widespread with the opening of 13 vaccination clinics in London by the Royal Jennerian Society in 1803.

## VEGEMITE

was first prepared by Fred Walker of Melbourne in February 1923, using brewers' surplus yeast from the Carlton & United Brewery. Although part of the Australian staple diet, the Vegemite cult has failed to spread beyond our shores.

## VEGETARIAN RESTAURANT

was the Vegetarian Café, established in March 1904 by the Sanitarium Health Food Co, a Seventh Day Adventist organization, in Royal Chambers at the corner of Castlereagh and Hunter Streets in Sydney. At first the carnivores of Australia seemed reluctant to patronise an enterprise where 'steak and eggs' was conspicuous only by its absence, but with the publication of Upton Sinclair's *The Jungle*, exposing the horrors of the Chicago meat-packing houses, business suddenly picked up. Pioneer Australian vegetarians were nearly all men — for some reason women were unwilling to eat at the Vegetarian Café, nor were they responsive when the café started cookery classes to teach them how to prepare health foods for their husbands.

## VETERAN CAR RALLY

was held at Melbourne in April 1933.

## VICTORIA CROSS

was won during the Boer War by Lt (later Sir) Nevill Reginald Howse of the NSW Medical Staff Corps on 24 July 1900 at Vredefort, South Africa, for rescuing a wounded man under heavy fire.
**The first VC won by an Australian airman** was awarded to Lt F. H. McNamara of No 1 Squadron, Australian Flying Corps, on 20 March 1917. This was the AFC's only VC of World War I.

Members of the Australian forces have won a total of 96 Victoria Crosses: 6 in the Transvaal War, 64 in World War I; 2 in the North Russia Campaign of 1919; 20 in World War II; and 4 in Vietnam.

# The first . . .

## VINEYARD

was planted in the Governor's garden at Parramatta in 1789. Governor Phillip wrote to Sir Joseph Banks in December 1791: ' . . . from the few cuttings I brought from the Rio and the Cape, we now have many thousand young vines, here and at Norfolk Island. I had two or three bunches of grapes the year before last and last year several good bunches, at present the old vines in my garden are loaded with very fine fruit.'

See also Wine

## VOTE BY BALLOT

in Parliamentary elections anywhere in the world was introduced by the Legislative Council of the Colony of Victoria under the Electoral Act which became law on 19 March 1856. Proposals to adopt a secret ballot had been rejected five years earlier by E. Deas Thomson, then Colonial Secretary, who said the very notion was 'not only unconstitutional, but un-British'. The man who finally succeeded in securing its adoption was William Nicholson, a Cumberland grocer who had emigrated to Victoria in 1841, was Mayor of Melbourne in 1850, and was to be Premier of the Colony in 1859. His motion in favour of the secret ballot was carried by 33 votes to 25 on 18 December 1855 and in consequence the Government was obliged to resign. Although returned to office, they were forced to respond to the majority will and allow for the passage of the measure.

*The first Parliamentary election to be held by secret ballot* was the General Election for the Victorian Legislative Council held on 27 August 1856. In the meantime, South Australia had introduced its own ballot law, which received the Governor's Assent on 2 April 1856, and the other Australian colonies followed suit — New South Wales and Tasmania in 1858, Queensland in 1859, and Western Australia somewhat tardily in 1879.

## VOTES AT 18

were pioneered by South Australia with effect from 30 June 1972. In Federal elections the 18-year old vote was introduced under the Commonwealth Electoral Act of 28 February 1973. The first General Election at which teenagers were able to vote was held on 18 May 1974, Labor being returned to power.

## VOTES FOR ALL ADULT MALES

were introduced by the Colony of South Australia under an Act which received the Governor's Assent on 24 June 1856. Other colonies had a property qualification. The first election in which all adult males were able to go to the polls was held for the South Australian Assembly on 10 March 1857. Victoria introduced universal male suffrage in November of that year, NSW in 1858 and Tasmania very belatedly in 1900. Britain lagged behind her Australian offspring, only abolishing property qualifications in 1918.

## VOTES FOR WOMEN

were introduced in South Australia under an Act passed on 18 December 1894, little more than a year after New Zealand had become the first country in the world to grant women the franchise. Women were also enabled to stand for both houses of the South Australian Parliament, though none was elected until 1959. The first general election under the new franchise was held on 25 May 1896, when 39,355 out of 59,044 eligible women voted. William Pember Reeves, in his *State Experiments in Australia and New Zealand* (1902), observed that, contrary to the fears of its opponents, the introduction of women's suffrage in NZ and SA had not led to 'any wearing of knickerbockers, smoking of cigarettes or scorning of marriage. Enfranchisement has led neither to divided households nor divided skirts.'

Western Australia granted women the vote in 1899, New South Wales and the Commonwealth of Australia in 1902, Tasmania in 1903, Queensland in 1905 and Victoria in 1908. No country in Europe introduced women's suffrage until 1907 (Finland) and Britain did not succumb until 1918.

*The first Federal election in which women voted* was held on 16 December 1903.

## VOTING, COMPULSORY

in the world was introduced in Queensland by Act on 24 December 1914 and first applied at a General Election on 22 May 1915, when Labor won their first overall majority.

*Compulsory voting in Federal elections* was enacted on 17 July 1924. The first General Election at which it applied was held on 14 November 1925.

Compulsory voting usually produces an average poll of some 90%, compared to an average of 59% before the system was introduced.

## WALTZING MATILDA

was performed for the first time at the North Gregory Hotel at Winton, Queensland on 6 April 1895. The author of the song was 'Banjo' Paterson, who had written it at Dagworth Station, near Winton, in January of that year. He set the words to a traditional Scottish air, 'Craigelea', which he had heard played on an old autoharp by Christine Macpherson, daughter of the station owner. She had first heard it played by the band at a race meeting held at Warrnambool, Vic, the previous year. The incident portrayed in the song was based on reality. Dagworth's proprietor, Robert Macpherson, related to the poet how he had been out riding accompanied by two mounted troops and an aboriginal when he came across a swagman camping beneath a Coolabah tree by Combo waterhole. The swagman had killed a sheep (the 'jumbuck' of the song) belonging to Macpherson and on seeing the troopers, dived into the waterhole (the 'billabong' of the song), whereupon he was pulled down by the weight of his clothes and drowned.

## WAR CORRESPONDENT

was Howard Willoughby, who reported the Maori War of 1863-64 for the Melbourne *Argus*.

## WAR MEMORIAL

was erected by members of the 99th Regiment of Foot at Hobart, Tas in 1850 in memory of 'those brave men of the Regiment who fell in the service of their Queen and Country during the campaigns in New Zealand, 1845-6'.

**The first war memorial to Australian troops** was erected in St Andrew's Cathedral by 'the officers, non-commissioned officers, gunners, drivers and trumpeters of the Field Battery, New South Wales Artillery, Soudan, 1885'. It bears the names of Captain Willows, Gunners Coburne and Lewis, and Driver Robertson.

## WATER FLUORIDATION

was introduced at Beaconsfield, Tas, in 1953.

## WATER SKIING

came to Australia in 1936 when Carl Atkinson skied on Darwin Harbour. He tried skiing on Sydney Harbour later the same year, but was stopped by the water police.

**The first club** was the Sackviller Water skiing Club, established at Sackville on the Hawkesbury River, NSW, in 1950. The founders, car trial drivers 'Wild Bill' McLachlan and 'Gelignite Jack' Murray, had been instrumental in establishing water skiing in Australia in 1946, Carl Atkinson's pioneer effort of ten years earlier having come to nought. Their equipment consisted of little more than sandshoes nailed to planks, but after seeing a film of American pioneer waterskiers they realised the necessity of fins and a turned up nose to ski.

**The first barefoot water-skier in the world to mount a ramp, jump and land upright on the water** was Geoff Nichols at Manly Dam in 1963.

## WATER SPEED RECORD

The first Australian to hold the world water speed record was Ken Warby, who drove his jet-powered *Spirit of Australia* at an average speed of 317.18 mph (510.45 km/h) at Blowering Dam, near Tumut, NSW, on 8 October 1978. Warby's record has not been broken.

## WEDDINGS

were conducted by the Rev. Richard Johnson at Sydney Cove on Sunday 10 February 1788. Those married were William Parr to Mary MacCormack, William Haynes to Hannah Green, William Bryant to Mary Brand, Simon

# The first ..

Burn to Fanny Anderson and Henry Cable to Susannah Holmes. Seven of the ten were unable to sign their names in the register and made a mark only. Lieutenant Ralph Clark, who was present, wrote that he was sure that some of those getting married had left wives or husbands behind in England.

**The first marriage of a white Australian** is believed to have been that of Rebecca Small, who was born at Sydney on 22 September 1789 and married Francis Oakes, Chief Constable of Parramatta, on 17 January 1806. Her 14 children were among the earliest second generation Australians. Rebecca outlived her 'bold rough creature of a husband', as the local schoolmaster called him, by nearly 40 years, dying at Parramatta in 1883 at the age of 94.

## WHALE

to be caught in Australasian waters was landed at Sydney by Captain Thos Melville of the *Britannia* on 10 November 1791. 'The oil and head matter of this fish, he extolled as an extraordinary fine quality.'

## WHALER

built in Australia was the *King George*, built by James Underwood and launched at Sydney on 19 April 1805.

## WHALING STATION

was established at Ralph Bay, on the Derwent Estuary in Tasmania, by William Collins in 1806. Whales were then so numerous in the Derwent during the whaling season that the Hobart chaplain, 'Bobby' Knapwood, declared that he had to sail close to the shore line to avoid colliding with them.

## WHISKY

was imported into Australia by J. B. Were, who brought several puncheons of Murphy's Irish Whiskey with him when he arrived at Melbourne from England aboard the *William Metcalfe* on 15 November 1839.

*World water speed record being made by Ken Warby.*

## WHO'S WHO IN AUSTRALIA

was first published in Melbourne in 1922.

## WIDOWS' PENSIONS

in the world were introduced by the NSW Labor Government of Jack Lang with effect from 24 February 1926 at the rate of £1 for the widow and 10s for each child under the age of 14. There was a means test limiting eligibility to widows with incomes of less than £78 pa.

## WINDMILL

was in course of construction when Governor Hunter wrote to the Duke of Portland on 12 November 1796: 'We are also erecting on the high ground over Sydney a strong substantial and well-built windmill with a stone tower, which will last for two hundred years . . .' (Would that it had still been standing for the Bicentenary celebrations). The stonework was completed on 21 December and the windmill was in operation grinding wheat for the convicts by the following March. The convicts employed at the mill failed to demonstrate a proper sense of gratitude for the benefits conferred on them. As soon as the miller was absent one day, they stole the sails of the windmill.

## WINE

The earliest reference to Australian wine is contained in a letter from Captain Paterson, acting Governor, to Sir Joseph Banks dated 17 March 1795: 'Old Chiffer has made this year from a small vineyard (30 Rod) ninety Gallons of wine in about two years more I expect we will not want to purchase either wine or Brandy for common use, the vines I think produce better than at the Cape.' 'Old Chiffer' was most probably Philip Schaffer, the first German to settle in Australia, who had a farm 'on the Creek leading to Parramatta' where he had planted vines in 1791. A Hessian by birth, he had been a lieutenant in a corps of 'Yagers' in America before coming to Australia. Captain Tench said of him: 'He never was professionally, in any part of life, a farmer, but he told me, that his father owned a small estate on the banks of the Rhine, on which he resided, and that he had always been fond of looking at, and assisting in his labours, particularly in the vineyard.'

Wine was first produced on a commercial scale by Capt. John Macarthur, who started cultivating vines at Camden Park and on the Nepean in 1817 and within ten years was producing 20,000 gallons of wine annually. In the meantime the first shipment of wine overseas (London) had been made by Gregory Blaxland of Parramatta, whose red wine won the Gold Ceres Medal of the Society of Arts on 2 June 1828. The South Australian and Victorian wine industries both began in 1838. The oldest vineyard in Australia is Minchinbury, NSW, planted by Dr McKay in 1821.

*The first champagne made in Australia* was exhibited by the manufacturers, J. & T. Fallon, at their wine cellars in Albury, NSW, on 28 November 1875.

*The first wine sold in cardboard 'casks'* was marketed by Tolley's of Hope Valley, SA, in 1967.

## WIRELESS TRANSMISSION

was made by the Marconi Co. from Queenscliff, Vic, to Melbourne on 18 May 1901 as the Duke and Duchess of York entered Port Phillip Heads in the Royal Yacht.

*The first permanent wireless installation* was made by the Marconi Co. in mid-1903 to connect the Cape Moreton Lighthouse on Moreton Island, Queensland, with Brisbane.

*The first interstate wireless telegraphy service* was established by the Marconi Co. on 12 July 1906 between Queenscliff, Vic and Devonport, Tas.

*The first direct wireless message from Britain* was received by (Sir) Ernest Fisk at Wahroonga, near Sydney, from Carnarvon, Wales, on 22 September 1918.

See also Ship's Radio.

## WOMAN AIRLINE PILOT

was Debbie Wardley of Ansett, who made her maiden commercial flight co-piloting a Fokker Friendship from Alice Springs to Darwin on 22 January 1980.

## WOMAN ARCHITECT

was Florence Taylor, who gained her certificate in building construction, architecture and quantity surveying from the Sydney Technical College in 1903, having served her articles as an architect with E. S. Garton from 1899. She had designed 100 houses before she was 26 and later became chief draughtsman to John Buchan Clamp, diocesan architect for all Anglican church buildings in NSW.

# The first . . .

Fifty years after qualifying she was still active as editor of *Building, Lighting, Engineering, The Australasian Engineer* and *Construction* — all at the same time. Among her many distinctions was a world first nothing to do with architecture — in 1909 she became the first woman to pilot a glider.

## WOMAN ARTIST
known by name was Jane Elizabeth Currie, wife of the first postmaster of Western Australia, who painted a watercolour titled 'Our First Hut on Garden Island' in June 1829. A view of Cockburn Sound is believed to date from about the same time. Mrs Currie also executed a considerable number of studies of the wild life of Western Australia during the early 1830s.

*The first Australian-born woman artist to paint professionally* was Adelaide Ironside (1831-1867), daughter of a Sydney commission agent, who began 'a *siege* and a *battle*' to become an artist in Rome in 1856, working up to 18 hours a day. Her first major work was *The Pilgrim of Art, Crowned by the Genius of Art* of 1859 and subsequently William Wentworth and the Prince of Wales each purchased a painting for £500. Later in London she was a pupil of John Ruskin and they formed a deep relationship. He told her: 'I cannot separate the nonsense from the sense in you — there is a good deal of both'. She died in Rome at the age of 35 from tuberculosis.

*The first woman to win the Archibald Prize for Portraiture* was Nora Heysen in 1938 for her *Mme Elink Chuurman*.

## WOMAN DENTIST
was Mrs Hierons of Napier Street, South Melbourne, who was practising in 1884. She advertised that ladies 'would be visited at their own residences if preferred'. Her late husband, Dr Hierons, was also a dentist and it is likely that she learned dentistry by serving as his assistant, as there was no formal medical training of any kind available to women in Australia at this date. Australia's pioneer woman dentist preceded the first in Britain by some six years.

## WOMAN DOCTOR
was Dr Constance Stone, who was born in Hobart and studied medicine first at Philadelphia and then at Toronto, where she qualified in 1888, after being refused admission to the medical faculty of Melbourne University. She became the first woman to be registered as a medical practitioner in Australia on 7 February 1890 and entered private practice in Melbourne. Her sisters Mary and Clara (see below) also became doctors and all three were honorary medical officers of the Queen Victoria Memorial Hospital for Women and Children, Melbourne, established in 1896 as the first hospital in Australia run entirely by women.

*The first women doctors to qualify in Australia* were Margaret Whyte and Grace Clara Stone at the University of Melbourne Medical School in 1891; and Laura Margaret Fowler at the University of Adelaide the same year.

## WOMAN ELECTRICAL ENGINEER
was Florence Violet Wallace McKenzie, who graduated from Sydney Technical College in 1923 and set up a wireless shop in Royal Arcade, Sydney. She was the first Australian woman to be granted an amateur radio operator's licence (station VK 2FV); formed the electrical Association for Women; founded the Women's Emergency Signalling Corps in 1939; was instrumental in persuading the Royal Australian Navy to establish the WRANS in 1941; and was responsible for the training in communications of 12,000 servicemen during World War II. The day before she died aged 90 in 1982 she said: 'It is finished, and I have proved to them all that women can be as good or better than men.'

## WOMAN LAWYER
was Miss Greta Flos Matilda Greig, who was admitted to the degree of Bachelor of Laws at Melbourne University on 28 March 1903 and called to the Victorian Bar on 1 August 1905. A special Act of Parliament was needed for her to be eligible: the Legal Profession Practice Act of 1903, known in the profession as the 'Flos Greig Enabling Bill'. In neighbouring New South Wales, Ada Emily Evans had graduated from Sydney University Law School in 1902 but could not be called to the NSW bar until 1921, when she had completed her term as student-at-law after the passing of the Women's Legal Status Act of 1918.

*The first woman QC* was Roma Mitchell, who took silk at Adelaide on 20 September 1962.

*The first woman judge* was Roma Mitchell, appointed to the Supreme Court of South Australia on 23 September 1965, at a salary of

£4,800 pa. It was decreed that she should be addressed as 'Your Honour, Mr Justice Mitchell'.

## WOMAN MAGAZINE EDITOR

was Cora Anna Weekes, who began editing *The Spectator* in July 1858 shortly after her arrival in Sydney from California. She was assisted in the endeavour by 'an Association of Ladies'.

## WOMAN MINISTER OF RELIGION

in the British Commonwealth was Miss Martha Turner, who was born in England in 1839, educated at Dijon, where she 'early developed high intellectual qualities', and emigrated to Australia to join her brother Henry Gyles Turner in October 1870. Turner was a lay preacher at the Unitarian Church in Melbourne, and during a period in 1872 when the minister was absent on sick leave, was one of six men who volunteered to conduct the services. In a memoir he wrote: 'I preached my first sermon on the 11th February and four more before the end of the year. But the work was a great labour to me owing to my sincere self-criticism, and the limited time I could spare from my anxious business. Happily my sister came to my assistance, and with such general approval, that she was formally called upon to take the position permanently.'

The Rev. Higginson being unable to resume his duties, a special meeting of the congregation of the church was held on 26 October 1873, and Martha Turner was elected as their first permanent minister. On Sunday, 23 November Miss Turner gave her inaugural address on accepting the pastorate — for the second lesson she read 1 Cor. 14, in which occurs the verse (34): 'Let your women keep silence in the churches.'

Miss Turner solemnized her first marriage at the Unitarian Church, Grey Street, Melbourne on 2 November 1876. The couple joined in Holy Matrimony were Joseph Howgate, hotel-keeper, of 38 Swanston Street, Melbourne, and Adelaide Jeanette Wustermann of Shelley Street, Richmond.

Two years later Miss Turner was herself married to John Webster, and planned to resign her office, but the congregation persuaded her to continue and she did so until 1883, when she resigned in order to make a journey to England with her husband.

The only country with women clergymen prior to Australia was the USA, where the first, a Congregationalist, was ordained in 1853.

## WOMAN MINISTER OF THE CROWN

was Dame Florence Cardell-Oliver, who became Honorary Minister without Portfolio in Western Australia's Liberal-Country League government on 2 April 1947. She was subsequently Honorary Minister for Supply and Shipping (1948-9) and Minister for Health, Supply and Shipping (1949-53) in the McLarty coalition government.

***The first woman minister in the Commonwealth Government*** was Dame Enid Lyons, who became Vice-President of the Executive Council (with ministerial rank) in the Menzies-Fadden coalition government on 19 December 1949. She retired in 1951.

The first woman minister in the Commonwealth Government to head up a Department of State was Senator Dame Annabelle Rankin, who became Minister of Housing in Harold Holt's first ministry on 26 January 1966. She retired from office in 1971 to become High Commissioner to New Zealand.

## WOMEN MPs

The first country in the world to confer on women the right to stand for parliament was the self governing colony of South Australia by the Suffrage Act which received assent on 9 February 1895. The only other country with women's suffrage at this date, New Zealand, did not admit women MPs. Ironically the measure was tacked on to the Suffrage Bill by its opponents in an effort at wrecking — it was thought that such an unlikey prospect as women in parliament would cause the whole Bill to be rejected — but to their chagrin the bill was passed in its entirety. Even more ironically, South Australia was the last State in the Commonwealth to actually elect a woman MP.

***The first woman to be elected to parliament*** was Mrs Edith Cowan, who won West Perth from the Western Australian Attorney-General Tom Draper in WA's General Election of 12 March 1921. She stood as a representative of the National League of Western Australia. The other States elected their woman MP as follows: NSW — 1929; Queensland — 1929; Victoria — 1933; Tasmania — 1948; South Australia — 1959.

***The first Labor woman MP*** was May Holman, who succeeded her father as the representative for Forrest, WA, in a by-

# The first . . .

election to the State Parliament on 3 April 1925. When she died in 1939 she was herself succeeded by her brother Edward Holman.

**The first Women MPs in the Commonwealth Parliament** were Miss Dorothy Tangney, who was elected as a Senator for Western Australia, and Dame Enid Lyons, who was elected a member of the House of Representatives for Darwin, both in the General Election of 21 August 1943.

## WOMAN NEWSPAPER EDITOR

was Elizabeth Macfarrell, Government Printer of Western Australia, who edited the *Perth Gazette* 1846-1847. Her husband, whom she succeeded as editor on his death, had founded the paper in 1833.

## WOMAN PILOT

See Aeroplane pilot.

## WOMAN SCULPTOR

was English-born Margaret Thomas of Melbourne, who exhibited a portrait bust of Sir Redmond Barry at the first exhibition of the Victorian Society of Fine Arts in 1857.

**The first Australian-born woman sculptor**

was Thea Cowan (1868-1949), who was trained in Florence and returned to Sydney in 1895 aware 'that there is a good deal of prejudice here against a woman sculptor'. Early works executed in Australia included portrait busts of premiers Sir Henry Parkes and Sir Edmund Barton and a bas-relief panel for Mr F. White's house at Armidale commemorating a family tragedy in which one sister lost her life to save another from drowning.

## WOMAN TO SERVE IN THE AUSTRALIAN FORCES

was Lady W. I. E. MacKenzie, MB, BS, who was commissioned into the Australian Army Medical Corps as Deputy Assistant Director-General of Medical Services on 25 September 1940. Confusingly she had three titles — Major, Dr and Lady.

**The first of the women's services** was the Women's Auxiliary Australian Air Force, whose nucleus was the 37 teleprinter operators and telegraphists who reported for duty on 15 March 1941 at No I Training Depot, Malvern, Vic. They were paid two thirds of the money earned by RAAF men in the same trade groups. By 1944 their number had swelled to 18,038.

Enrolment for the Women's Royal Australian Naval Service began on 28 April 1941.

*Woolworths opened their first store in this Sydney basement.*

Woolworths

The Australian Women's Army Service and the Australian Army Medical Women's Service were both established in 1942.

**The first servicewomen to serve overseas** were 500 AWAS who took up signals and clerical duties in New Guinea early in 1945. (NB: During World War I, 2030 Australian nurses served overseas, but were classified as civilians.)

**The first woman to join the Royal Australian Navy** (as opposed to the WRANS) was dental student Erica Jean Yates, who entered as a midshipman on 8 March 1977.

## WOMAN TO MAKE A SPEECH IN PUBLIC

was Mrs Delgarno, wife of a ship's captain, who spoke from the platform at the first annual meeting of the Melbourne Total Abstinence Society in 1842.

## WOMAN SERGEANT-AT-ARMS

of the Federal Parliament was Lyn Simmons, appointed 21 February 1985.

## WOMAN SPEAKER OF THE HOUSE OF REPRESENTATIVES

was Labor MHR and ex-factory worker Mrs Joan Child, who presided over the House for the first time on 11 February 1986.

## WOMAN UNION LEADER

of a mixed union was mother-of-two Mrs Diana Sonenberg, who became Victorian secretary of the Australian Insurance Staffs Federation on 21 June 1968. She was responsible for 4,000 members.

## WOMAN TO WEAR TROUSERS

in Australia was Miss Alice Leamar of London's Gaiety Theatre Company, who outraged convention with a baggy pantsuit sported for the first time in Sydney in December 1895.

## WOOLWORTHS

The first branch of Woolworths Stupendous Bargain Basement opened in a basement of the Imperial Arcade, between Pitt Street and Castlereagh Street, Sydney, on 5 December 1924. Then as now Woolworths had no connection with the chain stores of the same name in the USA and Britain. The founders of the Australian chain were astute enough to take advantage of the fact that F. W. Woolworth had never registered the name Woolworth in Australia.

## WORKMEN'S COMPENSATION

for industrial injuries was introduced under statute by Western Australia in 1894.

## WRAPPED BREAD

was raisin bread baked by the Victorial Railways bakery in Melbourne in 1925 for supply to their station refreshment rooms. Some 600 wrapped loaves a day were produced, consuming two tons of raisins a month. By 1928 three Sydney bakers were offering wrapped bread, despite the fact that the master bakers had denounced the practice on the grounds of cost, uncertainty of hygienic benefit, total lack of public demand and the prospect of its 'forcing trade into the hands of monopolies'.

## X-RAY

was made by Sir Thomas Ranken, Professor of Natural Philosophy at the University of Melbourne, on 3 March 1896. The technique had been discovered the previous November by Wilhelm Röntgen of Wurzburg, Germany.

**The first clinical use of X-Rays in surgery** took place at Melbourne Hospital in June 1896, when Prof. T. R. Lyle located a needle that had been embedded in a patient's hand.

**Radiation in the treatment of cancer** using X-Rays, was pioneered by Dr Clever Woods at Albury, NSW, in October 1896.

# The first . . .

### YACHT

registered in Australia was a three-tonner with gunter sails acquired by pioneer Sydney merchant Robert Campbell in or before 1827 and which he moored at Campbell's Wharf on Sydney Cove.

### YACHT CLUB

was the Australian Aquatic Racing Club, founded by Captain Barkus, proprietor of the *Australian Hotel*, Sydney, at a meeting held at his premises on 15 February 1830. The first races under the auspices of the club were held from Dawes' Battery round the Sow and Pigs on the Saturday after Easter.

### YACHT RACING

probably began in 1824, the year that the *Hobart Town Gazette* makes passing reference to a regatta of sorts, though no details are given. Scarcely more is known about the regatta held on the Derwent River on 5 January 1827. The first of which any details survive took place on Sydney Harbour on 28 April 1828, and this definitely included one yacht race. It was sailed over a course from Sydney Cove, around the Sow and Pigs and back and won by Lieutenant Preston's *Black Swan*. The other competitors are unrecorded, but were probably also Royal Naval officers, as the regatta had been organ-

Roger Garwood

Australia II, *skippered by John Bertrand, was the first non-American yacht to take the America's Cup.*

ised by the captains of two warships in port, HMS *Success* (Captain Stirling) and HMS *Rainbow* (Captain H. J. Rous). The prize was a purse of 50 Spanish dollars, worth £12 10s. The other events in the regatta were rowing races.

**The first ocean race** was held over a 28 nautical mile course from Sydney Harbour to Botany Bay and back on 26 January 1861. Sydney Yacht Club, the organisers of the race, put up the very considerable sum of £300 as a first prize (worth many thousands in today's currency) and this was won by the dock master Captain J. S. Rountree in his 15 ton *Annie Ogle*, which was named after his daughter. The gallant captain was modest enough to attribute his victory on handicap to good fortune and generous enough to divide £100 of his prize among the crew and donated the remainder to charity.

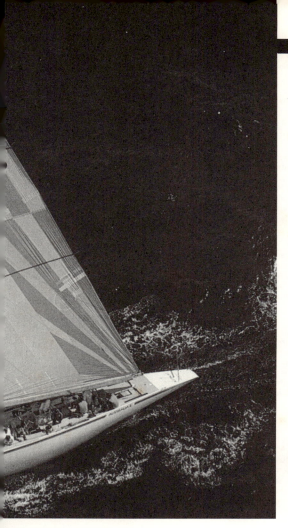

The first Sydney-Hobart race started on 26 December 1945 and was won by the British vessel *Rani* under the captaincy of Capt. J. Illingworth in 6 days, 14 hours and 22 minutes. *Rani* was so far ahead of her competitors that search planes, sent out after a bouncing southerly gale had wreaked chaos amongst the nine vessels, did not travel far enough south to locate her and it was feared in the newspapers that she had sunk.

Australia made its **first challenge in the America's Cup** in 1962, being only the fourth nation to do so in the 111 years of the event's history. Australia's 12 metre sloop *Gretel*, owned by Sir Frank Packer, was defeated by Henry Mercer's *Weatherly* (USA) by four races to one in the best of seven series which began on 9 September 1962.

Australia became the first country to wrest the America's Cup from the Americans when Alan Bond's *Australia* II, skippered by John Bertrand, defeated *Liberty* in the deciding race at Newport, R I, on 26 September 1983.

## YMCA

branch was founded at Adelaide in 1850, six years after the organization was first established in England. Australia's first YWCA was opened in Geelong, Vic, in 1872.

**The first long distance ocean race** was sailed from Sydney to Newcastle and back, a distance of 140 nm, for a purse of 250 gold sovereigns in 1864. Charles Parbury's Sydney-built 30 ton cutter *Xarifa* trounced William Walker's English-built 70 ton iron hulled schooner *Chance*, crossing the line four hours ahead of her much more favoured rival.

**The first international yacht races in which Australia competed** were held in September 1898 between Mr Mark Foy's 22 footer *Irex*, out of Sydney, and the English 24 ft vessel *Maid of Kent*. The contest was held in England on the River Medway and consisted of three races over a 12 mile course. The English roundly defeated their challengers by 10 mins 53 secs, 3 mins 25 secs, and 22 mins, a drubbing for the Australians that was made no more palatable by the fact that *Maid of Kent* was skippered by a woman no less, Mrs Maud Wyllie — albeit she was one of the skilfull helmsmen on the Medway.

## ZOO

was established in Hyde Park, Sydney, as an adjunct to the Australian Museum in 1848.

The first open zoo was the 300 ha Western Plains Zoo at Dubbo, NSW, opened in February 1977.

# CHRONOLOGY

## CHRONOLOGY

**1788**
| | |
|---|---|
| 18 Jan | European inhabitants |
| 21 Jan | Christening *Botany Bay*, NSW |
| 26 Jan | Settlement *Sydney* |
| 26 Jan | White Australian born *Port Jackson* |
| 28 Jan | Magistrate *Sydney* |
| 29 Jan | Garden *Sydney* |
| 30 Jan | Hospital *Sydney* |
| 1 Feb | Farm *Port Jackson*, NSW |
| 3 Feb | Church service *Sydney* |
| 7 Feb | Band performance *Sydney* |
| 10 Feb | Wedding *Sydney* |
| 11 Feb | Criminal court *Sydney* |
| 18 Feb | Dental operation *Sydney* |
| 19 Feb | Magistrate's court *Sydney* |
| 21 Feb | Free settler *Sydney* |
| 27 Feb | Brick manufacture *Sydney* |
| 27 Feb | Execution *Sydney* |
| Feb | Bridge *Sydney* |
| Feb | Vegetables cultivated *Sydney* |
| 15 May | Brick dwelling house *Sydney* |
| May | Buildings (permanent) *Sydney* |
| 4 June | Banquet *Sydney* |
| 1 July | Civil court *Sydney* |
| 12 July | Cemetery *Sydney* |
| July | Observatory (permanent) *Sydney* |
| 12 Aug | Duel *Sydney* |
| Sept | Road *Sydney* |
| 14 Dec | Coroner's court *Sydney* |
| | Pottery *Sydney* |

**1789**
| | |
|---|---|
| Feb | Barracks *Sydney* |
| 8 May | Piano *Sydney* |
| 4 June | Play performed *Sydney* |
| 7 July | Police force *Sydney* |
| 5 Oct | Boat *Sydney* |
| 17 Oct | Foster child *Sydney* |
| 21 Nov | Farm (private) *Parramatta*, NSW |
| | School *Sydney* |
| | Vineyard *Parramatta*, NSW |

**1790**
| | |
|---|---|
| May | Salt production *Sydney* |
| June | French settler *Sydney* |

**1791**
| | |
|---|---|
| 31 Oct | Suicide *Sydney* |
| 10 Nov | Whale caught in Australian waters |
| 3 Dec | Apples *Parramatta*, NSW |
| 16 Dec | Doctor to settle in Australia *Sydney* |

**1792**
| | |
|---|---|
| Feb | Shop *Sydney* |
| April | Market *Parramatta*, NSW |
| Oct | Licensed premises *Sydney* |

| | |
|---|---|
| 1 Nov | Americans to visit Australia *Sydney* |
| 24 Nov | Play set in Australia [*Paris*] |

**1793**
| | |
|---|---|
| 16 Jan | Government assisted immigrants |
| 25 Aug | Church *Sydney* |
| Dec | Distillery *Parramatta*, NSW |
| | Ferry Service (regular) *Sydney-Parramatta* |
| | Society *Sydney* |

**1794**
| | |
|---|---|
| 5 Jan | Murder *Parramatta*, NSW |
| July | Prison *Sydney* |
| 8 Dec | Auction *Concord*, NSW |
| | Highway *Sydney-Parramatta* |
| | Oil painting *Sydney* |

**1795**
| | |
|---|---|
| 23 March | Export cargo *Hawkesbury*, NSW |
| March | Australian wine *Parramatta*, NSW |
| Aug | Plough *Parramatta*, NSW |
| | Carriage *Parramatta*, NSW |
| | Printing *Sydney* |

**1796**
| | |
|---|---|
| 16 Jan | Theatre *Sydney* |
| May | Coal discovered *Port Stephens*, NSW |
| June | Court House *Sydney* |
| 23rd July | Advertisement *Sydney* |
| 21 Dec | Windmill *Sydney* |
| | Beer production *Sydney* |
| | Public houses *Sydney* and *Parramatta* |
| | Road bridge *Duck River*, NSW |
| | Soap manufacture *Sydney* |

**1797**
| | |
|---|---|
| | Merino sheep *Parramatta*, NSW |
| | Military hospital *Sydney* |
| | Platypus, first sighting *Hawkesbury*, NSW |

**1798**
| | |
|---|---|
| 31 Jan | Public clock *Sydney* |
| 18 May | Lawyer *Sydney* |
| 19 Sept | Bush pubs *Eastern Boundary* and *East Plain*, NSW |
| 19 Sept | Auctioneer (licensed) *Sydney* |
| 15 Dec | Custody order *Sydney* |
| Dec | Elections *Sydney* |
| | Koala, sighting of *Mittagong*, NSW |
| | Military Hospital |

**1799**
| | |
|---|---|
| 1 June | Textiles woven in Australia *Sydney* |
| Aug | Coal exported *Hunter River*, NSW |

**1800**
| | |
|---|---|
| 3 Jan | Ladies' fashions imported *Sydney* |
| Jan | Taxes *New South Wales* |
| 6 Sept | Military forces raised in Australia *Sydney* and *Parramatta* |
| Sept | Racehorse *Sydney* |
| 10 Oct | Shipping dues *Sydney* |
| 27 Oct | Licensing hours *New South Wales* |
| Oct | Textile mill *Sydney* |
| | Citrus fruits grown commercially *Parramatta*, NSW |
| | Furniture making (recorded) *Sydney* |
| | Hotel (residential) *Parramatta*, NSW |
| | Masonic lodge *Norfolk Island* |

**1801**
| | |
|---|---|
| June | Coal mine *Newcastle*, NSW |
| 8 Aug | Orphanage *Sydney* |
| | Doctor to qualify in Australia *Sydney* |
| | Factory *Sydney* |
| | Ship built in Australia *Sydney* |

**1802**
| | |
|---|---|
| 17 Sept | Freemason admitted *Sydney* |
| 31 Oct | Town map [*Paris*] |
| | Book *Sydney* |

**1803**
| | |
|---|---|
| 5 Mar | Newspaper *Sydney* |
| 5 Mar | Newspaper advertisement *Sydney* |
| April | Boxing match *Sydney* |
| 7 May | Roman Catholic wedding *Sydney* |
| 15 May | Roman Catholic mass *Sydney* |
| May | Jeweller *Sydney* |
| 8 May | Stationer *Sydney* |
| 6 June | Restaurant *Sydney* |
| Aug | Accountant *Sydney* |
| 12 Oct | Numbering of houses *Sydney* |
| Dec | Cricket match *Sydney* |
| | Shark attack, fatal *Hamelin Harbour*, WA |
| | Solicitor *Sydney* |
| | Tannery *Sydney* |

**1804**
| | |
|---|---|
| 4 Mar | Poem published *Sydney* |
| 27 Mar | Stone bridge *Sydney* |
| 6 May | Vaccination *Sydney* |
| 2 June | Stud *Sydney* |
| June | Children's entertainment *Sydney* |
| 29 July | Poem with Australian subject matter *Sydney* |
| 19 Aug | Boarding school *Parramatta*, NSW |
| Sept | Letter box *Sydney* |

| | | | | | |
|---|---|---|---|---|---|
| 1 Oct | School, purpose-built *Windsor, NSW* | | Art school *Sydney* | | Book of poetry *Sydney* |
| 14 Oct | Medical treatise *Sydney* | | Autobiography *Newcastle* | | Wine, commercial |
| | Cabinet maker *Sydney* | | Soldier, Australian-born | | production *Camden, NSW* |
| | Engravings *Sydney* | **1813** | | | |
| | Hops *Ryde, NSW* | 11 Mar | Cattle fair *Parramatta, NSW* | **1820** | |

**1805**

**1813**

**1820**

| | | | | | |
|---|---|---|---|---|---|
| 19 April | Whaler, Australian-built *Sydney* | 8 May | Charity founded *Sydney* | Jan | Schoolmaster, Australian-born *Sydney* |
| | | May | Sunday school *Parramatta, NSW* | 15 Aug | Driving on left enforced *New South Wales* |
| **1806** | | July | Cargo of mixed goods exported *Sydney* | | Jewish worship *Sydney* |
| 1 Jan | Book published commercially *Sydney* | 16 Aug | Race-card *Sydney* | | Pharmacist *Sydney* |
| 5 Jan | Triplets *Sydney* | 24 Dec | Architect's plan *Sydney* | | Silverware, Australian-made *Sydney* |
| 22 Sept | Bride, Australian-born *Parramatta, NSW* | | Coins bearing Australian inscription | | |
| 17 Nov | Evening classes *Sydney* | | Engravings published Aus *Sydney* | **1821** | |
| | Beer brewed from hops *Ryde, NSW* | | Illustrated book *Sydney* | 8 Mar | Stage coach *Sydney-Parramatta* |
| | Whaling station *Ralph Bay, Tas* | | Schoolteacher, Australian born *Sydney* | May | Magazine *Sydney* |
| | | | | 27 June | Learned society *Sydney* |
| **1807** | | **1814** | | Dec | Jewish free settler *Sydney* |
| 1 Feb | Furnished lodgings *Sydney* | 7 Jan | Prize fight *Sydney* | | Church choir *Hobart* |
| Feb | Naval officer, Australian-born | May | Portrait painting *Sydney* | | Flush lavatory *Sydney* |
| 29 May | Peal of church bells *Sydney* | 1 Oct | Freight carrier (scheduled service) *Sydney-Richmond* | | Hymn book *Sydney* |
| 25 June | Firework display *Sydney* | | | | Lithography *Parramatta, NSW* |
| | Salt-works *Newington, NSW* | **1815** | | | Orchestra *Hobart* |
| | Town map (published Aus) *Sydney* | 18 Jan | School for Aboriginals *Parramatta, NSW* | | |
| | Wool exported | 27 Jan | Clockmaker *Sydney* | **1822** | |
| | | 29 May | Steam engine *Cockle Bay, NSW* | Jan | Agricultural society *Tasmania* |
| 1808 | Girls' boarding school *Sydney* | 10 June | 'Australians' used to describe native born | Jan | Fire engine *Sydney* |
| | | 15 Aug | Methodist minister *Sydney* | 22 July | Solicitor to qualify in Aus *Sydney* |
| **1809** | | | Aborigines' reservation *George's Head, NSW* | July | Pottery figurine *Sydney* |
| 25 April | Post office *Sydney* | | General practitioner *Sydney* | | Roman Catholic school *Sydney* |
| 16 July | Fiction published Aus *Sydney* | | | | Sugar production *Port Macquarie, NSW* |
| Aug | Church, stone-built *Sydney* | **1816** | | | |
| | Billiards *Sydney* | 16 Mar | Methodist worship *Sydney* | **1823** | |
| | Dressmaker *Sydney* | Oct | Insurance agent *Sydney* | 15 Feb | Gold discovery *Bathurst, NSW* |
| | | Oct | Mail service between towns *Hobart-Launceston* | May | Presbyterian minister *Sydney* |
| **1810** | | | Botanic gardens *Sydney* | | Book of verse by Australian-born poet [London] |
| Jan | School book *Sydney* | | | | Doctor, Australian born |
| 22 Mar | Public school *Parramatta, NSW* | **1817** | | | Iron foundry *Sydney* |
| 23 April | Fair *Sydney* | 8 April | Bank *Sydney* | | |
| 30 April | Race meeting *Parramatta, NSW* | 8 April | Banknotes *Sydney* | **1824** | |
| 11 Aug | Planning permission *Sydney* | 7 Oct | Methodist chapel *Castlereagh, NSW* | 20 Feb | Australian boxer to defeat overseas opponent *Windsor, NSW* |
| Aug | Congregational service *Sydney* | 16 Dec | Lighthouse *Port Jackson, NSW* | July | Distillery (commercially operated) *Sydney* |
| 6 Oct | Coroner *Sydney* | 21 Dec | Name 'Australia' used officially | 11 Aug | Parliament *Sydney* |
| 6 Oct | Public park *Sydney* | | Sydney Harbour ferry | 10 Sept | Barristers *Sydney* |
| 15 Oct | Running races *Sydney* | | | 28 Sept | Act of Parliament *Sydney* |
| 17 Oct | Public ball *Sydney* | **1818** | | 7 Oct | Agricultural show *Parramatta, NSW* |
| 19 Oct | Australian song performed *Sydney* | April | Paper manufacture *Sydney* | 2 Nov | Trial by jury *Sydney* |
| | | | American to open a business in Aus *Sydney* | 16 Dec | Infant school *Sydney* |
| **1811** | | | Biography published *Hobart* | | Australian to receive official appointment overseas [London] |
| 1 Jan | Police officers, salaried *Sydney* | | Dentists *Sydney* | | Gin *Sydney* |
| 10 April | Toll road *Sydney-Parramatta* | **1819** | | | Music shop *Sydney* |
| June | Hat manufacture *Sydney* | 1 Jan | Orphanage, boys' *Parramatta, NSW* | | Stage coach, long-distance *Sydney-Bathurst* |
| 19 Aug | Rowing race *Sydney* | 17 June | Savings bank *Sydney* | | |
| Nov | Hunt *Nepean River, NSW* | 31 May | Sporting trophy (annual) *Sydney* | **1825** | |
| | | | Book by Australian-born author [London] | 5 Jan | Country newspaper *Launceston, Tas* |
| **1812** | | | | | |
| May | Glass manufacture *Sydney* | | | | |

5 July — Naturalization of foreign settler *Sydney*
19 Nov — Grammar school *Sydney*
Dam *Mount Gilead, NSW*
Hairdresser (known) *Parramatta, NSW*
Literature, full-length work *Sydney*
Music composed in Aus *Sydney*
Organ *Hobart*

## 1826
7 Mar — Library open to public *Sydney*
7 June — Concert *Sydney*
19 July — Gas lighting *Sydney*
July — Presbyterian church *Sydney*
Book of verse by Australian-born poet published Aus *Sydney*
Chamber of Commerce *Sydney*
Colour printing *Sydney*
Cricket club *Sydney*
Lithographs published *Sydney*

## 1827
10 Feb — Life assurance *Sydney*
20 April — Copper discovered *Macquarie Harbour, Tas*
Iron rails *Newcastle, NSW*
Yacht *Sydney*

## 1828
1 Jan — Book reviews *Sydney*
7 April — Street lamps *Sydney*
21 April — Auction catalogue (known) *Sydney*
28 April — Yacht race (recorded) *Sydney*
Aug — Ploughing match *Bong Bong, NSW*
13 Sept — Bank robbery *Sydney*
Census *New South Wales* and *Tas*
Hymn book, Anglican *Sydney*
Hymn book, Roman Catholic *Sydney*
Jewish marriage *Sydney*
Maps, printed *Sydney*
Postman *Sydney*
Apples exported *Sydney*

## 1829
June — Woman artist *Perth*
July — Football *Sydney*
17 Aug — Circuit court *Maitland, NSW*
20 Aug — Public concert *Sydney*
28 Aug — Greeks *Sydney*
29 Sept — Gunpowder *Sydney*
Bookshop *Sydney*
Statistical yearbook *Sydney*
Technical school *Hobart*

## 1830
Jan — Literary society *Perth*
15 Feb — Yacht club *Sydney*
15 Nov — Cab *Sydney*
Dental treatise *Sydney*
Friendly society *Sydney*
Museum *Sydney*

Novel published *Hobart*
Rabbi *Sydney*
Stud farm (racehorses) *Sydney*
Swimming pool *Sydney*

## 1831
31 Jan — Insurance company *Sydney*
24 April — Baptist service *Sydney*
17 June — Steamship *Port Jackson, NSW*
23 July — Steamship, Australian-built *Neutral Bay, NSW*
31 July — Migrant ship *Sydney*
Post office letter boxes *Sydney*
Sculpture *Bothwell, Tas*
Synagogue *Sydney*

## 1832
12 Feb — Quaker meeting *Hobart*
Cricket: overarm bowling *Sydney*
Woman novelist *Hobart*
Piano manufacture *Sydney*
Steeplechase *Coogee, NSW*

## 1833
15 Feb — Congregational chapel *Sydney*
1 Mar — Illustrated magazine *Hobart*
1 Mar — Short stories written and published in Aus *Hobart*
23 July — Fire insurance *Sydney* and *Hobart*
5 Oct — Theatre, professional *Sydney*
Bathroom *Camden, NSW*
Dancing school *Sydney*
Gymnastics *Sydney*
Police force, uniformed *Sydney*
Shop with plate glass windows *Sydney*
Trade union *Sydney*

## 1834
6 May — Temperance society *Sydney*
29 May — Play written and performed in Aus *Hobart*
1 Sept — School magazine *Sydney*
4 Sept — Opera *Sydney*
1 Dec — Baptist minister *Sydney*
Dec — Teacher training college *Sydney*
Woman to be naturalized in Aus *Sydney*
Wool auctions *Sydney*

## 1835
17 Jan — Ballet *Sydney*
17 Feb — Hunt (regularly established) *Sydney*
Feb — Play by Australian-born playwright *Sydney*
May — School cricket match *Sydney*
June — Agricultural journal *Sydney*
13 Sept — Roman Catholic bishop *Sydney*
1 Nov — Quaker meeting house *Sydney*
28 Nov — Baptist chapel *Sydney*
Law book *Sydney*
Newspaper cartoons *Launceston, Tas*

## 1836
5 Jan — Fire and life insurance company *Sydney*
Mar — Music school *Sydney*
9 May — Roman Catholic priest ordained in Aus *Sydney*
5 June — Anglican bishop *Sydney*
28 June — Snowfall (recorded)
29 June — Cathedral *Sydney*
28 Dec — Olive tree *Adelaide*
Aboriginal newspaper *Flinders Is*
American firm to open Australian branch *Sydney*
Bus *Sydney*
Diaries *Sydney*
Music composed by Australian-born composer *Sydney*
Sculpture: portrait bust *Sydney*

## 1837
June — Aqueduct *Sydney*
1 July — Railway *Norfolk Bay-Long Bay, Tas*
Cattle drive *Murray River-Port Phillip, Vic.*
Fire brigade *Sydney*

## 1838
1 Jan — Building regulations *Sydney*
2 Jan — Sydney-Melbourne mail service.
26 Jan — Australia Day (public holiday)
31 Jan — Music festival *Sydney*
19 Sept — Flower show *Sydney*
1 Nov — *Prepaid postage *Sydney*
25 Nov — Lutheran service *Port Adelaide, SA*
30 Dec — Nuns *Sydney*
Gardening book *Hobart*
Geological map *Sydney*
Municipal government *Perth*
Novel by woman writer published in Aus *Sydney*
Police force, native *Dandenong, Vic*
Postmistress *Cassilis, NSW*
Public Health Office *Sydney*
Shorthand *Adelaide*
Street paving *Sydney*

## 1839
15 Jan — American consul *Sydney*
15 Nov — Whisky imported *Melbourne*
Nurses, trained *Parramatta, NSW*
Prickly Pear *Scone, NSW*

## 1840
8 Jan — Trade union to call a strike *Sydney*
15 Feb — Ascent of Mount Kosciusko
19 Aug — City (legally incorporated) *Adelaide*
1 Oct — Daily newspaper *Sydney*
31 Oct — Mayor *Adelaide*
31 Oct — Municipal elections *Adelaide*
Oct — Archery club *Port Melbourne, Vic*
Oct — Camel *Port Adelaide, SA*

| | | | | | |
|---|---|---|---|---|---|
| Nov | Archery tournament *Port Melbourne, Vic* | 8 Sept | RC bishop consecrated in Aus *Adelaide* | Dec (?) | Gold nugget found *Daisy Hill, Vic* |
| 1 Dec | Steamship, sea-going *Sydney-Melbourne* | 26 Nov | Bowling green *Hobart* Sculpture: full-length figure *Sydney* | | Opals discovered *Angaston, SA* |
| Dec | Trade union closed shop *Sydney* | | Society granted prefix 'Royal' *Hobart* | **1850** | |
| | Book of verse by woman poet *Sydney* | | Trade surplus | 1 Jan | Postage stamps, adhesive *New South Wales* and *Victoria* |
| | Chess club *Sydney* | | | | Biscuit factory *Adelaide* |
| | Flush lavatory in private home *Maitland, NSW* | **1845** | | | *Brick veneer *Swan Hill, Vic* Geological map of Australia |
| | Medical text book *Sydney* | 1 Jan | Century scored in cricket match (recorded) *Melbourne* | | *Refrigeration plant *Rodey Point, Vic* |
| | Organ, Australian-built *Windsor, NSW* | 6 Jan | Art exhibition *Hobart* | | War memorial *Hobart* |
| | | Feb | Exhibition of sculpture *Sydney* | | YMCA *Adelaide* |
| **1841** | | 15 Sept | Play by Australian-born playwright performed *Melbourne* | **1851** | |
| 13 May | Photograph *Sydney* | | | 24 May | Gold prospector's licence *Bathurst, NSW* |
| 24 May | Gas supply, public *Sydney* | 25 Sept | Romantic ballet *Melbourne* | 3 Dec | Mormons *Sydney* |
| 7 July | Trans-Australian crossing | 10 Nov | Bowls club *Surry Hills, NSW* | | Olive oil *Adelaide* |
| Oct | Orchestral music composed in Aus *Sydney* | | Brass band *Launceston, Tas* | | Screw-driven steamship, Australian-built *Melbourne* |
| | Children's book *Sydney* | | Foxes *Upper Werribee, Vic* | | |
| | Mineral exports *Adelaide* | | School text book (full-length) *Hobart* | **1852** | |
| | Racing classic *Homebush, NSW* | | Short stories, collection of *Sydney* | 3 Aug | Liner to arrive Aus *Sydney* |
| | Sugar refinery *Canterbury, NSW* | | | 25 Sept | Money order *Tasmania* |
| | | **1846** | | 11 Oct | University *Sydney* |
| **1842** | | 17 Jan | Convent *Perth* | Nov | Coins minted in Aus *Adelaide* |
| 26 Jan | Circus *Sydney* | 26 Jan | Convent school *Perth* | | *Eucalyptus oil *Dandenong, Vic* |
| 9 April | Roman Catholic archbishop *Sydney* | 14 Feb | Swimming race *Sydney* | | Stockbroker *Sydney* |
| 11 April | Statue *Sydney* | Mar | Wine exported | | |
| 16 April | Bus service *Sydney* | 24 May | Art gallery *Hobart* | **1853** | |
| 4 May | Drag artiste *Sydney* | May | Song book *Sydney* | 30 Jan | Cobb & Co coach service *Melbourne-Castlemaine* |
| 27 May | Jewish periodical *Sydney* | 1 Aug | Medical journal *Sydney* | Feb | Iron steamship, Australian-built *Sydney* |
| Aug | Vehicular ferry *Sydney* | 30 Sept | Canned food *Sydney* | | |
| 12 Dec | Photographic studio *Sydney* | Dec | Theological college *Sydney* | Aug | Newspaper printed on power presses *Sydney* |
| | Country house lit by gas *Mulgra, NSW* | | Maths text book for schools *Hobart* | 30 Oct | Unitarian church *Sydney* |
| | Rifle club *Sydney* | | Woman newspaper editor *Perth* | | Billiard tables, Australian-made *Melbourne* |
| | Scientific journal *Hobart* | | | | Manly ferry |
| | Type foundry *Sydney* | **1847** | | | Novel by Australian-born writer [*London*] |
| | Woman to make a speech in public *Melbourne* | 3 Feb | Art exhibition: one man show *Adelaide* | | |
| | | 3 May | Opera, Australian *Sydney* | **1854** | |
| **1843** | | 7 June | Anaesthetic *Launceston, Tas* | Feb | Cotton exported *Brisbane* |
| 11 Mar | Tin discovered *Beechworth, Vic* | | Art society *Sydney* | 3 Mar | Electric telegraph *Melbourne-Williamstown* |
| 17 May | Warship, Australian-built *Port Arthur, Tas* | | Canning factory *Newcastle, NSW* | 13 Mar | Telegrams *Melbourne* |
| June | Italian opera *Sydney* | | Golf course *Melbourne* | 12 Sept | Steam railway *Melbourne* |
| 2 Aug | Elected parliament *Sydney* | | Medical insurance *Hobart* | Nov | Play by woman playwright written and performed in Aus *Ballarat, Vic* |
| 24 Aug | Monastery *Sydney* | | Photographer, Australian-born *Hobart* | | |
| Nov | Stripper harvesting machine *Adelaide* | | | | Steel production *Sydney* |
| | Atlas *Sydney* | **1848** | | | Town Hall *Melbourne* |
| | Branded product to be advertised regularly | 6 Jan | Foreign language newspaper *Adelaide* | | |
| | Unemployment figures *Sydney* | 2 Oct | Evening newspaper *Sydney* | **1855** | |
| | | | Gazetteer *Sydney* | 4 April | Warship built in Australia for home defence *Sydney* |
| **1844** | | | Iron produced from Australian ore *Mittagong, NSW* | 14 May | Mint *Sydney* |
| 1 Jan | Bowls *Hobart* | | Police detectives *Melbourne* | 15 May | Overseas exhibition of Australian art [*Paris*] |
| 8 Jan | Copper mine *Kapunda, SA* | | Zoo *Sydney* | 26 Sept | State-owned railway *Sydney* |
| 2 Mar | Working class newspaper *Sydney/Parramatta* | | | Sept | Eight hour day *Sydney* |
| 2 April | Synagogue, purpose-built *Sydney* | **1849** | | 28 Nov | Premier *Victoria* |
| 30 May | Operetta, Australian *Sydney* | Jan | Lottery *Sydney* | | Advertising agency *Victoria* |
| 1 June | Woman's magazine *Sydney* | 2 Feb | Convent *Parramatta, NSW* | | Australian to attain flag rank in Royal Navy |
| 11 June | Scheduled mail service to UK | 17 June | Sunday newspaper *Sydney* | | Eisteddfod *Ballarat, Vic* |
| 21 Aug | Fancy dress ball *Sydney* | 21 July | Clipper ship to arrive Aus *Sydney* | | Opera House *Sydney* |
| | | | | | Patents *Victoria* |

Publishing house *Melbourne*
Roadside letter boxes *Sydney*

## 1856

| | |
|---|---|
| 11 Feb | Public li|
| 12 Mar | Knighthood conferred on Australian |
| 19 Mar | *Vote by ballot *Victoria* |
| 26 Mar | Inter-State cricket match *Melbourne* |
| 30 April | Legislative Assembly elections *New South Wales* |
| 22 May | Parliament under responsible government *Sydney* |
| 31 May | Naval vessel, Australian *Melbourne* |
| 24 June | Votes for all adult males *South Australia* |
| 2 Aug | Joke cartoon *Melbourne* |
| 19 Aug | Maternity hospital *Melbourne* |
| | Weather bureau *Adelaide* |
| | Woman artist, Australian-born [*Rome*] |
| Nov | Hansard *Victoria* |

## 1857

| | |
|---|---|
| 10 Mar | Elections under universal suffrage *South Australia* |
| 31 Dec | Children's book, illustrated *Sydney* |
| | Dam, masonry *Melbourne* |
| | Novel by Australian-born woman writer |
| | Nuns, Australian order *Sydney* |
| | University graduates *Sydney* |
| | Woman sculptor *Melbourne* |

## 1858

| | |
|---|---|
| 27 Jan | Land Registration *South Australia* |
| 1 Feb | Balloon ascent *Melbourne* |
| 1 Feb | Trade union journal *Melbourne* |
| 9 Feb | *International swimming championship *Melbourne* |
| 1 July | Woman magazine editor *Sydney* |
| 10 July | Railway fatality *Lidcombe, NSW* |
| 7 Aug | Australian Rules football *Melbourne* |
| 29 Oct | Electric telegraph: Sydney-Melbourne-Adelaide |
| | Divorce *South Australia* |
| | Million population |
| | Photographic exhibition *Sydney* |

## 1859

| | |
|---|---|
| 22 Mar | Political party representing working class *Victoria* |
| 26 Aug | *Labor MP *Melbourne* |
| 3 Sept | Rowing club *Melbourne* |
| Sept | *Photolithography *Melbourne* |
| Oct | Stock exchange *Melbourne* |
| 25 Dec | Wild rabbits (mainland Aus) *Geelong, Vic* |
| | *Freezers *Sydney* |
| | *Mobile libraries *South Australia* and *Victoria* |
| | Oratorio, Australian *Melbourne* |

## 1860

| | |
|---|---|
| 21 Jan | Trotting meeting *Melbourne* |
| June | Insurance salesman *Sydney* |
| 7 Nov | Army Engineers *Melbourne* |
| 19 Dec | Australian forces on active service [*New Zealand*] |
| 29 Dec | Australian forces to engage in battle [*Kairu, NZ*] |
| | School for the blind *Melbourne* |
| | School for the deaf *Sydney* |

## 1861

| | |
|---|---|
| 26 Jan | Ocean yacht race *Sydney* |
| 25 Mar | Opera company *Melbourne* |
| July | Skiing *Kiandra, NSW* |
| 7 Nov | Melbourne Cup *Melbourne* |
| 23 Dec | Trams *Sydney* |
| | Jam factory *Hobart* |
| | Pearls gathered commercially *Nichol Bay, WA* |

## 1862

| | |
|---|---|
| 1 Jan | Cricket team from overseas to tour Aus *Melbourne* |
| 3 Nov | Interstate rifle shooting match *Melbourne* |
| | History of Australia *Sydney* |
| | *Newspaper with children's section *Adelaide* |

## 1863

| | |
|---|---|
| 4 Feb | Interstate rowing race *Sydney* |
| 11 June | Electric lighting *Sydney* |
| 1 July | Post Office Savings Bank *Perth* |
| 23 Oct | Australian soldier killed on active service [*Mauku, NZ*] |
| | Medical School *Melbourne* |
| | Ski races *Mt Hotham, Vic* |
| | War correspondent [*New Zealand*] |

## 1864

| | |
|---|---|
| 5 May | Trout hatched in Aus *Tasmania* |
| 24 Dec | Public picture gallery *Melbourne* |
| | Cookery book *Hobart* |
| | Ocean yacht race, long-distance *Sydney-Newcastle* |
| | Rugby football *Sydney* |
| | Silver mine *Moruya, NSW* |
| | Sugar mill *Brisbane* |

## 1865

| | |
|---|---|
| 21 April | Bronze sculpture cast in Aus *Melbourne* |
| | Export cargo to Japan |
| | Magazine with coloured illustration *Sydney* |
| | Oil production *Hartley Vale, NSW* |
| | Oil refinery *Alexandria, NSW* |

## 1866

| | |
|---|---|
| 1 Nov | Treasury notes *Queensland* |
| | Army cadet corps *Liverpool, NSW* |
| | Historical novel *Sydney* |
| | Saturday half-holiday *Sydney* |

## 1867

| | |
|---|---|
| 20 May | Reformatory *Sydney* |
| 18 Oct | Antisepsis *Parramatta, NSW* |
| 30 Oct | Member of Royal Family to visit Aus *Adelaide* |
| | *International advertising agency *Melbourne* |
| | Bicycle *Bathurst, NSW* |
| | Bowls, Australian-made *Parramatta, NSW* |
| | Diamond mine *Mudgee, NSW* |
| | Glass bottles manufactured *Sydney* |

## 1868

| | |
|---|---|
| 8 Feb | Cricket team to tour overseas |
| 11 March | Sculling championship *Melbourne* |
| Mar | Hospital nurses (trained) *Sydney* |
| 1 May | Submarine telegraph cable *Bass Strait* |
| 30 Nov | Anglican cathedral *Sydney* |
| | Croquet *Kapunda, SA* |
| | *Granny Smith apples *Ryde, NSW* |

## 1869

| | |
|---|---|
| 22 Jan | Reformatory for girls *Newcastle, NSW* |
| 4 May | Sydney Show |
| 10 July | Cycle race *Melbourne* |
| 26 July | Classified advertising *Sydney* |
| Nov | School examinations (external) *Sydney* |

## 1870

| | |
|---|---|
| 1 Jan | State to introduce free education *Queensland* |
| 4 Feb | State flag *Victoria* |
| 7 Feb | Science museum *Melbourne* |
| 14 Sept | Payment of MPs *Victoria* |
| Sept | Children's hospital *Melbourne* |
| 4 Nov | Army signallers *Melbourne* |
| 16 Dec | Death duties *Victoria* |
| 20 Dec | Rowing race between eights *Melbourne* |

## 1871

| | |
|---|---|
| 1 Jan | Regular Army *Victoria* |
| 17 May | Newspaper wire services *Sydney* and *Melbourne* |
| 20 Nov | Overseas telegram received *Darwin* |
| | Children's book with colour illustrations *Melbourne* |
| | Detective stories *Melbourne* |
| | *Sheepdog trials *Forbes, NSW* |
| | *Woman detective writer *Melbourne* |

## 1872

| | |
|---|---|
| 1 July | Electric telegraph: Australia-UK |
| | Athletics club *Sydney* |
| | Gas stove manufactured *Melbourne* |
| | Opals (precious) discovered *Avadale, Qld* |

Tin mine Inverell, NSW
YWCA Geelong, Vic

## 1873

1 Jan   Compulsory education
Victoria
April   Canoe trip
Seymour-Echuca, Vic
Oct   Drying-out clinic Melbourne
23 Nov   Woman minister of religion
Melbourne
Locomotive foundry
Ballarat, Vic
*Share ownership scheme
for company employees
Sydney

## 1874

Department store Sydney
Lacrosse Melbourne
Tree-felling contest
Ulverstone, Tas
Women's cricket match
Bendigo, Vic

## 1875

2 Sept   *Complete meal cooked
from frozen food Lithgow,
NSW
1 Oct   Postcards New South Wales
8 Nov   Polo match Melbourne
28 Nov   Australian champagne
Albury, NSW
Ostrich farm Swan Hill, Vic
Typewriter Sydney

## 1876

27 June   Sportsman to win world
championship Sydney
Aug   *Stump-jump plough
Kalkabury, SA
2 Nov   Marriage solemnized by
woman minister Melbourne
Diamond drill

## 1877

15 Mar   Test match Melbourne
Chorus girls Adelaide
Electric lighting (permanent)
Footscray, Vic
Elevator Melbourne
Lager, Australian-brewed
Sydney

## 1878

2 Jan   Telephone Melbourne
9 Jan   Long distance telephone
call Geelong-Queenscliff, Vic
13 June   Record player Melbourne
30 Nov   Advance Australia Fair
performed Sydney
Lawn tennis court Melbourne
Lawn tennis club Sydney
Ski club Kiandra, NSW
Superphosphate
Yarraville, Vic

## 1879

14 April   Parachute descent
Melbourne
28 April   National Park
Port Hacking, NSW

July   Telephone number
Melbourne
17 Sept   International exhibition
Sydney
28 Sept   Trams, self-propelled
Sydney
28 Oct   Frozen meat shipment
Sydney
Oct   Trades Union Congress
Sydney
Stamp collecting journals
Sydney and Adelaide
Steam carriage Adelaide

## 1880

1 Feb   Fashion journal Melbourne
23 Mar   Female undergraduate
Melbourne
14 April   Interstate bowls match
Annandale, NSW
10 May   Telephone exchange
Melbourne
3 Aug   Soccer club Sydney
14 Aug   Soccer match Parramatta,
NSW
Aug   Telephone directory
Melbourne
5 Sept   Salvation Army meeting
Adelaide
6 Sept   Test match played overseas
[London]
Artesian bore
Riverina district, NSW
Lawn tennis tournament
Melbourne
Military medal Victoria
Oranges exported
Paper dress patterns
Richmond, Vic

## 1881

Feb   Salvation Army Corps
Adelaide
3 April   Census, national
April   Totalisator Perth
Oct   Women's bowls Stawell, Vic
Incandescent electric lights
Sydney and Melbourne
Play, Australian, performed
overseas [London]
Tattersall's Lottery Sydney

## 1882

31 Oct   Parachute jump Ashfield,
NSW
10 Dec   Strike by women Melbourne
15 Dec   Women's trade union
Melbourne
Bookmaker, on-course
Morphettville, SA
Clay target shooting
Melbourne
Concrete road gutters
Sydney
Hockey Adelaide
Teaching hospital Sydney

## 1883

21 Aug   Railway line:
Melbourne-Sydney
9 Sept   Australian Ballet, Melbourne
1 Dec   Woman graduate Melbourne
College of Music Adelaide
State secondary schools
Sydney, Bathurst,
Goulburn, NSW

Statue to a private citizen
Sydney
Typists Sydney

## 1884

Feb   *Combine harvester
Raywood, Vic
May   Cyclist to ride from Sydney
to Melbourne
26 July   Heavyweight boxing
champion of Australia
Melbourne
Apples and pears exported
*Athletics: crouch start
Income tax South Australia
Passenger lifts Sydney and
Melbourne
*Salvation Army social
worker Melbourne
Woman dentist Melbourne

## 1885

3 Feb   Agricultural college
Olive Hill, SA
3 Mar   Expeditionary Force
[NSW-Sudan]
June   Seventh Day Adventists
Melbourne
1 July   Floodlit football match
Adelaide
27 July   Cardinal Sydney
15 Aug   General Sydney
Sept   Stamp collecting society
Sydney
3 Dec   Digger hat Melbourne
Female medical student
Sydney
Gas supply, municipal
Bega, NSW
Returned servicemen's
organization New South Wales
*Shearing machine
Melbourne
War memorial to Australian
troops Sydney
Women's cycle race Adelaide

## 1886

Jan   Seventh Day Adventist
church Melbourne
28 June   Privy Councillor Sydney
Detective novel Melbourne
Gas fires Melbourne
Telephone trunk line
Adelaide-Port Adelaide

## 1887

31 Jan   Co-educational secondary
school Hobart
*Cricket: six ball over
Snooker Sydney
*Theatre with sliding roof
Melbourne
*Women church choristers
Melbourne

## 1888

1 Jan   Art journal Sydney
26 Jan   Commemorative stamps
New South Wales
10 May   State athletics
championship Sydney
Oct   Halftone photograph Sydney

| 9 Nov | Electric street lighting *Tamworth, NSW* |
| | Municipal power station *Tamworth, NSW* |
| | *Combine harvesters manufactured |
| | Kindergarten *Sydney* |
| | Newspaper with women's column *Sydney* |
| | Shearing by machine, complete *Louth, NSW* |
| | Symphony orchestra *Melbourne* |
| | Woman B.Sc *Sydney* |
| | Women's bicycle race *Ashfield, NSW* |

**1889**

| 1 Feb | Foster's lager *Collingwood, Vic* |
| 15 April | Municipal electricity supply (domestic) *Young, NSW* |
| 20 Aug | *Electric drill *Melbourne* |
| | Cross-country running *Sydney* |
| | Pneumatic tyres *Melbourne* |

**1890**

| 7 Feb | Woman doctor *Melbourne* |
| 25 Mar | St John Ambulance Association *Sydney* |
| April | *Juvenile court *Adelaide* |
| May | Boys' Brigade *Melbourne* |
| Sept | Labor Party *Queensland* |
| | Cotton mill *Ipswich, Qld* |

**1891**

| 2 Jan | Athletics: world record |
| 4 Jan | Advertising photograph *Sydney* |
| 11 May | Rodeo *Wodonga, Vic* |
| 4 July | Golf caddies *Melbourne* |
| 20 Oct | Children's magazine *Sydney* |
| 19 Dec | Cremation legalised *South Australia* |
| | *Call girls *Melbourne* |
| | Canned fruit *Hobart.* |
| | Golfer, professional *Melbourne* |
| | Women doctors to qualify in Aus *Melbourne* and *Adelaide* |

**1892**

| 6 Feb | Woman surgeon *Adelaide* |
| 18 Feb | Employment exchange *Sydney* |
| 5 July | *Preferential voting *Queensland* |
| | Athletics: 100 yds in under 10 secs *Melbourne* |
| | District nurse *Melbourne* |
| | Milking machine *Bodalla, NSW* |

**1893**

| 16 Feb | *Box-kite *Bulli, NSW* |
| 8 Mar | Public telephone box *Sydney* |
| 11 Mar | Appendicectomy *Toowoomba, Qld* |
| 18 Aug | *Racing: starting gate *Melbourne* |
| 9 Sept | Ballet, Australian *Melbourne* |
| Sept | Electric trams *Sydney* |

| | Ambulance service *Brisbane* |
| | Hydro-electric station *Thargomindah, Qld* |
| | Motor cycle *Brisbane* |

**1894**

| 28 April | Street collection for charity *Sydney* |
| April | Newspaper set on Linotype machines *Sydney* |
| 29 Aug | Golf championship *Geelong, Vic* |
| 18 Dec | Votes for women *South Australia* |
| Dec | Arbitration court *South Australia* |
| | Life saving clubs *Bronte* and *Waverley, NSW* |
| | Motor car *Sydney* |
| | Workmen's compensation *Western Australia* |

**1895**

| 6 April | *Waltzing Matilda* performed *Winton, Qld* |
| Dec | Woman to wear trousers *Sydney* |
| | Dictionary of Australian English *Melbourne* |
| | Hydro-electric station, municipal *Launceston, Tas* |
| | Woman sculptor, Australian-born *Sydney* |

**1896**

| 3 Mar | X-ray *Melbourne* |
| 7 April | Olympic gold medallist [*Athens*] |
| 25 May | Election at which women were able to vote *South Australia* |

**1896**

| June | Clinical use of X-rays *Melbourne* |
| 22 Aug | Films screened before paying audience *Melbourne* |
| 23 Sept | Adoption legally recognised *Western Australia* |
| 28 Sept | Cinema *Sydney* |
| 28 Sept | Australian-made films shown *Sydney* |
| Oct | Radiation treatment for cancer *Albury, NSW* |
| | Greek Orthodox priest *Sydney/Melbourne* |
| | Motor car with pneumatic tyres *Armadale, Vic* |
| | Motor car, imported *Melbourne* |
| | Motor cycle, imported *Sydney* |
| | Reinforced concrete *Annandale, NSW* |

**1897**

| 16 Feb | Four-wheeled motor car built in Aus *Melbourne* |
| | Anglican archbishop *Sydney* |
| | Ballet school *Melbourne* |
| | Beet sugar *Maffra, Vic* |
| | Dramatic film *Melbourne* |
| | Home movie outfit *Melbourne* |

| | *Motor vehicle with differential gear *Mannum, SA* |
| | Motoring conviction *Sydney* |
| | *Rugby football: numbering of players *Brisbane* |

**1898**

| 29 May | Greek Orthodox church *Sydney* |
| May | Picture postcards *Adelaide* |
| 3 June | Referendum |
| 13 Aug | Army nurses *Sydney* |
| Sept | International yacht race [*R. Medway*] |
| 16 Dec | Women's bowls club *Melbourne* |
| | *Anthropological film *Torres Strait Is* |
| | Christian Science *Melbourne* |
| | *Crawl *Sydney* |
| | Dental school *Melbourne* |
| | Paperback novels *Sydney* |
| | *Teleprinter *Sydney* |

**1899**

| 1 Aug | Colour photographs *Sydney* |
| 24 Aug | Commonwealth army regiment |
| 28 Nov | *Labor premier *Queensland* |
| 1 Dec | *Labor government *Queensland* |
| | Pneumatic tyres, Australian-made *Melbourne* |

**1900**

| 24 April | Open hearth steel furnace *Lithgow, NSW* |
| 24 July | Victoria Cross *Transvaal* |
| Dec | Motor car journey: Sydney-Melbourne |
| | Badminton *Fremantle, WA* |
| | Natural gas discovered *Roma, Qld* |
| | Public housing *Sydney* |

**1901**

| 1 Jan | Commonwealth Prime Minister |
| 1 Jan | Governor-General |
| 1 Jan | Motorcycle racing *Sydney* |
| 1 Jan | Old age pensions *Victoria* |
| 29 Mar | Federal elections |
| 8 May | Labor Party, Federal |
| 9 May | Federal Parliament *Melbourne* |
| 18 May | Wireless transmission *Queenscliff, Vic* |
| 3 Sept | Australian national flag *Melbourne* |
| 23 Sept | Australian manufactured car sold *Melbourne* |
| | *Documentary film with sound *Charlotte Waters, NT* |
| | Motor van *Sydney* |

**1902**

| 31 Oct | Electric telegraph: Pacific cable |
| 28 Dec | Fingerprints *Sydney* |
| | Health food shop *Sydney* |
| | Interstate telephone trunk line *Nelson, Vic*-*Mt Gambier, SA* |
| | *Notepads *Launceston, Tas* |

**1903**

20 Mar — Motoring association
9 April — Ship's radio *Brisbane*
16 Dec — Federal elections in which women were able to vote
— Car designed for outback *Melbourne*
— Car driver convicted for speeding *Melbourne*
— Crematorium *Adelaide*
— Motor buses, Australian-built *Geelong, Vic*
— Motor racing *Adelaide*
— Wireless installations *Moreton Is* and *Brisbane*
— Woman architect *Sydney*

**1904**

Mar — Vegetarian restaurant *Sydney*
27 April — Labor government (Commonwealth)
April — Motor fire engine *Sydney*
3 Sept — Australian Open Golf Championship
1 June — Patents, Commonwealth
15 Dec — Commonwealth Arbitration Court
— Cigarette cards *Melbourne*
— Jehovah's Witnesses *Melbourne*
— Motor coach *Devonport, Tas*
— Motor cycle manufacture *Prahran, Vic*
— Motorcycling clubs *Perth, Melbourne* and *Sydney*
— Speed limit (motor vehicles) *South Australia*
— Taxis *Sydney*

**1905**

21 Feb — Motor rally *Melbourne-Sydney*
17 July — Australian challenge in Davis Cup [*London*]
1 Aug — Woman lawyer *Melbourne*
11 Nov — Australian runner to break world record *Sydney*
— Canned fish *Hobart*
— Motor bus service *Hobart*
— Reinforced concrete bridge *Richmond, NSW*
— White collar trade union *Adelaide*

**1906**

28 Jan — Motorcycle racetrack *Aspendale, Vic*
12 July — Interstate wireless telegraphy service *Victoria-Tasmania*
4 Aug — Reinforced concrete used in a building *Sydney*
10 Sept — Driving licence *Woodville, SA*
10 Sept — Motor vehicle licence plates *South Australia*
23 Dec — *Life-saving reel *Bondi, NSW*
24 Dec — *Feature film *Melbourne*
31 Dec — *Rescue with life saving reel *Bondi, NSW*
— Motor car, fully enclosed *Melbourne*
— Natural gas supply *Roma, Qld*

— Surf life saving club *Bondi, NSW*
— Trade agreement, international

**1907**

1 May — Comic strip *Sydney*
4 July — Australian to win Wimbledon
10 July — Telephone trunk line: Melbourne-Sydney
23 July — Australian victory in Davis Cup
8 Nov — Basic wage
— Legal aid *Queensland* and *New South Wales*
— Motor van, Australian-built *Melbourne*
— Women's rowing club *Melbourne*

**1908**

8 Jan — Rugby League club *Newtown, NSW*
Jan — Surf boat race *Manly, NSW*
14 Mar — Industrial film *Sydney*
20 Aug — Transcontinental motor car journey *Adelaide-Darwin*
2 Nov — Labor daily newspaper *Broken Hill, NSW*
— Motor racing track *Sydney*
— Scout troop *Mosman, NSW*
— Seismograph *Adelaide*
— Surf board *Curl Curl Beach, NSW*
— Tennis balls manufactured *Port Melbourne, Vic*

**1909**

Mar — Tabloid newspaper *Sydney*
12 April — Marathon *Sydney*
5 Dec — Glider flight *Narrabeen Heads, NSW*
5 Dec — *Woman glider pilot *Narrabeen Heads, NSW*
9 Dec — Aeroplane flight, powered *Sydney*
15 Dec — Safety matches manufactured *Richmond, Vic*
— Film studio *Caulfield, Vic*
— Medical research institute *Townsville, Qld*
— Motor mail van *Nowra-Ulladulla, NSW*
— Tractor, Australian-made *Melbourne*
— Uranium mine *Radium Hill, SA*

**1910**

1 Jan — Driving tests *Sydney* and *Melbourne*
22 Jan — Australian diplomat
1 Mar — Commonwealth of Australia coinage
17 Mar — Aeroplane flight, controlled and sustained *Bolivar, SA*
13 April — Labor government elected to power (Commonwealth)
June — Ante-natal clinic *Adelaide*
1 July — Newspaper to carry front page news *Sydney*
16 July — Flight by Australian-built aeroplane *Mia Mia, Vic*

21 July — Newsreel *Sydney*
Sept — Aerodrome *Penrith, NSW*
— Cinema, purpose-built *Sydney*
— Girl Guide troops *Hawthorn* and *Richmond, Vic; Powelltown, Tas*
— Steel-framed building *Sydney*

**1911**

3 Jan — *Gaol to hold film shows *Sydney*
18 Feb — Bush-nurse *Beech Forest, Vic*
20 Feb — Cross-country aeroplane flight *Altona Bay-Geelong, Vic*
23 Feb — Woman to fly in aeroplane *Altona Bay, Vic*
25 April — Australian to qualify as pilot
15 May — *Cinema to present double bill *Melbourne*
27 June — Military college *Duntroon, ACT*
21 Oct — Comic strip in colour *Sydney*
15 Nov — Ships commissioned in Royal Australian Navy
5 Dec — Pilot to qualify in Aus *Sydney*
— Dirt track racing *Sydney*
— Motor trucks, Australian-built *Auburn, NSW* .
— Police patrol car *Perth*

**1912**

3 Jan — Flying school *Penrith, NSW*
6 Jan — Film magazine *Sydney*
13 April — Transcontinental motor car journey: west-east *Fremantle-Sydney*
29 June — Air race *Sydney-Parramatta*
6 July — Automatic telephone exchange *Geelong, Vic*
13 July — Woman to win Olympic gold medal [*Stockholm*]
15 July — Commonwealth Bank Savings Department *Victoria*
Aug — Motor show *Melbourne*
20 Sept — Air force
9 Oct — Maternity benefit
— Canoe club *Melbourne*
— Car with self-starter imported
— Children's library *Sydney*

**1913**

Jan — Commonwealth postage stamps
13 Feb — Free university *Perth*
1 Mar — Naval college *Geelong, Vic*
20 Mar — Lifesaving instructor (qualified) *Sydney*
May — Newspaper comic strip *Perth*
21 June — Overseas ballet company to perform in Aus *Melbourne*
13 July — Commonwealth banknotes
July — Squash court *Melbourne*
— Progressive school *Mittagong, NSW*

**1914**

1 Mar — Flight by military aircraft *Point Cook, Vic*
6 May — Submarines *Darwin*
8 May — Seaplane *Sydney*
4 July — Airship *Sydney*

155

| | | | | | | |
|---|---|---|---|---|---|---|
| 16 July | Air mail *Melbourne-Sydney* | **1920** | | 7 Nov | Commercials *Sydney* | |
| 16 July | Air freight *Melbourne-Sydney* | 22 Jan | Country Party formed | 29 Nov | *Broadcast racing commentary *Adelaide* | |
| 4 Aug | Shot fired by British forces in WWI *Port Phillip, Vic* | | *Melbourne* | 5 Dec | Woolworths *Sydney* | |
| 17 Aug | Military flying school *Point Cook, Vic* | 18 Feb | *Bathing beauty contest *Maroubra Beach, NSW* | 23 Dec | Labor politician to become State Governor *Tasmania* | |
| 14 Sept | Australian ship lost in action [*New Britain*] | Mar | State lottery *Queensland* | | Business school *Melbourne* | |
| | | 13 Oct | Radio broadcast by live performer *Melbourne* | | *Car radio *Alexandria, NSW* | |
| 12 Nov | Military pilot to qualify *Point Cook, Vic* | 30 Oct | Communist Party formed | | City with one million inhabitants *Sydney* | |
| | Open prison | 6 Nov | Night trotting meeting *Adelaide* | | Corn flakes *Sydney* | |
| | PABX telephone system *Sydney* | 2 Dec | Transcontinental flight: east-west | | Disc records, Australian *Sydney* | |
| | Paid annual holidays *Western Australia* | 16 Dec | Transcontinental flight: west-east | | | |
| | | | Boys' paper *Melbourne* | **1925** | | |
| **1915** | | | Petrol pumps *Melbourne* | 1 Jan | Airline service: Adelaide-Sydney | |
| 22 May | *Compulsory voting *Queensland* | | *Rotary hoe *Gilgandra, NSW* | 21 Mar | Play written for radio *Melbourne* | |
| 12 June | *Aspro *Melbourne* | **1921** | | 24 Mar | *Broadcast from Parliament *Sydney* | |
| 1 July | Policewomen *Sydney* | 12 Mar | Woman MP *Perth* | 3 April | Woman Labor MP *Forrest, WA* | |
| 30 July | Pilot killed in warfare [*Mesopotamia*] | 31 Mar | Royal Australian Air Force founded | 27 July | Radio newscaster *Brisbane* | |
| 10 Aug | Flight by Australian-built military aircraft *Point Cook, Vic* | 21 April | Rotary Club *Melbourne* | 14 Nov | Federal elections at which voting was compulsory | |
| | | Oct | Broadcasts, regular | | | |
| 15 Aug | Air-conditioned shop *Sydney* | 5 Dec | Airliner crash *Murchison River, WA* | 4 Dec | *Broadcast cricket commentary *Sydney* | |
| 13 Sept | Income tax, Federal | | | | | |
| 12 Nov | Nobel Prize winner *Adelaide* | 5 Dec | Airmail service, regular *Geraldton-Derby, WA* | 30 Dec | Round-Australia motor car journey *Perth-Perth* | |
| | *Brick veneer cladding *Melbourne* | **1922** | | | Coal briquettes *Yallourn, Vic* | |
| | Woman surfboarder *Freshwater, NSW* | 3 Mar | Passenger airline service *Geraldton-Derby, WA* | | Encyclopaedia, Australian *Sydney* | |
| | | 13 Mar | Airliner, Australian-built *Sydney* | | Hire purchase finance company *Perth* | |
| **1916** | | | Abolition of capital punishment *Queensland* | | Jazz recording | |
| 16 Mar | Air Force squadron on active service | | Bottled milk *Camden, NSW* | | Wrapped bread *Melbourne* | |
| 26 Mar | 'Six o'clock swill' *South Australia* | | Legacy Club *Hobart* | | | |
| | | | *Prime Minister to broadcast *Bendigo, Vic* | **1926** | | |
| 30 Sept | Cruiser, Australian-built *Sydney* | | Rice cultivated *Leeton, NSW* | 24 Feb | *Widows' pensions *New South Wales* | |
| | Dolls, Australian-made *Adelaide* | | *Rotary hoe manufactured *Moss Vale, NSW* | Mar | Women's athletics *Manly, NSW* | |
| | Totalisator, automatic *Perth* | | Who's Who in Australia *Melbourne* | 25 June | 'Miss Australia' contest *Sydney* | |
| | Town planner *Adelaide* | | | 1 July | Gift tax *Queensland* | |
| | | **1923** | | 22 Nov | Film directed by a woman *Sydney* | |
| **1917** | | Feb | *Vegemite *Melbourne* | 25 Nov | Exhibition of Australian modern art *Sydney* | |
| 22 Oct | Transcontinental railway *Sydney-Perth* | Mar | Diabetic treated with insulin *Melbourne* | 20 Dec | Underground railway *Sydney* | |
| 8 Dec | Aeroplane to take off from ship | April | Drug trafficking conviction *Melbourne* | | Blood transfusion service | |
| 12 Dec | Commonwealth Police Force | May | Police radio patrol cars *Melbourne* | | Bookmatches, Australian-made *Richmond, Vic* | |
| | | 20 July | Electric locomotive, Australian-built *Newport, Vic* | | Electric refrigerators | |
| **1918** | | 23 Nov | Broadcasting station *Sydney* | | Glider club *Granville, NSW* | |
| 7 Feb | Peer of the Realm, Australian-born *Perth* | 5 Dec | Play to be broadcast *Sydney* | | Processed cheese *Melbourne* | |
| 22 Sept | Wireless message from England *Wahroonga, NSW* | | Refrigerator, domestic *Sydney* | | | |
| Sept | Trade Commissioner to represent Aus overseas | | Unemployment benefit *Queensland* | **1927** | | |
| 6 Oct | Electric railway *Melbourne* | | Woman electrical engineer *Sydney* | Feb | Child benefit *New South Wales* | |
| | | | | 23 Mar | Woman pilot *Sydney* | |
| **1919** | | **1924** | | 9 May | Talking film shot in Aus *Canberra* | |
| 25 April | ANZAC Day *Western Australia* | 7 April | *Rotary clothes hoist *East Malvern, Vic* | 9 May | Parliament to sit at Canberra | |
| 13 Aug | Radio broadcast *Sydney* | 4 June | Airmail service: Adelaide-Melbourne-Sydney | 28 May | Greyhound track racing *Epping, NSW* | |
| 10 Dec | England-Australia flight | 7 Aug | Earl, Australian-born *Toogoom, Qld* | 5 Sept | Overseas broadcast *Sydney* | |
| 12 Dec | Transcontinental flight | | | | Electric refrigerators, Australian-made | |
| 16 Dec | Flight across Bass Strait | | | | | |
| | Abstract paintings *Sydney* | | | | | |

156

**1928**

| 19 Mar | Woman to fly England-Australia |
| 31 Mar | Australian Grand Prix Phillip Is, Vic |
| 9 May | Daily airline service Brisbane-Toowoomba |
| 15 May | *Flying doctor Cloncurry, Qnd |
| 9 June | Trans-Pacific flight |
| 9 Aug | Transcontinental flight, non-stop |
| Aug | Woman to compete in Olympic track event [Amsterdam] |
| 1 Sept | Television journal Melbourne |
| 11 Sept | Australia-NZ flight |
| 29 Dec | Feature-length talking film released Sydney |
| | Film club Sydney |
| | Junior Farmers Club Glen Innes, NSW |
| | Martial arts club Brisbane |
| | Traffic lights Melbourne |

**1929**

| 10 Jan | Television transmission Melbourne |
| 2 June | Airline service: Perth-Adelaide |
| 9 Sept | Radiophotographs Melbourne |
| Sept | Tanks Randwick, NSW |
| 2 Nov | Sound newsreel |
| | Air freight England-Australia |
| | Exhibition of Aboriginal art Melbourne |
| | Hospital almoner Melbourne |
| | Neon lighting Sydney |
| | School broadcasts |

**1930**

| 30 April | Australian-UK telephone service |
| 1 June | Feature-length talkie, Australian-made Sydney |
| 1 June | Airline service: Melbourne-Sydney |
| | Sales tax |

**1931**

| 1 Jan | Sound newsreel, Australian produced |
| 19 Jan | Airline service: Melbourne-Hobart |
| 22 Jan | Governor-General, Australian-born |
| 21 Mar | Airliner crash involving passenger fatalities |
| Mar | Exhibition of abstract sculpture Melbourne |
| 25 April | Airmail: England-Australia |
| April | *Plastic bowls Melbourne |
| 14 May | Airmail: Australia-England |
| 26 Sept | All-talkie feature films, Australian-made Melbourne |
| 4 Nov | Ballet company (permanent Sydney |
| Dec | Film musical, Australian-made |

**1932**

| 15 May | Premier dismissed from office New South Wales |
| 1 July | ABC radio stations |

| 4 Nov | Trans-Pacific flight: west-east |
| | Colour film, Australian-made Melbourne |
| | Golf balls, Australian-made Melbourne |
| | Tobacco auction Brisbane |

**1933**

| April | Veteran car rally Melbourne |
| | *Milk bar Sydney |

**1934**

| 22 Jan | Trolley buses Sydney |
| 17 Feb | Airmail: NZ-Australia |
| 11 April | Airmail: Australia-NZ |
| 20 April | Airline service: Australia-England |
| 6 May | Television, electronic Brisbane |
| 17 Oct | Radiophotographs, international Melbourne-London |
| | *Pavlova Perth |
| | *Utility truck Geelong, Vic |

**1935**

| 22 Feb | Broadcasting round the clock Sydney |
| | Manmade fabric Brunswick, Vic |

**1936**

| 1 Jan | Service pensions |
| 5 Aug | Gastronomic society Melbourne |
| 11 Sept | World champion dirt-track racer [London] |
| 31 Dec | Paid annual holidays (Federal Award) |
| | Diplomatic representative of overseas country |
| | Lighthouse with fully-automatic flashing light Wollongong, NSW |
| | Water skiiing Darwin |

**1937**

| Jan | Petrol pump, automatic Enfield, NSW |
| 20 April | Airmail: Australia-USA |
| 23 Nov | Air-conditioned train Melbourne-Albury |
| | Children's museum Adelaide |
| | Diplomat to serve in USA |

**1938**

| | Coca Cola Sydney |
| | Submachine gun Wollongong, NSW |
| | Woman artist to win Archibald Prize. |

**1939**

| 27 Mar | Flight by Australian-designed warplane |
| 29 May | Airline service: night flights Sydney-Brisbane |
| 3 Sept | Shot fired by British forces in WWII Port Phillip, Vic |
| | Instant coffee |
| | Japanese car imported |

| | Multi-storey car park Melbourne |
| | Ready-mixed concrete Sydney |
| | *Shepherd castors Melbourne |
| | Sliced bread Newtown, NSW |

**1940**

| 8 Jan | Australian legation [Washington] |
| Mar | Radar Sydney |
| 1 Aug | Minesweeper, Australian-built Sydney |
| 25 Sept | Woman to serve in Forces |
| Nov | Woman radio announcer |
| | Comic book Sydney |

**1941**

| 15 March | Women to serve in Air Force Malvern, Vic |
| 28 April | Woman to serve in Navy |
| 30 June | Pay-roll tax |
| 8 July | Professional ballet company (permanent) Sydney |
| 29 July | Child benefit (national) |

**1942**

| 19 Feb | Air raid on Australian territory Darwin |
| 30 Mar | Food rationing |
| Aug | Tank, Australian-built Melbourne |
| | Air-warning radar Darwin |
| | Softball Victoria |
| | Submachine gun manu-factured Port Kembla, NSW |

**1943**

| Feb | PAYE |
| 7 June | Butter rationing |
| 21 Aug | Woman Senator Western Australia |
| 21 Aug | Woman Member of the House of Representatives Darwin |
| Dec | *Penicillin for civilian use Melbourne |
| | Platypus bred in captivity Healesville, Vic |

**1944**

| 17 Jan | Meat rationing |
| 11 Sept | Aerogrammes |
| 16 Dec | Liberal Party founded Albury, NSW |
| | Aboriginal army officer |
| | Unemployment benefit (national) |

**1945**

| 1 Jan | State to introduce paid annual holidays for all New South Wales |
| 5 Feb | Artifical rainfall Blue Mountains, NSW |
| 24 Dec | Cardinal, Australian-born Sydney |
| 26 Dec | Sydney-Hobart Yacht Race |
| | Servicewomen to serve overseas [New Guinea] |

**1946**

| | |
|---|---|
| 16 Mar | Photo-finish camera *Canterbury*, NSW |
| June | Jet aircraft *Laverton*, *Vic* |
| 5 July | Parliamentary broadcasting, regular *Canberra* |
| 15 Sept | Airline service: trans-Pacific |
| | Australian Embassy [*Washington*] |
| | Ballpoint pens *Launceston*, *Tas* |
| | Bikini *Bondi*, NSW |
| | Dubbed film |
| | Parking officers *Sydney* |
| | University to award PhDs *Melbourne* |

**1947**

| | |
|---|---|
| 11 Mar | Governor-General of working class origin |
| 26 Mar | Australian Peer to sit in House of Lords |
| 2 April | Woman Minister of the Crown *Western Australia* |
| 1 Aug | Air Force college *Point Cook*, *Vic* |
| 3 Oct | Helicopter *Laverton*, *Vic* |
| Nov | Train with fluorescent lighting *Perth-Bunbury* |
| | Anglican monastery *Adelaide* |
| | National Trust *New South Wales* |

**1948**

| | |
|---|---|
| 1 Jan | 40 hour week (standard) |
| April | Marriage Guidance Council *Sydney* |
| Aug | Woman to win Olympic medal for track event [*London*] |
| 29 Nov | All-Australian car to be mass produced *Melbourne* |

**1949**

| | |
|---|---|
| 26 Jan | Australian citizenship |
| 29 June | Jet aircraft, Australian-built *Bankstown*, NSW |
| 19 Dec | Woman Minister in Federal Government |
| | Australian ballet company to tour overseas |

**1950**

| | |
|---|---|
| Jan | Frozen food *Sydney* and *Orange*, NSW |
| 8 June | Field Marshal |
| Aug | Guide dog for the blind *Perth* |
| | Motor truck to be mass produced *Melbourne* |
| | Water skiing club *Sackville*, NSW |

**1951**

| | |
|---|---|
| Feb | Myxomatosis epidemic *Murray Valley* |
| 1 July | Paid sick leave *New South Wales* |
| 1 July | *Long service leave *New South Wales* |
| 22 Sept | Diesel locomotive, mainline *Port Pirie-Port Augusta*, SA |
| | Computer *Sydney* |

| | School of the Air broadcasts *Alice Springs*, NT |

**1952**

| | |
|---|---|
| Jan | Guide dog training centre *Perth* |
| 22 July | Woman to win Olympic gold medal in track event [*Helsinki*] |
| 3 Oct | Nuclear explosion *Monte Bellow Is*, WA |
| | Rotary lawn mower *Concord*, NSW |

**1953**

| | |
|---|---|
| 11 Aug | Supersonic flight *Avalon*, NSW |
| | Water fluoridation *Beaconsfield*, *Tas* |

**1954**

| | |
|---|---|
| 3 Feb | Reigning monarch to visit Aus *Sydney* |
| 21 June | Australian to run 4 min mile [*Turku, Finland*] |
| 21 July | Railway mainline electrification *Dandenong-Warragul*, *Vic* |
| 13 Nov | Speaking clock *Sydney* |
| | Feature film in colour *Sydney* |
| 16 Dec | Malibu surf board *North Bondi*, NSW |
| | Newspaper to introduce photo-typesetting *Melbourne* |

**1955**

| | |
|---|---|
| 1 April | Parking meters *Hobart* |
| | Aluminium, Australian-produced *Bell Bay*, *Tas* |
| | 45rpm records |
| | Novel by Aboriginal |
| | Trampolines *Newtown*, NSW and *Oakleigh*, *Vic* |

**1956**

| | |
|---|---|
| 19 May | Helicopter in passenger service |
| May | Motel *Canberra* |
| 16 Sept | Television station *Sydney* |
| 16 Sept | Television news *Sydney* |
| 16 Sept | Television commercial *Sydney* |
| 5 Nov | Prime Minister on television *Sydney* |
| 5 Nov | Television play *Sydney* |
| 22 Nov | Olympic Games *Melbourne* |
| Nov | Sports telecast *Sydney* |
| Dec | Australian play on TV *Sydney* |
| | Credit cards |
| | Pearl culture farm *Kuri Bay*, WA |
| | Scientology |
| | STD telephone service *Sydney* and *Melbourne* |

**1957**

| | |
|---|---|
| July | Rock recording by Australian band |
| Nov | Christmas stamp |
| | Satellite tracking station *Woomera*, SA |

| | Station wagon, Australian-made *Melbourne* |
| | *Trousers with permanent creases |

**1958**

| | |
|---|---|
| 14 Jan | *Airline service: round-the-world |
| 28 Jan | British Prime Minister to visit Aus *Sydney* |
| 1 Mar | Air pollution control *Victoria* |
| 24 Mar | Freeway *Sydney* |
| 18 April | Nuclear reactor *Lucas Heights*, *Sydney* |
| | Australian pop song in British charts |
| | *'Black Box' flight crash recorder |
| | Skyscraper *Melbourne* |
| March | First all Australian Pop Music Charts |

**1959**

| | |
|---|---|
| 10 Jan | Television transmission: Sydney-Melbourne |
| 17 June | Shakespeare plays on TV *Sydney* and *Melbourne* |
| 29 July | Jet airline service *Sydney-San Francisco* |
| 20 Oct | Australian record No 1 in charts |
| 13 Dec | Australian to become World Champion Motor Racing Driver |
| Dec | Army truck, Australian-designed *Dandenong*, *Vic* |
| | Overseas symphony orchestra to tour Aus |
| | TV soap opera *Sydney* and *Melbourne* |

**1960**

| | |
|---|---|
| May | TABs *Victoria* |
| May | Tenpin bowling alley *Glenelg*, SA |
| 7 July | Kidnapping for ransom *Sydney* |
| Nov | Computer for commercial use *Sydney* |
| 20 Dec | Heliport *Melbourne* |
| | Australian TV series in Top Ten ratings |
| | Guided missiles |

**1961**

| | |
|---|---|
| 1 Jan | Reverse charge telephone calls |
| Feb | Contraceptive pill |
| 16 Sept | Baha'i temple *Sydney* |
| Nov | Breathalyser tests *Victoria* |
| 3 Dec | Oil well *Moonie*, Qld |
| | Guided missile base *Williamstown*, NSW |
| | Pizza *Sydney* |

**1962**

| | |
|---|---|
| 9 Sept | Australian challenge in America's Cup |
| 20 Sept | Woman QC *Adelaide* |
| Sept | Australian pop song in US charts |

## 1963

| | |
|---|---|
| April | Aluminium produced from Australian bauxite *Geelong, Vic* |
| | Australian to win Wimbledon Women's Singles |
| | *Barefoot waterski jump *Manly, NSW* |
| | Telephone counselling service *Sydney* |

## 1964

| | |
|---|---|
| 8 April | Oil pipeline *Moonie-Brisbane* |
| May | Australian to become world surfing champion *Manly, NSW* |
| 15 July | National daily newspaper |
| July | Topless sunbather *Mona Vale, NSW* |
| | Aboriginal university graduate |
| | *Container ship, fully-cellular |
| | Skateboards *Sydney* |

## 1965

| | |
|---|---|
| 7 Jan | Hydrofoil *Sydney* |
| 18 Feb | Offshore oil field *Gippsland Basin* |
| 8 Mar | Non-stop airline service to USA |
| 25 Mar | Air Chief Marshal |
| 7 Aug | Australian to swim English Channel |
| 23 Sept | Woman judge *Adelaide* |
| Sept | Symphony orchestra to tour overseas |
| 1 Oct | Overseas debut of the Australian Ballet [*London*] |
| | Record to sell 1 million |

## 1966

| | |
|---|---|
| 26 Jan | Woman Minister to head Department of State |
| 28 Jan | Nickel mine *Kambalda, WA* |
| Jan | Maternity leave (statutory) |
| 7 Feb | Decimal postage stamps |
| 14 Feb | Decimal currency |
| Feb | Homosexual sauna *Bondi, NSW* |
| 7 July | Pizza restaurant *Melbourne* |
| Oct | US President to visit Aus *Canberra* |
| 24 Nov | International TV transmission |
| Dec | Film based on TV series *Melbourne* |

## 1967

| | |
|---|---|
| Mar | Natural gas pipeline *Roma-Brisbane* |
| 29 May | $5 banknotes |
| July | Oil rig, Australian-built *Whyalla, SA* |
| July | Postcodes |
| 19 Nov | Space satellite *Woomera, SA* |
| 31 Dec | Quintuplets *Brisbane* |
| | Pantihose |
| | Wine sold in cardboard casks ('bladders') |

## 1968

| | |
|---|---|
| 27 April | Kentucky Fried Chicken *Guildford, NSW* |
| 21 June | Woman trade union leader *Melbourne* |
| June | Homosexual disco *Sydney* |
| 23 Oct | Heart transplant *Sydney* |

## 1969

| | |
|---|---|
| 6 Jan | Railway: double-decker passenger carriages *Sydney* |
| 1 Mar | P plates *Victoria* |
| Aug | Orienteering *Upper Beaconsfield, Vic* |

## 1970

| | |
|---|---|
| 8 Jan | Abortion (legal) *South Australia* |
| 1 Mar | Transcontinental through passenger train *Sydney-Perth* |
| 19 April | Pizza Hut *Belfield, NSW* |
| 30 Nov | Pope to visit Aus *Sydney* |
| 22 Dec | Seat belts (compulsory) *Victoria* |
| | *Laser beam lighthouse *Point Danger, NSW* |

## 1971

| | |
|---|---|
| 18 Mar | Woman High Commissioner [*New Zealand*] |
| 24 April | Ombudsman *Western Australia* |
| 13 June | *Nonuplets *Sydney* |
| 16 Aug | Jumbo jet *Sydney* |
| Oct | Sex shop *Sydney* |
| 30 Dec | McDonald's *Yagoona, NSW* |
| | Aboriginal Member of Parliament |
| | Green Ban *Sydney* |
| | Sex change clinic *Sydney* |
| | Votes at 18 *South Australia* |

## 1972

| | |
|---|---|
| 2 June | Aboriginal knight *Adelaide* |
| Nov | Nude male centrefold *Sydney* |
| Dec | Animated feature film |
| | Homosexual hotel *Sydney* |

## 1973

| | |
|---|---|
| May | Women's trotting race *Adelaide* |
| July | *Government adviser on women's affairs |
| 9 Oct | $50 banknotes |
| 18 Oct | Nobel Prize for Literature |
| | Australian TV series to top ratings overseas |
| | Casino *Hobart* |
| | Film school *Sydney* |

## 1974

| | |
|---|---|
| Mar | Rape Crisis Centre *Sydney* |
| 18 May | Federal election at which 18-year olds able to vote |
| 1 July | Metric road signs *Victoria* |
| Aug | Parliament televised *Canberra* |
| Nov | Bankcards |

## 1975

| | |
|---|---|
| Feb | Nude bathing beach *Maslin Beach, SA* |
| 1 Mar | Colour TV programmes |
| May | Freepost |
| May | Aboriginal RC priest |
| 14 June | Decoration or Honour, Australian |
| 14 June | Medal for gallantry, Australian |
| 11 Nov | Prime Minister dismissed from office |
| | State Film Corporation *South Australia* |

## 1976

| | |
|---|---|
| 5 Jan | Divorce by mutual consent |
| 1 April | International STD |
| 24 May | Knight of the Order of Australia |
| 1 July | Random breath tests *Victoria* |
| 12 July | General strike |
| 30 Nov | Rape in marriage as criminal offence *South Australia* |
| 1 Dec | Aboriginal State Governor *South Australia* |
| | Awards for TV commercials |
| | Skateboard track *Albany, WA* |

## 1977

| | |
|---|---|
| Feb | Open zoo *Dubbo, NSW* |
| 8 Mar | Woman to serve in Royal Australian Navy |
| May | Newspaper to introduce computer typesetting *Canberra* |
| 22 June | Uniting Church founded |
| June | State with fully automatic telephone network *Tasmania* |
| 3 Aug | Sydney International Piano Competition |

## 1978

| | |
|---|---|
| Mar | Woman TV newsreader |
| 12 April | Contemporary ballet, full-length *Sydney* |
| 8 Oct | Australian to hold world water speed record *Tumut, NSW* |
| | Play by Aboriginal playwright published *Sydney* |
| | Women's boxing tournament *King Is, Tas.* |
| | Aboriginal Barrister *Sydney* |

## 1979

| | |
|---|---|
| 9 Mar | Maternity leave (Commonwealth) |
| 5 Nov | Lotto *New South Wales* |
| | *Bionic ear *Melbourne* |

## 1980

| | |
|---|---|
| 22 Jan | Woman airline pilot *Alice Springs-Darwin* |
| 4 Feb | Teletext |
| 22 June | Test tube baby *Melbourne* |
| 1 Aug | International bankcards |
| 24 Oct | Ethnic TV channels *Sydney* and *Melbourne* |
| | Music synthesiser, Australian-made *Sydney* |

**1981**

| | |
|---|---|
| 21 June | Australian golfer to win US Open |
| 17 Dec | Terrorist assassination *Sydney* |
| Dec | Sex problems clinic *Perth* |

**1982**

| | |
|---|---|
| 8 April | High-speed XPT passenger train *Sydney-Dubbo* |
| 18 Aug | *Solo Atlantic helicopter flight |
| 19 Oct | Australian to win Booker Prize |
| Dec | AIDS *Sydney* |
| | State to abolish corporal punishment in schools *Victoria* |

**1983**

| | |
|---|---|
| April | Four day working week |
| 8 July | Death from AIDS *Melbourne* |
| 26 Sept | Australian yacht to win America's Cup [*Newport*, RI] |
| Oct | Divorce-by-mail |

**1984**

| | |
|---|---|
| 1 Feb | Medicare |
| 26 Mar | $100 banknotes |
| 28 Mar | *Frozen embryo baby *Melbourne* |
| 14 May | Dollar coins |
| 22 May | Legalised brothels *Victoria* |
| 3 Oct | Ascent of Everest by Australians |

**1985**

| | |
|---|---|
| 21 Feb | Woman Sergeant-at-Arms *Canberra* |
| 19 Sept | Fringe Benefits Tax |
| 3 Nov | World Championship motor race *Adelaide* |

**1986**

| | |
|---|---|
| 11 Feb | Woman Speaker of the House of Representatives *Canberra* |
| Oct | Pedicabs *Adelaide* |

**1987**

| | |
|---|---|
| July | Automated stock exchanges *Sydney* and *Melbourne* |
| 31 Dec | Monorail public transport system *Sydney* |